Grenadier Divisions of the Waffen-SS

Rolf Michaelis

Schiffer Publishing Ltd
4880 Lower Valley Road • Atglen, PA 19310

Library of Congress Control Number: 2014958495

Designed by Robert Biondi and Rolf Michaelis
Type set in Times New Roman/Gill Sans Std

ISBN: 978-0-7643-4837-2
Printed in China

Published by Schiffer Publishing, Ltd.
4880 Lower Valley Road
Atglen, PA 19310
Phone: (610) 593-1777; Fax: (610) 593-2002
E-mail: Info@schifferbooks.com

Translated from the German by David Johnston.

This book was originally published under the title,
Die Grenadier-Divisionen der Waffen-SS,
© 2013 by Michaelis-Verlag, Berlin, Germany.

Contents

Foreword

More than 350,000 Germans, *Volksdeutsche* [ethnic Germans who lived in or were citizens of other countries] and foreigners served in the *Grenadier-Divisionen* of the armed SS military formations. Initially, these formations relied upon voluntary enlistments, but as a result of the enormous losses in the war, more and more, almost the entire cohort of men born in a year, at home and abroad, were called up for compulsory service in the *Waffen-SS*.

This book is intended to provide a clearly presented account of these eighteen *SS-Grenadier-Divisionen.* When were they formed, how were the personnel assembled, and where were they trained, what occurred in their deployment? These and other questions will be discussed in what follows, in which I have attempted to provide an objective and balanced description. This includes, among other things, addressing the problems that occurred due to differing mindsets.

This work is not just intended to further illuminate the history of the *Waffen-SS*, but also to offer new information to those interested in this historical period.

I want to thank everyone who helped me accomplish this work. The interviews with contemporary eyewitnesses were interesting and repeatedly provided information that I could not obtain from the archives.

It was difficult to treat such a broad topic comprehensively within 250 pages. Additions and further perspectives would be gladly received.

Rolf Michaelis
Berlin, March 2013

14. Waffen-Grenadier-Division der SS (*ukrainische Nr. 1*)

After Hitler had already approved the formation of an *SS-Gebirgs-Division* [SS Mountain *Division*] using Bosnian Croat volunteers,[1] a second so-called *fremdvölkischer Verband* [Foreign Peoples' formation] followed in the spring of 1943, with the establishment of an *SS-Freiwilligen-Division Galizien* [SS Volunteer *Division* Galician]. This was to be made up of of young Ukrainians, from the some 3.5 million people of Greek Catholic faith, who inhabited the district of Galicia (*Generalgouvernement* [General Government: Third Reich-occupied regional governments]). Ukrainian *Freiwilligen* of Greek Orthodox faith, who lived in the Lublin district in smaller numbers, were mainly recruited into the newly formed *Regimenter* regiments] of the *Ordnungspolizei* [Nazi Germany regular police]. The press published the following about this development on April 29, 1943:

> *"It has been made possible for the Galician-Ukrainian population to actively participate in the European freedom struggle against the Soviet Union, in their own military formation!"*

There was recruitment potential for both *Divisionen*, Bosnian and Galician, among the men who had already served in the Austro-Hungarian Army up until 1918. For these men, service on the German side under an Austrian *Führer* was not something entirely unknown. Within four weeks, about 80,000 volunteers reported for duty; of these, by the end of the first round of physicals on June 3, 1943, some 50,000 were provisionally accepted. The physicals were not intended to be strict and did not meet the standards of so-called *SS-Tauglichkeit* [SS physical fitness]. A meeting on April 12, 1943, established the following for this issue:

> *"In the light of the average inferior qualities of the local human material, particularly in racial terms, members of Rassegruppen [racial groups] II and IV will also be recruited."*

[1] These involved the later *13. Waffen-Gebirgs-Division der SS Handschar (kroatische Nr. 1)*. Cf.: Michaelis, Rolf: *Die Gebirgs-Divisionen der Waffen-SS*, Barsinghausen, 2008.

Himmler inspecting Ukrainian SS Freiwilligen [volunteers]. The minimum soldiers' height was reduced to 1.60m at the end of 1943.

Map exercise in the trenches.

In terms of racial groups, the *Rasse- und Siedlungshauptamt* [Race and Settlement Central Bureau], made a distinction between:

I	pure Nordic,
II	predominantly Nordic or false
III	Nordic, or false with slight Alpine, Dinaric or Mediterranean additional features
IV	mixed race, mainly of eastern or Alpine origin
V	mixed race of non-European origin.

Initially, the *Freiwilligen* were supposed to be between 17-30 years old and at least 1.65m tall. However, since surprisingly it was only possible to recruit about 8,000 volunteers, a second draft followed immediately, for which the age range was expanded to 16 to 36 years, and the minimum height reduced to 1.60m.

On July 30, 1943, the *SS-Führungshauptamt* [Operational Headquarters] (*SS-FHA*) issued a decree calling for forming the infantry *Divisionen* at *SS-Truppenübungsplatz* [troop training grounds] Heidelager, organized as follows:

Divisionsstab [*Division* Staff]
Galizisches SS-Freiwilligen-Regiment 1 [Galician SS Volunteer Regiment] (*I. – III. Bataillon* [Battalion])
Galizisches SS-Freiwilligen-Regiment 2 (*I. – III. Bataillon*)
Galizisches SS-Freiwilligen-Regiment 3 (*I. – III. Bataillon*)
Galizisches SS-Freiwilligen-Artillerie-Regiment [Volunteer Artillery Regiment] (*I. – IV. Abteilung* [Detachments])
SS-Panzerjäger-Abteilung [Anti-Tank Detachment]/*Galizische SS-Freiwilligen-Division*
SS-Pionier-Bataillon [Engineer Battalion]/*Galizische SS-Freiwilligen-Division*
SS-Nachrichten-Abteilung [Communications Detachment]/*Galizische SS-Freiwilligen-Division*
SS-Feldersatz-Bataillon [Field Replacement Battalion]/*Galizische SS-Freiwilligen-Division*
SS-Flak-Abteilung [Anti-Aircraft Detachment]/*Galizische SS-Freiwilligen-Division*
SS-Füsilier-Bataillon [Infantry Battalion]/*Galizische SS-Freiwilligen-Division*
SS-Wirtschafts-Bataillon [Supply Unit]/*Galizische SS-Freiwilligen-Division*
SS-Sanitäts-Abteilung [Medical Unit]/*Galizische SS-Freiwilligen-Division*

Former *SS und Polizeiführer* [SS and Police Commander] for *Weißruthenien* ["White Ruthenia," Byelorussia], *SS-Brigadeführer* [Brigade Commander], and

Generalmajor [Brigadier General] *der Waffen-SS und Polizei* [Police] Schimana was initially responsible for the formation. The language for giving orders was to be Ukrainian, and the language of the unit command, German.

On October 22, 1943, within the serial numbering of *Waffen-SS* formations, the unit was designated the ***14. Galizische SS-Freiwilligen-Infanterie-Division***.

Initially reduced to *Regimenter* [Regiments] due to lack of personnel, they designated as *SS-Freiwilligen-Infanterie-Regimenter 29-31 (galizische Nr. 1 - 3).*[2]

In the same month, Schimana handed the formation over to *SS-Oberführer* [Brigadier General] Freitag and himself became *Höherer SS- und Polizeiführer Griechenland* [Higher SS and Police Commander for Greece]. *SS-Oberführer* Freitag had previously led *Waffen-SS Brigaden* and *Divisionen*, but had apparently (no longer) had the mental strength to lead such a large formation. Six months earlier, Himmler had removed him from command of *8. SS-Kavallerie-Division* [Cavalry *Division*] due to incapacity. Possibly due to the lack of any alternative, however, he was again entrusted by Himmler with a *Divisionenkommando* [*Division* Command].

Through the second draft, the *Division* in any case reached by year's end a strength of:

	Führer	***Unterführer***	***Männer***	**Total**
Actual	256	499	11,929	12,634
	2%	3.5%	94.5%	100%
Authorized	480	2,587	11,682	14,749
	3.3%	17.5%	79.2%	100%

To bring the formation up to authroized strength again, nearly 2,000 Greek Orthodox Ukrainians in the ranks of the *Ordnungspolizei* [Nazi Germany regular police] were ordered to report to *Galizischen SS-Freiwilligen-Regimenter 6* and *7* of the *Division*. However, this did not change the relationship of the *Führerkorps* [Officers' Corps] to the men. Instead of a ratio of over 20% *Führer* [officers] and *Unterführer* [non-commissioned officers], only about 5% were available. The background for this was the lack of trained Ukrainian *Führer* and *Unterführer*. After the Polish-Soviet War of 1920-21, Galacia became part of Poland, and the Ukrainian population was thereafter given extremely restrictive treatment. This included discrimination in the Polish Army. It was almost impossible for them to reach a service rank. As a result, it was especially the older men drafted into the *Division*, who had already served in the *k.u.k.* [*kaiserlich und königlich*: imperial and royal] – *Armee Osterreich-Ungarn* [Austrian-Hungarian Army] as officers or non-commissioned officers. These men, at 50 to 60 years of age, were not only far too old, but also – since they had not been in active service for at least twenty-five

[2] Organization of the *III. Battalione* started in May 1944 but due to the losses in the von Brody pocket, it was already disbanded in the summer of 1944.

Inspection of SS-Nachrichten-Abteilung 14 and constructing a foxhole for Grenadiere.

SS-Brigadeführer Freitag presents the Division Führerkorps to Reichsführer-SS [Reich SS Commander] Himmler.

years – had none of the knowledge necessary for a modern war at all. Since also the German *Rahmenpersonal* [cadre staff] were often not motivated to serve with foreign soldiers, it was virtually impossible to use the unit successfully in a front line deployment.

In early February 1944, a *Regiment*-strength *Kampfgruppe* [combat task force] was transferred to the *Höheren SS- und Polizeiführer Ost* to fight partisans in the Lublin district. This was a motorized *Grenadier-Bataillon* and a *schweres Bataillon* [heavy battalion], which was, starting February 16, 1944, to combat the approximately 2,000 partisans suspected to be in the local forests of the greater Zamosc area. On March 20, 1944, the so-called *SS-Kampfgruppe Beyersdorff* rejoined the *Division*; it had meanwhile been transferred from the *SS-Truppenübungsplatz* Heidelager (Debica) to *SS-Truppenübungsplatz* Neuhammer.

At the same time, there was a third draft of troops, which conscripted some 1,000 recruits. One of them was Myron Pryjma:

> *"I was born in March 1929 as son of the pastor Myron Pryjma in Lviv [German: Lemberg]. My father was editor of the parish newsletter Neta (Goal) and collected information on the famine of 1932-1933. He published a book about this tragedy, under the initials M.P. Not publishing this work under his full name saved his life later on. He was arrested on November 25, 1940 by the Bolsheviks and exiled to Siberia for fifteen years.*
>
> *When the German troops arrived in Lemberg, my mother, grandmother and I – like thousands of others – sought for him in the many prisons. We saw hundreds of corpses, but did not find him. We learned later that he had been sent to Siberia before the war. I attended grade school and then a Gymnasiumn [academic high school] that was closed in March 1944, when the Red Army was already close to Galicia. I then volunteered for the 14. Galizischen SS-Freiwilligen-Division. To be taken at all, I said that I was two years older than I was. In the first days of April 1944, I was already in SS-Feldersatz-Bataillon 14 at Truppenübungsplatz Neuhammer.*

About a year after it was formed, Himmler visited the *Division* on May 6, 1944, with the *Gouverneur* of the Galicia District. The troops demonstrated combat exercises and various military units held a parade for the visit. Himmler appeared very pleased and stated that the *Division* would soon be ready for action. The lack of *Rahmenpersonal* was also documented by later *SS-Obersturmführer* [SS First Lieutenant] Dornbusch, who came from the *SS-Ärztlichen Akademie* [Medical Academy] in Graz, and was assigned to be adjutant of *II./SS-Freiwilligen-Regiment 29*:

> *"On Sept. 1, 1940, I began studies at the SS-Ärztlichen Akademie in Graz, which were finished off by attending the SS-Junkerschule [Officers' Training*

School] at Tölz. I was actually assigned as a military doctor, however, I was given command of the 14. Galizischen SS-Freiwilligen-Division and was unceremoniously appointed Bataillon adjutant. I still remember well Himmler's visit to Truppenübungsplatz Neuhammer. After the combat exercises, during the parade before Himmler – on horseback – I was trying, to maintain the correct distance from my Bataillonskommandeur [Battalion Commander]. Then I went to the registry office at Lipschau-Dohm to get married, and then had to be back punctually in the evening for Himmler's speech at the Casino in Neuhammer. It was a very long evening and we were presented to Himmler. His speech was translated into Ukrainian and the next day, accompanied by a small escort, he left the Truppenübungsplatz.

Since I went ahead and took my wedding leave, I was replaced as adjutant and, after returning, was transferred to the schwere Kompanie [heavy company] of the Feldersatz-Bataillon."

The formation, renamed the ***14. SS-Waffen-Grenadier-Division (galizische Nr. 1)*** was, due to the Soviet summer offensive launched on June 22, 1944, brought up a few days later to a strength of:

	Führer	***Unterführer***	***Männer***	**Total**
Actual	346	1,131	13,822	15,299
	2.3%	7.4%	90.3%	100%
Authorized	480	2,587	11,682	14,749
	3.3%	17.5%	79.2%	100%

They were transferred to the *XIII. Armee-Korps (Heeresgruppe Nordukraine)* [Army Corps (Army Group North Ukraine)] on June 27, 1944. Since the formation still lacked about 50% of *Führer* and *Unterführer* and those it had were to a large extent unfit, its readiness for action was highly questionable. The *Division* moved initially into a second line about 12km west of Brody behind the *HKL [Hauptkampflinie*: main combat line] and was deployed against Soviet partisans in the Olesko-Podhorce-Konty region.

The Red Army attacked *Heeresgruppe Nordukraine* on July 13, 1944, in its Summer Offensive and two days later achieved a breakthrough between the *XIII. Armee-Korps* and *XXXXII. Armee-Korps*, which adjoined it to the south. Since the German troops in the *HKL* were unable to reestablish contact, *14. Waffen-Grenadier-Division der SS*, stationed in the area southeast of Olesko, was alerted. While still on the march to the front, *Waffen-Grenadier-Regiment der SS 30* was heavily attacked by Soviet artillery and strafed by low-flying aircraft; it was deemed wiped out just two hours later. Only the deployment of the other two *Grenadier-Regimenter* made it possible to initially seal off the enemy breakthrough south of Brody.

3.7cm Flak 36 [Flugabwehrkanone: Anti-aircraft gun] of SS-Flak-Abteilung 14.

The Divisionskommandeur [Divisional commander] instructing an SS-Freiwilliger [SS volunteer].

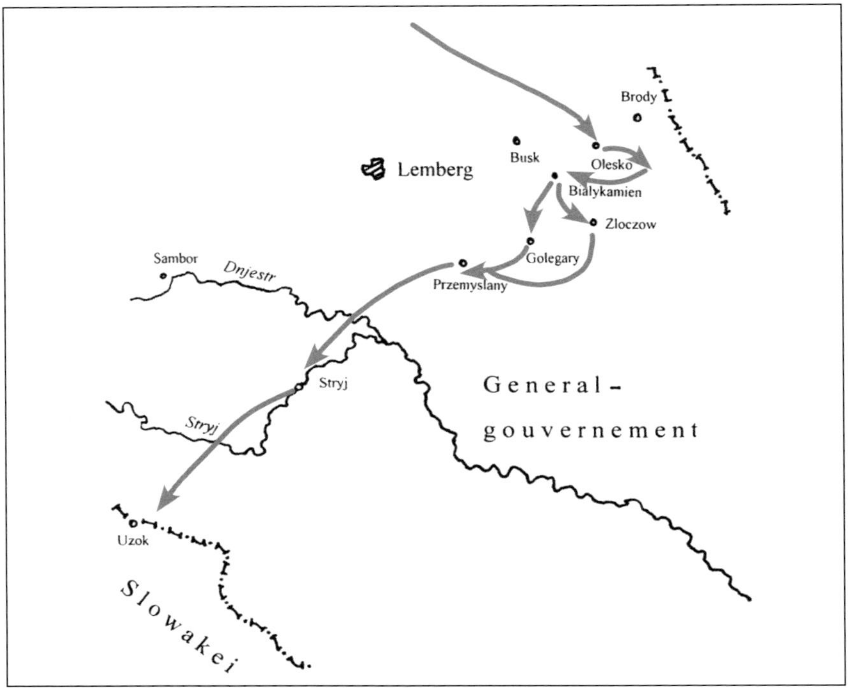

After the Red Army pushed forward in a broad sweep through Radziechow southwards towards Busk on July 17, 1944, and then on from the Zborow area towards Zloczow, it succeeded the next day at Busk to combine its armored advance guard and thus encircle large sections of the *XIII. Armee-Korps* in the Busk-Turze-Padhorce-Majdan-Opaki-Kruhow-Kniaze region into a pocket. The Ukrainian SS units were deployed on the hills to the east of the Padhorze-Zloczow road but, demoralized by the force of the attack, hardly showed any resistance.

When the *8. Panzer* and *20. Panzer-Grenadier-Division* relief attempt from the west failed, the encircled pocket was rapidly compressed into the Olesko-Bialykamien-Sassow area. At this point, the *XIII. Armee-Korps* were allowed to abandon their positions and fight their way back to the west.

On the morning of July 21, 1944, the units began their breakout from the Bialykamien area towards Kniaze, across the Bug River. The constant strafing and tank fire caused chaos and panic among the often almost leaderless units. In addition, *Divisionskommandeur SS-Brigadeführer* Freitag lost his nerve and declared himself that evening unfit to carry on with his command. As a result, the *Kommandierende General* [Commanding General] of *XIII. Armee-Korps* (*General der Infanterie* Hauffe) put the remnants of the *Division* under the command of the *361. Infanterie-Division (Generalmajor* Lindemann). When he was taken prisoner the next day, Freitag, as ranking officer, had to take over command of the remnants of both *Divisionen*. With the loss of all their heavy weapons, the soldiers, with no unit cohesion, attempted to break through, from Kniaze towards Gologory and Zloczow. Erich Rommel recalls:

> *"The Division was destroyed in the pocket west of Brody, including blatant collapse of the earlier strict discipline. At the end, we were a motley crew thrown together from the Heer [Army], Luftwaffe [Air Force], and Waffen-SS – without heavy weapons – with little ammunition and without air support. I spent the day in the pocket with SS-Unterscharführer [Junior Squad Leader] Daumann, the driver of our regimental commander, SS-Obersturmbannführer [SS Lieutenant Colonel] Dern, and we always kept calling out to each other during the constant low-flying aircraft attacks, asking if the other was still alive. Again and again we tried to crack the pocket open, in Kampfgruppen which had just been pulled together. For the present, all was in vain. In a village full of wounded, with Red Cross flag laid out, my comrade and I were separated when the Russian low-flying planes shot everything to pieces. The wounded all stayed in the pocket. The roadway was clogged with vehicles and men; nothing moved.*
>
> *On July 18, 1944, I was together with an SS man of my Division, a Ukrainian and a German Feldwebel [Sergeant]. The Feldwebel had an irrepressible persuasive power, and he said to me over and over: "We will surely get home, you have to really believe that!" Just as he wanted to look up over an embankment for the enemy, he was hit by a machine-gun burst and he rolled down right to my feet.*
>
> *On July 20, 1944, I was lying with a Kampfgruppe in a wheat field and shooting at single Russians with a carbine, but they were pretty far away. I suddenly felt a hit in my right heel: I had been hit by shrapnel. Since we were under constant fire, it took a long time before I got an emergency bandage. Then we went on, but I only had my left boot; they had cut off my right one.*
>
> *We lay for hours by the road, where Soviet armored reconnaissance cars were driving by at intervals, firing from all gun barrels.*
>
> *On the evening of July 21, 1944, I got out of the pocket with some comrades. In a small village, we met many Red Army soldiers who had surrendered. A badly wounded Russian was lying on a destroyed Panzerabwehrkanone [anti-tank gun] and held out both arms to me: in one a packet of ruble bills, in the other a family photo. Dead comrades and Red Army soldiers were lying in the little brooks; but we drank the water anyway because we were so thirsty. Shot horses were screaming like people in agony!"*

By July 24, 1944, 3,000 Ukrainians had reached Carpathian Ukraine, moving by way of Przemyslany-Stry-Sambor-Uzsok. Some 8,000 men had been killed, taken prisoner by the Soviets, or deserted to the UPA (Ukranian Insurgent Army – national Ukrainian partisans). The later *SS-Obersturmführer* Dornbusch recalls:

> *"The commander of the schwere Kompanie/SS-Feldersatz-Bataillon 14 was SS-Obersturmführer Schneller. There was an alarm on the day the Soviets broke through. We saw the Russians on the parallel street moving westwards – in no time, SS-Obersturmführer Schneller was gone (sic!).*
>
> *As the next ranking officer, I had to lead the Kompanie. This now consisted of only two German and two Ukrainian Unterführer – the rest were Ukrainian Mannschaften [other ranks]. You could at least exchange a few words with them in German, to the extent these were students or pupils. We were in Besbrody, near Busk, and had no contact with the enemy during the encirclement. But my successor as adjutant of II./Waffen-Grenadier-Regiment der SS 29 fell in the command post at Brody from a direct hit – the Bataillonskommandeur at that time was counted among the missing."*

A year after it was formed, the *Division* had been obliterated within ten days. The unit had come to the front about 11,000 strong, but only about 3,000 of them got back to the German lines. On August 7, 1944, despite his now negative view of the Ukrainian *Freiwilligen*, Himmler ordered *14. Waffen-Grenadier-Division der SS* to be newly reorganized.

He also ordered that about 1,000 Ukrainians be used to reorganize *III./SS-Panzergrenadier-Regiment 10 Westland.* Formed on *SS-Truppenübungsplatz Böhmen* [Bohemia], the newly formed *Bataillon* was transferred in September 1944 by train to Modlin and placed under command of the *5. SS-Panzer-Division "Wiking"* [SS Tank Division "Viking"]. Deployed in the area of Nowy Dvor, starting on October 10, 1944, the men were engaged in the heaviest fighting in the third defensive battle in front of Warsaw. After the Red Army halted their offensive on October 28, 1944, the *Führer* [commanding officer] of *5. SS-Panzer-Division "Wiking," SS-Standartenführer* Ullrich, on November 4, 1944, released the remaining 300 Ukrainians back to the *14. Waffen-Grenadier-Division der SS.* Former *Waffen-Grenadier* Ostap Hladkiwskyj (*11./SS-Panzergrenadier-Regiment 10 Westland*) recalls:

> *"I was born on May 15, 1926, in Galicia. Under Polish rule, we Ukrainians suffered a lot. My father, who worked for the Polish government, had to convert from Greek Catholic to the Roman Catholic faith, so as not to lose his job.*
>
> *In the summer of 1944, all 16- to 36-year-old men in our village were rounded up. At the Arbeitsamt [Labor Office], you could decide whether you wanted to go to work in Germany or fight with weapon in hand. To get as far away from the Russians as they could, many went to Germany.*

I signed up with about thirty others for the SS-Division and was seen off with flowers and song. In Lviv we were given a physical and sent by train in civilian clothes to Kirchbaum, near Neuhammer. In Lviv [German: Lemberg] we were given a physical and then sent by train in civilian clothes to Kirchbaum, near Świętoszów [German: Neuhammer]. There 1,000 men were initially pulled out and ordered to the Heidelager. Finally we got to the Protektorat Böhmen und Mähren [Protectorate of Bohemia and Moravia], in the Seltschan area. We now had real Knobelbecher [jackboots] instead of lace-up shoes, and better uniforms. We still had collar patches with a lion, however, as well as the rank designation of Waffen-Grenadier. We were very angry about this degradation in rank, in contrast to our German comrades, who became SS-Panzergrenadiere.

For our training, there were big problems with language, so we simply imitated what the others showed us. In September 1944, we were taken to the station by truck and from there went by train to Modlin, where the 5. SS-Panzer-Division Wiking was. We now knew that we were going to the front and we were afraid. On October 10, 1944, all hell broke loose. We were bombarded by artillery and Stalinorgeln [Stalin's "organ pipes": Soviet rocket launchers] and finally came masses of tanks. They overran us and we had to fight our way back in small groups. Our comrades kept calling: Quickly, quickly, keep coming! We finally reached our own Panzer and were saved. Soon it was announced that all Ukrainians were to be assembled, and sent to the 14. Waffen-Grenadier-Division der SS."

This *Division* was at *Truppenübungsplatz* Neuhammer and the around 8,000 men – including *III. Bataillone der drei Waffen-Grenadier-Regimenter* as well as the *Waffen-Grenadier-Ausbildungs- und Ersatz-Regiments der SS* [Training and Replacement Regiment] *14* – were used for reinforcements. By September 1944, *Division* strength was already back to:

	Führer	***Unterführer***	***Männer***	**Total**
Actual	261	673	11,967	12,901
	2%	5.2%	92.8%	100%
Auhorized	480	2,587	11,682	14,749
	3.3%	17.5%	79.2%	100%

However, around two-thirds of the *Führer* and *Unterführer* positions were unfilled making it impossible to deploy the *Division* as a cohesive formation.

After the Slovak National Uprising broke out on August 23, 1944, the *14. Waffen Grenadier Division der SS* was ordered to set up a *Kampfgruppe* on September 19, 1944, in the strength of a reinforced *Battalion*.

Training on the light 7.5cm Infanteriegeschütz [infantry gun] 18 ("Gypsy Artillery").

By 1943-44, old and young alike served together in the 14. SS-Freiwilligen-Division Galizien, as in purely German units.

This *SS-Kampfgruppe Wildner* reached western Slovakia on September 27, 1944, and was placed under command of *SS-Kampfgruppe* Schill, which was among the units in Nova Bana (Königsberg) -Sv. Kriz (Heiligenkreuz) -Bánska Bystrica (Neusohl) fighting against the insurgents.

On October 7, 1944, the order came that the entire *14. Waffen-Grenadier-Division der SS* was to be transferred to Slovakia – for use at least in limited security operations. On October 15, 1944, transport began from Neuhammer to Zilina and deployment under *Höherer SS- und Polizeiführer Slowakei* [Slovakia]. For this, *SS-Kampfgruppe Wittenmeyer* was formed from the reinforced *II./ Waffen-Grenadier-Regiment der SS 30*. The *Kampfgruppe* was deployed at times together with elements of *SS-Sonderregiment* [Special Regiment] *Dirlewanger* in the area of Poprad-Neudorf.

The *Division* itself moved into quarters in a 40km x 50km region:

Divisionstab [Division staff]	Zilina [German: Sillein]
Waffen-Grenadier-Regiment der SS 29	Kysucké N. Mesto
Waffen-Grenadier-Regiment der SS 30	V. Bytca
Waffen-Grenadier-Regiment der SS 31	Sv. Martin
Waffen-Artillerie-Regiment der SS 14	Vrtuky
SS-Feldersatz-Bataillon 14	Belá
SS-Flak-Abteilung 14	Vrutky
SS-Füsilier-Bataillon 14	Rajec
W.-Grenadier-Ausb. u. Ers.-Regiment der SS 14	Cadca
SS-Panzerjäger-Abteilung 14	Sv. Martin

In December 1944, the units were used to expand a number of defensive positions, including along the Váh River [German: Waag] or in Nitra position northwards from Sv. Martin via Vrutky.

When the Red Army crossed the Hungarian-Slovak border in late 1944 and advanced by way of Levice northwards to Schemnitz, a *Regiment*-strength *Kampfgruppe* was formed and sent to join *Armeegruppe Wöhler*, which was fighting about 60km distant. In January 1945, the *SS-Kampfgruppe* rejoined the *Division*, which, as a German concession was allowed as of January 15, 1945, to be called *"Ukrainian."* It was designated from then as ***14. Waffen-Grenadier-Division der SS (ukrainische Nr. 1)***.

Because of the Soviet thrust into Slovakia, the unit was ordered to move to Styria on January 26, 1945. Rather than have the relatively well-equipped formation reinforce the embattled front in the region, it was decided to allow it to march 400km southwest towards Marburg: a note on the German leadership's assessment of the fighting capacity and morale of the Ukrainians.

Placed under command of the *Höheren SS- und Polizeiführer Alpenland* to combat partisans, it secured the Bacher Mountains in the area of Cilli-Marburg. The former *Waffen-Grenadier* Ostap Hladkiwskyj recalls:

> *"In February 1945, we began to redeploy to Slovenia. First, we marched during the day, and when the bombers attacked us, only at night. In Slovenia, we moved into quarters in a few small villages and began Aufklärungsunternehmen [reconnaissance operations]. We were to hunt down the Tito partisans day and night. But usually they evaded us. Only once we got caught in an ambush and had a few wounded.*
>
> *We never had enough sleep and were always hungry. A soldier of our Bataillon was publicly executed because he had eaten his Eiserne Portion [emergency rations]. While the population in Slovakia was very nice, the Slovenes were just as hostile to us as the Czechs had been when I met them during my training in Protektorat Böhmen und Mähren."*

The lion from the Galician coat of arms was introduced starting 1943 for the 14. SS-Freiwilligen-Division "Galizien" and worn by most of the soldiers. (left center, Führer version.)

When the unit was renamed the 1. Division der Ukrainischen Nationalarmee [Ukrainian National Army], some metal cockades and collar patches with the Ukrainian trident were issued and worn.

At the beginning of March 1945, elements of the *Division* took part in a large operation of the *Höheren SS- und Polizeiführer Alpenland* north of Laibach in the Savinjske Alps and Boskovecz region. After traversing an approach route of about 100km, the Ukrainians climbed up the 1,500m high mountains and tried without success to apprehend the partisans in the Prassberg-Laufen-Sulzbach area. After three days, the men were ordered back to the Bacher Mountains. From March 18-22, 1945, the units scoured the Poßruck Mountains and, crossing the river Drava southwards, again the Bacher Mountains.

When Hitler the next day showed he was paying attention to accounts of the *14. Waffen-Grenadier-Division der SS* in the evening briefing, he explained:

> *"There are constant lies about a Galician Division. Is the same as the Ukrainian? If it is the same as the Austrian Ruthenians, you can do nothing other than immediately take away their weapons. The Austrian Ruthenians have become pacifists. They were lambs, not wolves. They were already miserable in the Austrian Armee. It's all self-deception."*

He failed to recall that two years before, he had given the command to form this *Division*. Anyway, he saw the *"self-deception"* of organizing numbers of formations that were of no use to Germany.

The *Division* had at this time:

2,400	*Pistolen* [pistols]
9,000	*Gewehre* [rifles]
610	*Maschinenpistolen* [submachine guns]
70	*Gewehre mit Zielfernrohr* [telescopic sights]
65	*Gewehre K 43* [K rifles]
434	*leichte Maschinengewehre* [light machine guns]
96	*schwere Maschinengewehre* [heavy machine guns]
22	*Flammenwerfer* [flame throwers]
1	*Panzerabwehrkanone 5cm*
11	*Panzerabwehrkanonen 7.5cm*
9	*Flugabwehrkanonen 3.7cm*
17	*leichte Infanteriegeschütze 7.5cm* [light infantry guns]
3	*schwere Infanteriegeschütze 15cm* [heavy infantry guns]
37	*leichte Feldhaubitzen 10.5cm* [light field howitzers]
6	*schwere Feldhaubitzen 15cm* [heavy field howitzers]
58	*Lastkraftwagen* [trucks]
4	*Schützenpanzerwagen* [armored personnel cars]

This meant that this unit was fully equipped – at a time when proven front *Divisionen,* after the fierce battles and heavy losses during retreats, had only a fraction of their equipment. As a result of this fact, at the end of March 1945 the decision was made to disarm the *Division* and split up the men, just as was done with many other foreign soldiers, into *Schanzkommando* [trench digging units] and to use them to build positions.

However, when on March 31, 1945, strong enemy forces broke through between the *IV. SS-Panzer-Korps (6. Armee)* and *XXII. Gebirgs-Korps* [Mountain Corps] *(2. Panzer-Armee)*, the *14. Waffen-Grenadier-Division der SS* was alerted and thrown into the 30km distant threatened area. During the day of April 1, 1945, it was able to close the gap in the front between Feldbach and Gleichenberg and hold on until the arrival of the *I. Kavallerie-Korps*.

Fierce fighting followed around the strategically important Stradnerkogel, in which the Ukrainians were repeatedly driven from the positions by heavy artillery fire, and then recaptured them in close combat. When this was no longer possible, *SS-Brigadeführer* Freitag – as he had earlier at Brody – lost his nerve.

Waffen-Grenadier-Regimenter der SS 29 and *30* were so decimated in the fighting that they had to be reduced from three to two *Bataillone* and reorganized. For this, the *Division* received 2,500 untrained *Luftwaffe* members as infantry. Since these men also had no weapons, *SS-Brigadeführer* Freitag intended to disarm 2,500 Ukrainian *Division* members. Since the *Luftwaffe* soldiers, inexperienced in ground combat, could not initially be expected to increase the unit's fighting power, about half of them were sent for a four-week training to *SS-Feldersatz-Bataillon 14*. Specialists (for example radio operators) were sent immediately to the units. Around 800 men re-formed the disbanded *III. Waffen-Grenadier-Regiment der SS 30.*

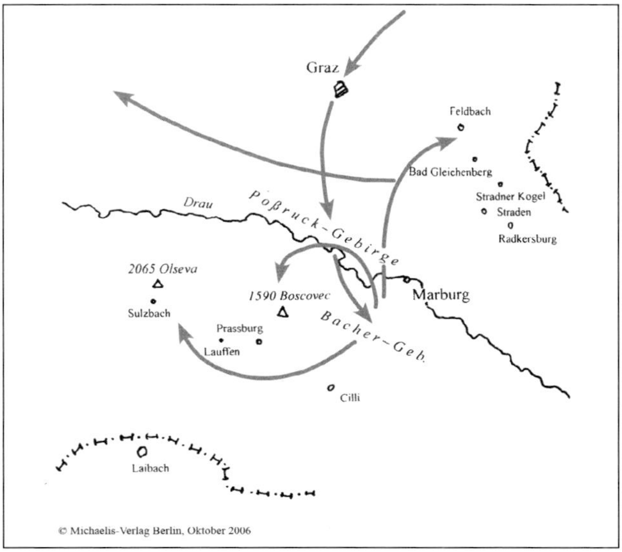

On April 11, 1944, *Waffen-Grenadier-Regiment der SS 299* was on both sides of the village of Trautmannsdorf. The other two *Grenadier-Regimenter* were behind the *3. Kavallerie-Division,* adjoining on the right side, in the area north of Straden. In mid-April 1945, it was placed under command of the *IV. SS-Panzer-Korps (6. Armee)*, to fix the about 20km long positions between Feldberg and Schloss Gleichenberg. While the three *Regimenter* were in the *HKL, SS-Pionier-Bataillon 14, SS-Füsilier-Bataillon 14,* and *SS-Feldersatz-Bataillon 14* formed the *Division* reserves.

The Ukrainian National Committee was established on March 17, 1945, and General Shandruk was appointed *Oberbefehlshaber* [Commander-in-Chief] of the Ukrainian National Army. Then, on April 27, 1945, *14. Waffen-Grenadier-Division der SS (ukrainische Nr. 1)* was renamed the ***1. Division der Ukrainische Nationalarmee***. Ostap Hladkiwskyj recalls:

> *"At the last, we were called the Ukrainian National Army. We had put down our weapons and after this symbolic gesture, we swore a new oath to Ukraine. Rearmed, we moved again into the HKL."*

Discipline was lost to some extent in the last days of the war. The Ukrainians plundered the houses in the surrounding villages, chanting repeatedly: *"Swoboda, Swoboda"* (Freedom, freedom). This demonstrated that they had felt exploited by Germany.

As British troops were advancing into the Klagenfurt area in early May 1945, the *Divisionkommando* made contact with them. At the command of the *IV. SS-Panzer-Korps*, however, the soldiers were marched via Tamsweg to Spittal and from there into the POW camp at Rimini.

Since the Ukrainians had had Polish citizenship in Galicia, they were not turned over to the Soviet Union, but after internment could choose whether they would be released home or to Germany, Austria, England, Canada, or even Australia.

Except for a certain propaganda effect, the formation of this unit brought virtually no benefit to Germany. The initial enthusiasm fell sharply after the first deployment due to the developing situation. After just a one-week deployment, the *Division* was again commanded to the front only about eight months later. For eight months, a 14,000-man-strong unit was given daily rations and equipped with all heavy weapons, while other *Divisionen* were in daily combat without any *Panzerabwehr* and *Artillerie*, against an enemy far superior in numbers and materiel. Possibly, a change in the *Divisionkommando* and sufficient training of the Ukrainian men as *Führer* and *Unterführer* could have created a more combat-ready unit.

Kommandeure [Commanders]:
04/43 – 10/43 *SS-Brigadeführer* Schimana
10/43 – 05/45 *SS-Brigadeführer* Freitag

Feldpost [Field Post] numbers:

*Divisions*stab [*Division* Staff]	15 000
Waffen-Grenadier-Regiment der SS 29 (galizische Nr. 1)	00 650
I. Bataillon	03 368
II. Bataillon	07 226
III. Bataillon	19 233
Waffen-Grenadier-Regiment der SS 30 (galizische Nr. 2)	05 330
I. Bataillon	09 084
II. Bataillon	10 227
III. Bataillon	23 374
Waffen-Grenadier-Regiment der SS 31 (galizische Nr. 3)	11 088
I. Bataillon	19 265
II. Bataillon	16 138
III. Bataillon	28 714
Waffen-Artillerie-Regiment der SS 14 (galizische Nr. 1)	02 002
I. Abteilung	21 985
II. Abteilung	15 107
III. Abteilung	20 213
IV. Abteilung	25 614
SS-Pionier-Bataillon 14	29 826
SS-Flak-Abteilung 14	57 966
SS-Panzerjäger-Abteilung 14	30 904
SS-Nachrichtentruppe 14	24 047
SS-Wirtschafts-Bataillon 14	06 771
SS-Nachschubtruppen 14	31 283
SS-Sanitäts-Abteilung 14	12 102
Waffen-Grenadier-Ausb.- u. Ers.-Regiment der SS 14	39 336
I. Bataillon	67 249
II. Bataillon	37 682
III. Bataillon	64 425

15. Waffen-Grenadier-Division der SS (*lettische Nr. 1*)

Excursus: Lettische SS-Freiwilligen-Legion [Latvian SS Volunteer Legion]

Since only about 8,000 Latvians had volunteered for the *Schutzmannschafts-Bataillone der Ordnungspolizei* [Auxilliary Police Battalions of the Nazi Police Force] from summer of 1941, and as a result of the tragedy of Stalingrad, Hitler authorized the organization of large military formations, including in Latvia.[3] As in the case of the Croatian and Galician *SS-Divisionen*, the *Waffen-SS* also took responsibility for recruitment, by which means they hoped to quickly recruit 50,000 men. Already on February 10, 1943, Hitler ordered the *SS-Hauptamt* [*SS* Central Office]:

> *"I order the formation of a Latvian SS-Freiwilligen-Legion. The size and type of unit depends on the number of available Latvian men."*

As a result of this order, after discussions with former Latvian General Bangerskis, who was appointed *Inspekteur* [Inspector] of the *Lettischen SS-Freiwilligen-Legion*, Himmler issued the guidelines for recruiting Latvians. Minimum heights were set for *Freiwilligen Polizei* personnel at 1.64m and for *Waffen-SS Freiwilligen* at 1.68m. The country's own administration, (*Generaldirektorat für Verteidigung* [Directorate General for Defense]) had to carry out the induction and physicals for the men. An *SS-Ergänzungskommando* [Supplementary or Replacement Command] was established in Riga, that eventually functioned as the *SS-Ersatzkommando Ostland* [*SS* Replacement Command for Eastern Lands] under the leadership of *SS-Standartenführer* Hierthes.

In the first draft, which followed quickly, men of the mandatory working ages, those born between 1919-1924, were registered for induction. Of the approximately 70,000 young Latvians registered, ultimately 30,000 volunteered for the *Lettische SS-Freiwilligen-Legion*. Himmler's expectations of 50,000 *Freiwilligen* were thus not met, due to the age limitations. However, they succeeded in forming a *Lettische SS-Freiwilligen-Division* with about 18,000 men and a *Lettische SS-Freiwilligen-Brigade* of about 8,000 men.

In contrast to the mostly *Bataillon*-strength *Freiwilligen* legions from western Europe (such as *Freiwilligen-Legion Flandern* [Volunteer Legion Flanders]), the title *Lettische SS-Freiwilligen-Legion* did not designate a military unit in itself, but was regarded as a collective name for all Latvian *SS Freiwilligen* who were

[3] In principle, Hitler had to date only allowed the formation of *Sicherungseinheiten* [security units], which could not be structured into *Bataillon* size. In addition to the fear that larger formations could become a security risk, the reluctance to have to deal with any associated political demands of respective foreign politicians, were the reasons for earlier refusal to take such a step.

Teofiis Dreimanis as a Kapralis [corporal] in 1939 in the Latvian Army and in 1943 as the Legions-Unterscharführer [SS Sergeant]. He served as a driving instructor in the Lettischen SS-Freiwilligen-Legion.

sent from that country to various military units. This also included those who, due to their limited capability, were sent to the *SS-Wachsturmbannen* [Camp Guard Units] for the *SS* concentration and labor camps.

Through a second wave of inductions in October 1943 (again of those born between 1919-1924 and 1912-1918), it was possible to draft about 5,000 more Latvians into the *Waffen-SS*. After those born in 1925 were also called up already a month later, on December 21, 1943, the *SS-FHA* [*Führungshauptamt*: Leadership Central Office] ordered the formation of the *SS-Freiwilligen-Grenadier-Ausbildungs- und Ersatz-Brigade 15* for these numerous recruits in Jelgava [German name Mitau]. Teofils Dreimanis was drafted in the fall of 1943. He remembers his service in the *Waffen-SS*:

> *"I was born in 1917 in Cesis and served 1939-1940 in the Latvian Army. In the fall of 1943, after the introduction of the Arbeitsdienstpflicht [Compulsory Labor Service] for my birth year, I was drafted and decided to enter the Militärdienst [Military Service]. First, I got my driving license for Vollkettenfahrzeuge [full-track vehicles] up to 40t and motorcycles and then worked briefly as a driving instructor for other recruits. In spring 1944, I was transferred to SS-Flak-Abteilung 19. My Kommandeur was Legion-Obersturmbannführer [Lieutenant Colonel] Harris Gusevs, who also commanded in summer 1944 the SS-Abteilung 106, made up of combined Flak-Abteilungen of both Latvian SS-Divisionen.*
>
> *Deployed to use the 8.8cm Flak, I took part in the retreat to the Velikaya River and then in the fighting in our homeland. In Sabile (Courland), I was taken prisoner by the Soviets. I lost my wristwatch and boots right away. I was allowed to work off my service in the Waffen-SS in forced labor in the Gulag in Karelia until 1959."*

In January 1944, in view of the imminent general mobilization, the order was issued for *2. Lettische SS-Freiwilligen-Brigade* to be used to reinforce the *19. Lettischen SS-Freiwilligen-Division*. Thus there were two *Grenadier-Divisionen*. In the wake of the collapse of the front in summer 1944 and the evacuation of many remnants of the *Polizei- und SS-Grenzschutz-Regimenter* [Police and *SS* Border Guard Regiments] to Germany, a Latvian *Feldersatz-Depot* [Field Replacement Depot] joined them, with a strength of about 10,000 men. Although there was a close relationship with the *Waffen-SS* – among other things, the *Kommandeur* was a member of the *Waffen-SS* – this did not appear in the unit designations. However, the *Lettische Feldersatz-Depot* had, at least in terms of organizational planning, an *Infanterie-Division 44*, thus constituting, purely in terms of numbers, a third Latvian *Division*.

15. Waffen-Grenadier-Division der SS (lettische Nr. 1)

Already on February 15, 1943, Hitler issued the order to form a ***Lettische SS-Freiwilligen-Division***. The unit, which – in contrast to the first two foreign national *SS-Divisionen* – was allowed to use Latvian as its command language and its members were given the ranks of the *Waffen-SS*, with the prefix *"Legions-,"*[4] was to be formed as an *Infanterie-Division* in the *Reichskommissariat Ostland* [Reich Commissariat Eastern Lands]. The troops were based as follows:

Divisionsstab	Riga
Lett. SS-Freiwilligen-Regiment 1 (I. - III. Bataillon)	Paplaka-Libau
Lett.SS-Freiwilligen-Regiment 2 (I. - III. Bataillon)	Vainode
Lett.SS-Freiwilligen-Regiment 2 *(I. - III. Bataillon)*	Wenden
Lett.SS-Freiwilligen-Artillerie-Regiment (I. – IV. Abt.)	Mitau
SS-Panzerjäger-Abteilung/Lett. SS-Freiw.-Division	Grobina
SS-Pionier-Bataillon/Lett. SS-Freiw.-Division	Mitau
SS-Nachrichten-Abteilung/Lett. SS-Freiw.-Division	Tukkum
SS-Feldersatz-Bataillon/Lett. SS-Freiw.-Division	Cekule
SS-Flak-Abteilung/Lett. SS-Freiw.-Division	Grobina
SS-Füsilier-Bataillon/Lett. SS-Freiw.-Division	Ventspils

Due to the lack of a suitable Division *Kommandeur*, initially, the *Inspekteur der Artillerie und Flak* in the *SS-FHA, SS-Brigadeführer* Hansen, was appointed *Kommandeur* of the *Aufstellungsstab* [Unit Formation Staff]. After about ten weeks, he handed command over to the former *Kommandeur* of the *Waffen-SS* in the *Protektorat Böhmen und Mähren, SS-Brigadeführer* [*SS* Brigadier General] Pückler-Burghaus. Something new in command of a *Division* was the appointment of an *Infanterieführer* [Infantry Commander], who received his orders from the *Division Kommandeur*, but was explicitly responsible for the deployment of the infantry. In order to give the Latvian *Grenadieren* the sense that they were being led by a fellow countryman, on March 1, 1943, Arturs Silgailis, with the rank of *Legions-Standartenführer*, was appointed *Infanterieführer* of the Latvian *SS-Freiwilligen-Division*.

The greatest difficulty in forming the new *Division* was arming it. After the losses, not just of troops, in Stalingrad and Africa, by spring 1943, the German armaments industry was no longer able to meet the constant demands of the *Wehrmacht* [Armed Forces], *Waffen-SS* and *Polizei*. Therefore, the newly formed *Division* also could not be outfitted with weapons and equipment, as had been announced as early as April 1943. In the next months, these material shortages made comprehensive training of the recruits as a formation, all the more

[4] Such as, *Legions-Rottenführer* [*SS* Corporal] or *Legions-Hauptsturmführer* [*SS* Captain].

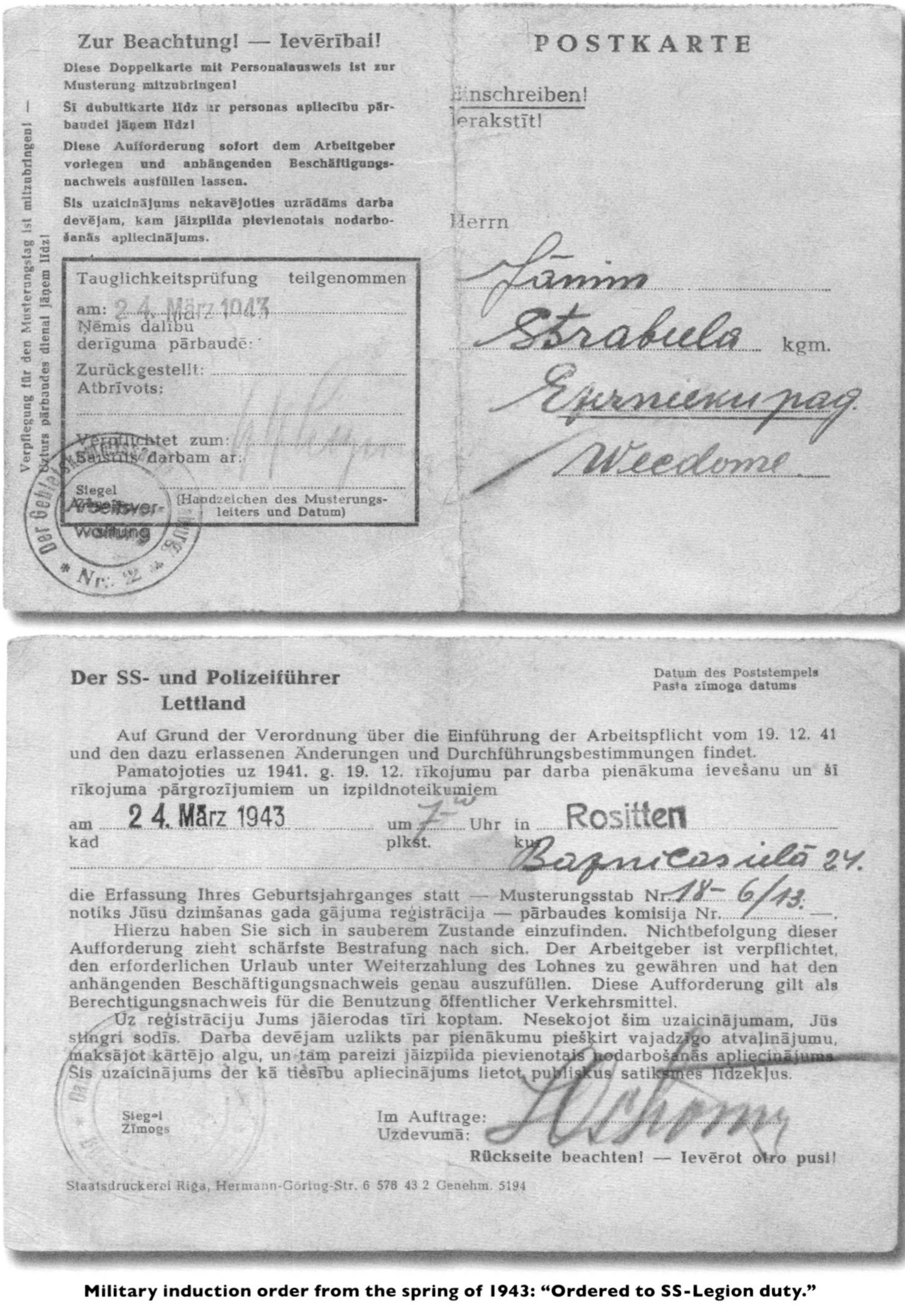

Zur Beachtung! — Ievērībai!

Diese Doppelkarte mit Personalausweis ist zur Musterung mitzubringen!

Šī dubultkarte līdz ar personas apliecību pārbaudei jāņem līdz!

Diese Aufforderung sofort dem Arbeitgeber vorlegen und anhängenden Beschäftigungsnachweis ausfüllen lassen.

Šis uzaicinājums nekavējoties uzrādāms darba devējam, kam jāizpilda pievienotais nodarbošanās apliecinājums.

Verpflegung für den Musterungstag ist mitzubringen! — Uzturs pārbaudes dienai jāņem līdz!

Tauglichkeitsprüfung teilgenommen am: 24. März 1943
Ņēmis dalību derīguma pārbaudē:
Zurückgestellt:
Atbrīvots:
Verpflichtet zum:
Saistīts darbam ar:
Siegel Zīmogs
(Handzeichen des Musterungsleiters und Datum)

POSTKARTE

Einschreiben!
Ierakstīt!

Herrn
Jānim
Strabula kgm.
Ezernieku pag.
Weedome

Der SS- und Polizeiführer Lettland

Datum des Poststempels
Pasta zīmoga datums

Auf Grund der Verordnung über die Einführung der Arbeitspflicht vom 19. 12. 41 und den dazu erlassenen Änderungen und Durchführungsbestimmungen findet.
Pamatojoties uz 1941. g. 19. 12. rīkojumu par darba pienākuma ievešanu un šī rīkojuma pārgrozījumiem un izpildnoteikumiem

am 24. März 1943 um 7[00] Uhr in Rositten
kad plkst. kur Baznīcas ielā 24.

die Erfassung Ihres Geburtsjahrganges statt — Musterungsstab Nr. 18–6/43.
notiks Jūsu dzimšanas gada gājuma reģistrācija — pārbaudes komisija Nr. ....
Hierzu haben Sie sich in sauberem Zustande einzufinden. Nichtbefolgung dieser Aufforderung zieht schärfste Bestrafung nach sich. Der Arbeitgeber ist verpflichtet, den erforderlichen Urlaub unter Weiterzahlung des Lohnes zu gewähren und hat den anhängenden Beschäftigungsnachweis genau auszufüllen. Diese Aufforderung gilt als Berechtigungsnachweis für die Benutzung öffentlicher Verkehrsmittel.
Uz reģistrāciju Jums jāierodas tīri koptam. Nesekojot šim uzaicinājumam, Jūs stingri sodīs. Darba devējam uzlikts par pienākumu piešķirt vajadzīgo atvaļinājumu, maksājot kārtējo algu, un tam pareizi jāizpilda pievienotais nodarbošanās apliecinājums. Šis uzaicinājums der kā tiesību apliecinājums lietot publiskus satiksmes līdzekļus.

Siegel
Zīmogs

Im Auftrage:
Uzdevumā:

Rückseite beachten! — Ievērot otro pusi!

Staatsdruckerei Riga, Hermann-Göring-Str. 6 578 43 2 Genehm. 5194

Military induction order from the spring of 1943: "Ordered to SS-Legion duty."

difficult, so that, later on, the *Division* was not entirely prepared for its upcoming deployment.

After a six-month training period, at the end of September 1943, around 1,000 soldiers were transferred to *2. Lettischen SS-Freiwilligen-Brigade*, which had suffered heavy losses during the fighting on the Volkhov River.

A month later, the *Waffen-SS* units were serially numbered. *Lettische SS-Freiwilligen-Division* was given number **15** and the *Regimenter* the designations:

*SS-Freiwilligen-**Grenadier**-Regiment **32** (lettische Nr. 3)*[5]
*SS-Freiwilligen-**Grenadier**-Regiment **33** (lettische Nr. 4)*
*SS-Freiwilligen-**Grenadier**-Regiment **34** (lettische Nr. 5)*
*SS-Freiwilligen-Artillerie-Regiment **15** (lettische Nr. 1)*

The unit formation was to be completed, in accordance with orders, within eight months,[6] and thus the *15. Lettische SS-Freiwilligen-Division* received its movement orders at the beginning of November 1943, to join *Heeresgruppe Nord* [Army Group North]. Placed under command of the *XXXXIII. Armee-Korps*, the formations moved first into a second line (Barbarossa position) north of Nevel, which was about 5km behind the actual *HKL* (*Hauptkampflinie*) [main front line]. The *Division* command post was set up in Novosokolniki. The *Grenadier Kompanien* were in turns inserted into *83.* and *205. Infanterie-Division* positions, to gain their first experience on the front. At the same time, *SS-Freiwilligen-Artillerie-Regiment 15* was placed under the command of *Artillerie-Regiment 205*. Elements of *SS-Freiwilligen-Grenadier-Regiment 34* took part in an anti-partisan operation near Ostrow until November 20, 1943, in the sector of the *281. Sicherungs-Division* [Security *Division*].

On December 31, 1943, the *Division* reported a strength of:

	Führer	***Unterführer***	***Männer***	**Total**
Actual	471	1,330	13,391	15,192
	3.1%	8.75%	88.15%	100%
Authorized	475	2,588	11,619	14,682
	3.2%	17.6%	79.2%	100%

Since almost half of the *Unterführer* positions were unfilled, the *Division* was still not fully combat-ready. Surprisingly, the *Führer* positions were filled to an extent almost corresponding to their authorized strength. This can be explained by the fact that after World War I until 1940, Latvia, like Estonia, had been a sovereign country for about twenty years and had its own army. In contrast to the *Galician*

[5] The two *Grenadier-Regimenter* of the *2. Lettischen SS-Freiwilligen-Brigade* were designated as *"lettische Nr. 1 und 2."*

[6] For an *Infanterie-Division*, an eight-month training period was generally considered sufficient.

SS-Freiwilligen-Division, in the Baltic countries, they could count on a modern, trained, and young *Führerkorps* [Officers Corps].

By the end of January 1944, it replaced the *21. Feld-Division (L)* in the sector of the *X. Armee-Korps* (*16. Armee*), south of Staraya Rusa. Here, the formation took over its own front sector, along a stretch that ran about 35km between Ratschi (about 40km west of Cholm) and Kamenka (about 20km northwest of Cholm), south of Lake Ilmen, along the Lovat River.

In the course of its winter offensive launched on December 24, 1943, the Red Army succeeded in breaking through *Heeresgruppe Nord* between the *18.* and *16. Armee*, the *Oberbefehlshaber* [Commander-in-Chief] of the *Heeresgruppe, Generalfeldmarschall* [Field Marshal] Model, ordered the withdrawal of his units to the Panther position on February 18, 1944.

Since the previous *Kommandeur*, *SS-Brigadeführer* Pückler-Burghaus, had been overwhelmed by leadership of a front line *Division*, the former first *Generalstabsoffizier (Ia)* [*1. Generalstabsoffizier*: 1st General Staff Officer] of the *VI. SS-Freiwilligen-Armee-Korps (lettisches)*, *SS-Oberführer* Heilmann, was put in charge of the unit.

The withdrawal of the *16. Armee* succeeded as planned. The few motorized units of the *15. SS-Freiwilligen-Division* drove unchallenged along the completely overcrowded roadway towards Ostrov. The remaining units, however, which were mostly redeployed along side roads through forest and marsh areas, were repeatedly attacked by partisans. At the end of February 1944, after marching around 140km, the men reached the Panther position in the area south of Ostrow to Novgorodka (about 30km south of Ostrow).

Here they joined the *2. Lettischen SS-Freiwilligen-Brigade* and *21. Feld-Division (L)* under the general command of the *VI. SS-Freiwilligen-Armee-Korps (lettisches)*. Now, in the *18. Armee* sector, they tried to hold off the Red Army in the relatively well-constructed position along the Welikaja. On March 11, 1944, the *Wehrmachtbericht* [Armed Services radio report] stated:

> *"In the north sector of the Ostfront [Eastern Front], the Bolsheviks attacked northwest of Newel, in the Ostrow region, at Pskov and Narva, with strong forces, supported by tanks and battle planes. Their attempted breakthrough was thwarted by the stubborn resistance of the troops of the Heer, the Waffen-SS, and Latvian and Estonian SS-Freiwilligen-Verbänd [units]. Localized breakthroughs were eliminated or sealed off by immediate counter-attacks. The enemy lost 101 tanks."*

When on March 16, 1944, the enemy was able to occupy height 93.4, at the boundary between the Latvian *SS-Division* and the Latvian *SS-Brigade*, a mixed Latvian *Kampfgruppe* launched a counterattack and was able to retake the heights in heavy fighting and hold it against further attacks. The *Wehrmacht* reported about in the newspapers:

The Latvian SS-Freiwilligen wore a Landesschild [country shield] initially on the right, and later on the left upper arm, and was produced in numerous versions.

As a so-called foreign-national unit, the men received special collar patches. Instead of Sigrunen ["victory" runes], these displayed a stylized sun and three stars for the regions of Kurzeme, Vidzeme, and Latgale.

> *"On the rest of the Ostfront, the Soviets attacked in the area west of Nevel, at Ostrow and along the Narva front. Latvian SS-Freiwilligen-Verbände made an outstanding contribution to the successful defense against these attacks."*

On March 26, 1944, the Red Army attacked again to force a breakthrough at the Panther position. In this attack, enemy troops were able to cross the Velikaya and form a three by five kilometer-deep bridgehead. The *Wehrmachtbericht* reported the next day, to downplay the drama of the situation:

> *"In the area southeast of Ostrow, Latvian SS-Freiwilligenverbände and German troops fought off the onslaught of several enemy divisions. A localized breakthrough was sealed off."*

The attempts to push in the bridgehead failed. Nevertheless, the newspapers reported on March 29, 1944, again:

> *"Even southeast of Ostrow and at the Narva front, violent attacks by enemy were smashed by German troops and Latvian SS-Freiwilligenverbände in hard fighting."*

On April 10, 1944, the Red Army ended its offensive along the Velikaya for the moment. It had achieved its goal of gaining a bridgehead. Since the *15. Latvian SS-Freiwilligen-Division* had been hit hard in the previous battles, *Heeresgruppe Nord* ordered its refitting and retraining under the *16. Armee*. It was transferred to the *VI. SS-Freiwilligen-Armee-Korps* sector in the area northeast of Opochka, where it was supplied replacements for men and materiel. In June 1944, it was renamed the ***15. Waffen-Grenadier-Division der SS (lettische Nr. 1).***

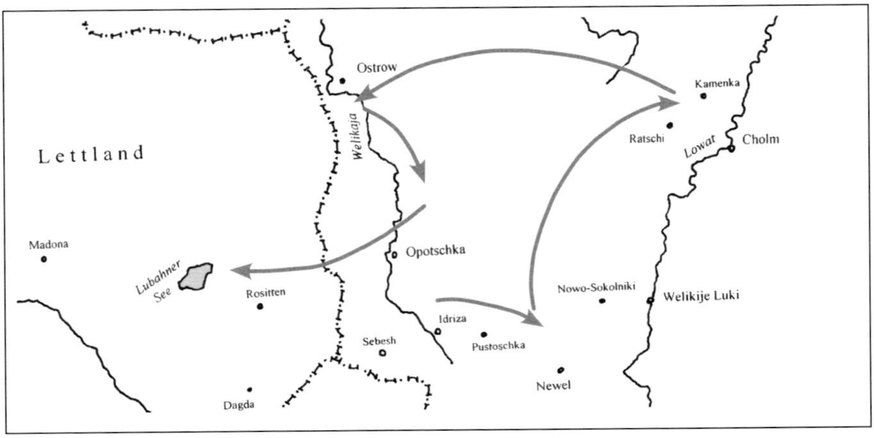

On July 10, 1944, the *VI. Waffen-Armee-Korps der SS (lettisches)*, deployed on the extreme left flank of the *16. Armee,* attacked on the 2nd Baltic Front during the Soviet summer offensive. The next day, the *Kommandierende General, SS-Gruppenführer* Treuenfeld, who was obviously not tactically experienced, ordered the units to pull back to the so-called Odenwald position.[7] Instead of creating unified resistance to the Soviet troops, this set the front in motion. Strong enemy armored units pushed immediately into the retreating troops, and unleashed chaos. On July 12, 1944, the Latvian *Armee-Korps* was already close to Opochka and crossed the Velikaya the next day, some swimming across, leaving behind large amounts of heavy weapons and equipment. Contact with its left neighbor to the north, the *L. Armee-Korps* of the *18. Armee*, was torn apart and the *15. Waffen-Grenadier-Division der SS*, despite brave defensive fighting by individual *Kompanien*, lost its solidarity.

The *Führer*, from the commanding General to the Regiments commanders, were demonstrably totally overwhelmed. Treuenfeld was ordered to the Heeres-gruppe command at Rositten and had to answer for his failure. Due to the chaotic flight of the *VI. Waffen-Armee-Korps der SS* (*lettisches*), the 23. and 93. *Infanterie-Divisions* were also almost completely wiped out. Himmler had him, and the first *Generalstabsoffizier* of the Korps and the *Kommandeur* of the *15. Waffen-Grenadier-Division* of the SS, *SS-Oberführer* Heilmann, immediately replaced. The latter had just had Latvian soldiers shot because they had lost their weapons and equipment in the retreat. The situation threatened to escalate. Hundreds of Latvian members deserted and tried to fight their way home.

What remained of *15. Waffen-Grenadier-Division der SS (lettische Nr. 1)* was first placed under command of the *23. Infanterie-Division* and again deployed in defensive positions. When on July 15, 1944, the Red Army pushed through the front between Sebesh and Opochka, the units got the order to retreat, to avoid being cut off. The next day they crossed the Issa at Kozenec. The *SS-Kampfgruppe Aperats*, formed from the remnants of *Waffen-Grenadier-Regimenter der SS 32* and *33*, and elements of *Grenadier-Regiment 159*, was crushed by Soviet tank forces south of Krasnoi on July 18, 1944. This left the *Division* without any organized combat units. Small groups tried to make contact with German troops. Of the formerly some 1,200 men of *SS-Kampfgruppe Aperats*, no more than 100 reached the positions of *Füsilier-Bataillon 93* by July 20, 1944.

Not all were taken prisoner or killed. As happened for the entire *Division*, hundreds left their units to fight their way to the west. To the extent that it was possible to hold the units together, they were sent to the Karsava area (about 30km northeast of Rositten), where the *Kommandeur* of the *19. Waffen-Grenadier-Division der SS (lettische Nr. 2)*. From here, they marched into the Lubahn area and on July 23, 1944, handed over their remaining heavy weapons to their brother unit.

[7] This ran in a line along the Alolja River-Beresovskoje Lake-Subowo-Schegino-Ljebedinjetza.

Heeresgruppe Nord described the two Latvian *Divisionen* on July 24, 1944, as "destroyed," and recommended the disbanding of *15. Waffen-Grenadier-Division der SS*. The remaining *Division* members were not and could not be deployed at the front any longer, but only used to build defensive positions. The Latvian unit had been completely shattered within a few days and had lost equipment for almost 15,000 men!

However, Himmler had decided already, for reasons of prestige, against disbanding the unit, and ordered on August 15, 1944, that it be re-formed in Germany. For this purpose, all available remnants of the formation, together with the numerically very strong *SS-Grenadier-Ausbildungs- und Ersatz-Brigade 15*, were ordered out of Riga, to *SS-Truppenübungsplatz Westpreußen* [West Prussia] at Zempelburg in the Bütow-Berent area. After they arrived at the *Truppenübungsplatz*, the *SS-Führungshauptamt* commanded the new *Division Kommandeur*, the former *Kommandeur* of *SS-Grenadier-Ausbildungs- und Ersatz-Brigade 15, SS-Oberführer* von Obwurzer, to make the unit again fit for duty by November 15, 1944. Von Obwurzer, however, could only be regarded as an interim solution, after it had already been shown repeatedly that he did not possess the ability to lead units in combat.

Through the acquisition of about 8,000 men from *SS-Grenadier-Ausbildungs- und Ersatz-Brigade 15*, the *Division* was able to report in Chojnice [German: Konitz] the following strength again on September 20, 1944:

	Führer	***Unterführer***	***Männer***	**Total**
Actual	292	1,522	15,056	16,870
	1.73%	9.02%	89.25%	100%
Authorized	475	2,588	11,619	14,682
	3.24%	17.63%	79.13%	100%

In addition to materiel, the unit lacked some 1,500 *Führer* and *Unterführer* to command about 15,000 men. It was no longer possible to make up this deficit, and this considerably reduced the unit's deployment capability.

Initially it was planned to transfer the *Division* back to Latvia in November 1944, after a three-month re-organization. However, since the supply of arms and equipment posed major problems and the physical condition of the men was very poor,[8] they decided to have the *Division* remain at *SS-Truppenübungsplatz Westpreußen*. Thus, the men were in Germany for the 1944-45 change of year, and heard their new *Division Kommandeur* for the first time make a definitive statement on the future of their homeland in his New Year's speech:

> *"You are fighting for the restoration of an independent Latvia. You are fighting for the liberation of the Latvian homeland, which will emerge as an independent state after the German victories!"*

[8] Due to overcrowding in the *SS-Truppenübungsplatz*, many men had to be quartered in tents. Lack of fuel and insufficient food led to a sharp deterioration of the men's physical strength.

Schiffer Publishing

This statement, however, by that time had no meaning at all, and it is questionable whether it was Obwurzer's own formulation or came from the *SS-Hauptamt*.

When the Red Army reached Bromberg on January 23, 1945, where there were hardly any German troops in this entire area anymore, the *Division* was alerted and placed under the command of the newly formed *XVI. SS-Armee-Korps (2. Armee)*. This was organized initially as follows:

15. Waffen-Grenadier-Division der SS (lettische Nr. 1)
SS-Freiwilligen-Panzergrenadier-Regiment 48 General Seyffart
combined *Artillerie-Abteilung (mot.)* [motorized] *Groß Born*
4./Flak Abteilung 325 (8.8cm)
Lettisches Feldersatz-Depot[9]
all the troops stationed in the Notec sector

Already the next day, except for:

elements of *Waffen-Artillerie-Regiments der SS 15*
II./Waffen-Grenadier -Regiment der SS 32
III./Waffen-Grenadier-Regiment der SS 33
II./Waffen-Grenadier-Regiment der SS 34
SS-Feldersatz-Bataillon 15

Most of *15. Waffen-Grenadier-Division der SS* marched to the front. They were to retake Naklo, already occupied by the enemy, which lay northwest of Bromberg, and then move into positions along the Notec connected to Bromberg.

Since *SS-Oberführer* von Obwurzer had been killed during a trip to the front, the chief of staff of the *XVI. SS-Armee-Korps*, *SS-Oberführer* Ax, took command of the *Division* on January 25, 1945. It was pushed back shortly afterwards towards Wiecbork-Sępólno Krajeńskie [German: Vandsburg-Zempelburg]. Both places were lost on January 28, 1945. Deployed on the right flank of the *2. Armee*, the *XVI. SS-Armee-Korps* failed to secure contact to the left flank of the *11. SS-Panzer-Armee.*

On January 30, 1945, the enemy overran *15. Waffen-Grenadier-Division der SS* and pressed it back towards Szczecinek [German: Neustettin]. Here, because of *SS-Oberführer* Ax's *Haltebefehl* [order to hold out to the last], the *Division* was quickly encircled in the Podgaje-Okonek [German: Flederborn-Ratzebuhr] area. Strict *Haltebefehle*, to a unit with no support on their left and right, always led to encirclement of the troops. Because he gave this order anyway to hold the area, he was nominated for the *Ritterkreuz* [Knight's Cross] of the *Eiserne Kreuz* [Iron Cross]. The former *SS-Obersturmführer* Knöringer recalls:

[9] The Latvian *Feldersatz-Depot* was itself instructed to quickly assemble with two *Regimenter* in the area of Chojnice and a *Regiment* near Schneidemühl.

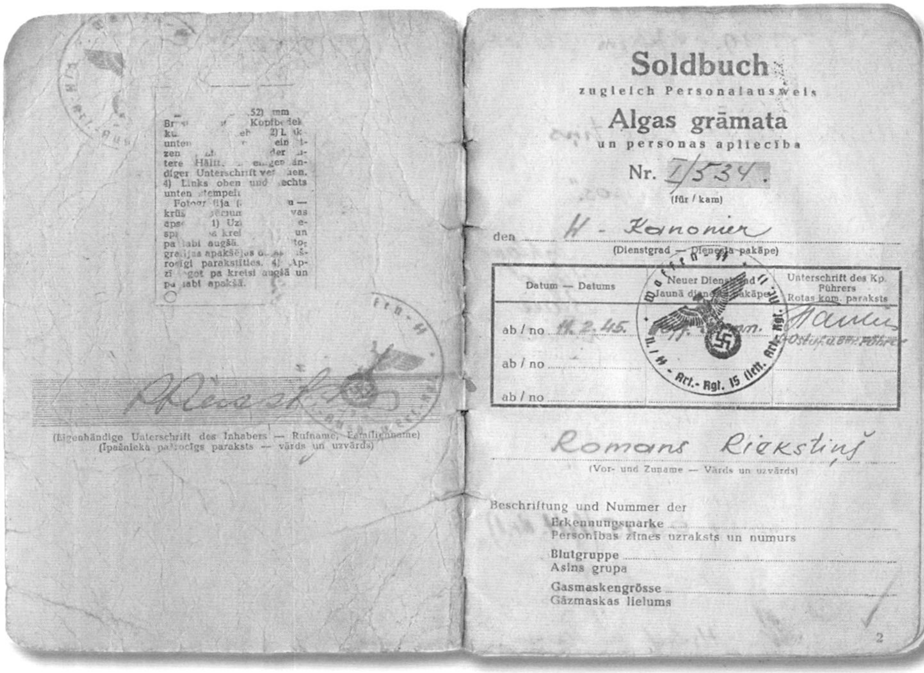

Romans Riekstins – a namesake of Ritterkreuz [Knight's Cross] holder Alfreds Riekstins – joined Waffen-Artillerie-Regiment der SS 15 (lettische Nr. 1) on August 5, 1944.

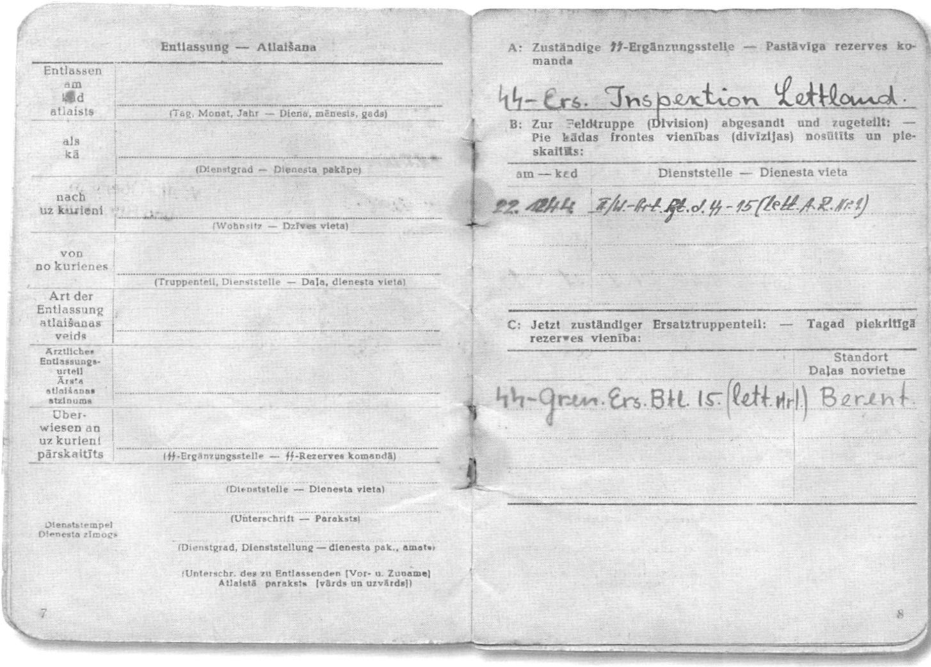

Entlassung — Atlaišana

Entlassen am kad atlaists	(Tag, Monat, Jahr — Diena, mēnesis, gads)
als kā	(Dienstgrad — Dienesta pakāpe)
nach uz kurieni	(Wohnsitz — Dzīves vieta)
von no kurienes	(Truppenteil, Dienststelle — Daļa, dienesta vieta)
Art der Entlassung atlaišanas veids	
Ärztliches Entlassungsurteil Ārsta atlaišanas atzinums	
Überwiesen an uz kurieni pārskaitīts	(ᛋᛋ-Ergänzungsstelle — ᛋᛋ-Rezerves komandā)

(Dienststelle — Dienesta vieta)

Dienststempel Dienesta zīmogs

(Unterschrift — Paraksts)

(Dienstgrad, Dienststellung — dienesta pak., amats)

(Unterschr. des zu Entlassenden [Vor- u. Zuname] Atlaistā paraksts [vārds un uzvārds])

7

A: Zuständige ᛋᛋ-Ergänzungsstelle — Pastāvīga rezerves komanda

ᛋᛋ-Ers. Inspektion Lettland.

B: Zur Feldtruppe (Division) abgesandt und zugeteilt: — Pie kādas frontes vienības (divīzijas) nosūtīts un pieskaitīts:

am — kad	Dienststelle — Dienesta vieta
22. 12.44	II/W.-Art. Rgt. d. ᛋᛋ-15 (lett. A.R. Nr. 1)

C: Jetzt zuständiger Ersatztruppenteil: — Tagad piekritīgā rezerves vienība:

	Standort Daļas novietne
ᛋᛋ-Gren. Ers. Btl. 15 (lett. Nr. 1)	Berent.

8

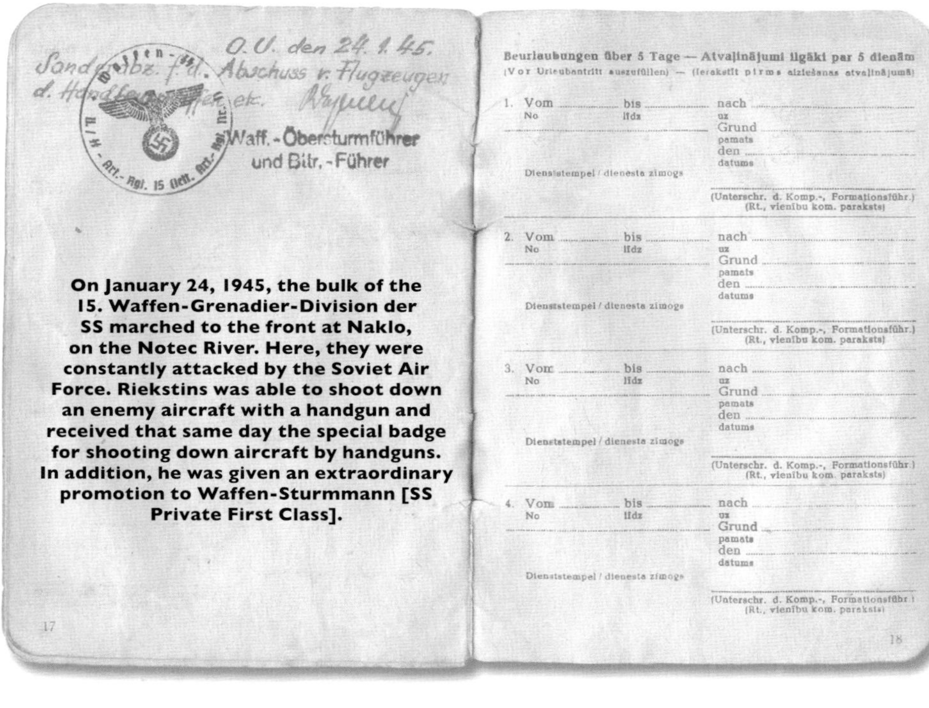

O.U. den 24.1.45.

Sonderabz. f. d. Abschuss v. Flugzeugen d. Handfeuerwaffen erh.

Waff.-Obersturmführer und Bttr.-Führer

17

Beurlaubungen über 5 Tage — Atvaļinājumi ilgāki par 5 dienām
(Vor Urlaubsantritt auszufüllen) — (Ierakstīt pirms aizlešanas atvaļinājumā)

1. Vom ... No ... bis ... līdz ... nach ... uz ... Grund ... pamats ... den ... datums ...
Dienststempel / dienesta zīmogs
(Unterschr. d. Komp.-, Formationsführ.) (Rt., vienību kom. paraksts)

2. Vom ... No ... bis ... līdz ... nach ... uz ... Grund ... pamats ... den ... datums ...
Dienststempel / dienesta zīmogs
(Unterschr. d. Komp.-, Formationsführ.) (Rt., vienību kom. paraksts)

3. Vom ... No ... bis ... līdz ... nach ... uz ... Grund ... pamats ... den ... datums ...
Dienststempel / dienesta zīmogs
(Unterschr. d. Komp.-, Formationsführ.) (Rt., vienību kom. paraksts)

4. Vom ... No ... bis ... līdz ... nach ... uz ... Grund ... pamats ... den ... datums ...
Dienststempel / dienesta zīmogs
(Unterschr. d. Komp.-, Formationsführ.) (Rt., vienību kom. paraksts)

18

On January 24, 1945, the bulk of the 15. Waffen-Grenadier-Division der SS marched to the front at Naklo, on the Notec River. Here, they were constantly attacked by the Soviet Air Force. Riekstins was able to shoot down an enemy aircraft with a handgun and received that same day the special badge for shooting down aircraft by handguns. In addition, he was given an extraordinary promotion to Waffen-Sturmmann [SS Private First Class].

"In mid-January 1945, the Division, then being refitted, was alerted and set in elements to march towards the advancing Russians. The emergency was so great that only elements of the Division could be moved to the south in motorized march. In Chojnice the vehicles were refueled. In unheated vehicles in the freezing cold, we passed Kamin [Polish: Kamien], Tempelburg [Polish: Czaplinek] and met the enemy near Vandsburg [Polish: Wiecbork]. At this time, the Russians used the following tactics: deliberately seeking an empty area, each time they would send a truck carrying soldiers and a second truck loaded with arms and ammunition on to the next place. So our men found only a few Russian soldiers and armed civilian volunteers. They were overpowered and soon our Batallione were in Nakel [Naklo]. The Treidelkanal [canal] formed the HKL. It was fatal that after a few days, our Division had no contact to other units, either on the left or right. So what we expected had to come!

After a few days, the enemy started the 'dance for survival' with a massive barrage for about two hours. The Division gave way after the loss of our Divisionkommandeur SS-Oberführer von Obwurzer, and, deploying all our remaining forces to put up some resistance, fell back to Vandsburg. Here we got the order to hold the town, in an all-round defense, to the last man. It would have been the death sentence for all of us, if it had not been rescinded in time. Obviously, there had to have been a higher authority than our Division staff. Very soon we realized that we were trapped and in a 'wandernder Kessel' ['moving surrounded pocket of troops'], but we fought our way further by way of Wilkenswalde, Flatow [Zlotow] to Jastrow [Jastrowie].

We were long since no longer masters of the situation. We could perceive initial signs of disintegration. Suddenly, there were strange troops among us. We were covered by separate heavy weapons and no one had the time and patience to ask, where they were from and where they were going. Our Regimenter were still reasonably intact and kept the Russians at bay. But it was only a matter of sheer survival. So the enemy forced us further, by Flederborn [Podgaje] and Wallachsee [Chwalimie] towards Landeck [Lądek-Zdrój], where our own troops were supposed to be. During these days, we encountered quite a few scattered units; of these I would particularly like to emphasize the SS-Freiwilligen-Panzergrenadier-Regiment 48. They led the breakthrough and cleared the way through the Russian lines. We called out all our thanks to them, that we had survived this chaos!

Just before Wallachensee, the last town before our own HKL, our Abteilungskommandeur, SS-Sturmbannführer Dostmann, ordered all men to come to him with all the available weapons. Only the drivers had to stay in the vehicles. About fifty men gathered on the edge of the woods. We observed the terrain ahead of us in the deepest darkness and knew: that's where the

Russian Paks are. We could divine the outlines of some buildings. At dawn, SS-Sturmbannführer Dostmann and a couple of men creep along the forest edge and reached the way out of the village opposite. Meanwhile, about 10 to 15 men rallied around me, and I took the same route with them, but was surprised as day broke. We took cover behind the trees and watched a forester's building in front of us. All stayed quiet. Slowly, we could see the buildings in front of us. Everything was quiet.

Far and wide, we could see and hear nothing of our other units of the Division. Suddenly there was a deafening noise of battle. The enemy was firing from all barrels, from the opposite heights, towards the meadow in front of us. With the ten to fifteen brave Latvians, who had been forced into battle with virtually no infantry training, we took the building east of the central street. The enemy stood fast in the houses opposite. Due to heavy losses, including the death of SS-Sturmbannführer Dostmann, we had to withdraw. Meanwhile, our vehicle convoys were in a jam on the road. An 8.8cm Flak-Geschütz was in position and kept the Russians at bay from us. There were no trees at all on the road to Landeck from here for two kilometers, and it was under full enemy fire. Therefore, our 1. Generalstabsoffizier [General Staff Officer], only let a few vehicles on the road, and these each attempted to reach the safety of the forest as fast as they could.

The staff car in which I was riding for a while on the fender, got a Pak hit and stopped on the open street. Besides my personal stuff, I lost all the detachment's personal documents (Wehrpässe [military service books]).

My driver and I got through with a few injuries and joined the column in the forest. A 7.5cm Pak of the SS-Freiwilligen-Panzergrenadier-Regiment 48 was at a small curve of the road, and it shot the way free for us. Despite many losses, most of us reached the saving bridge to Landeck and reached the HKL across the bridge."

By February 3, 1945, the unit had reached Landeck and a week later, the *XVIII. Gebirgs-Korps* took over command from the once-again disbanded *Generalkommando XIV. SS-Armee-Korps*. The badly hit *15. Waffen-Grenadier-Division der SS* was now again led as *Gruppe Ax*, and, without heavy weapons, was only deployed as infantry. The men fought with rifles, machineguns, and *Panzerfäuste* [literally "tank fists," German anti-tank weapons] against the Soviet Air Force, artillery and tank forces.

On February 15, 1945, the *32. Infanterie-Division* and *Gruppe Ax* nevertheless had to leave the region east of Szczecinek for a localized counter-attack to the east, and were able to consolidate the front at least for a short time. After that, *SS-Oberführer* Burk, who was in the *Führerreserve* [Officers Reserve], took command of the mixed *Gruppe* and led it three days later towards Prusinowo [German: Prützenwalde]. They were to strengthen the positions between Landeck and the Gwda River [German: Küddow]. When on February 24, 1945, the Red Army was able to break through the positions of the *32. Infanterie-Division*, deployed on the left wing, those positions had to be abandoned again.

The *SS-Grenadier-Ausbildungs- und Ersatz-Bataillon 15*, still stationed at the *Truppenübungsplatz* at Kościerzyna [German: Berent] (re-named from *SS-Grenadier-Ausbildungs- und Ersatz-Brigade 15*) was simultaneously placed under command of *Gruppe von Rappard* (*Kdr. 7. Infanterie-Division*) and like the elements of the *15. Waffen-Grenadier-Division der SS* remaining in Chojnice, was forced back into the Gdansk [German: Danzig] area.

On February 26, 1945, heavy fighting also started in Czarne [German: Hammerstein]. Here the unit was put under command of the *Korpsgrup*pe Tettau, which formed the left wing of *3. Panzer-Armee* up to the Baltic Sea. Marching by way of Gramenz towards Bialogard [German: Belgard], the *Korpsgruppe* was almost surrounded. In an attempt to re-establish contact with the German lines, chaotic conditions broke out again. With his units without any strong leadership, the *Kommandierende General* of the *Korpsgruppe*, *Generalleutnant* [Major General] von Tettau, saw no other option than to give the order to destroy all remaining weapons and vehicles, and break out in small groups to the west.

Briefly taking improvised defense positions between Lakes Wilmen and Dolgen and Steppen, the remnants of *15. Waffen-Grenadier-Division der SS*, moving by way of Siodłonie [German: Zedlin], reached the Dziwnow [German: Dievenow] bridgehead on March 11, 1945. Combat-ready elements were deployed in the bridgehead positions under command of *Korpsgruppe Munzel*. On March 19, 1945, the men left the combat zone and followed the other *Division* elements to

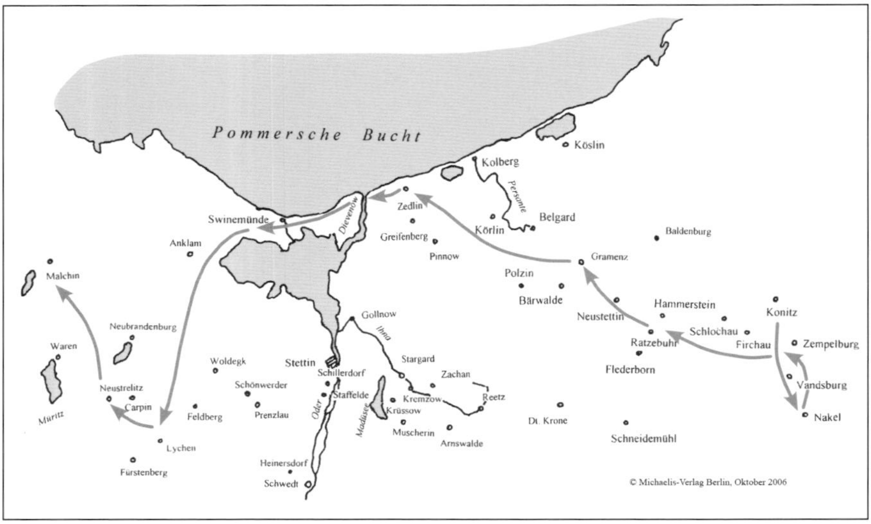

The retreat of 15. Waffen-Grenadier-Division der SS through Pomerania, February-March 1945.

Mecklenburg. With a combat strength of about 4,000 men, *15. Waffen-Grenadier-Division der SS (lettische Nr. 1)* still had an overall strength of about 8,000 men.

Ordered to the Fürstenberg-Feldberg-Lychen area, the Latvians were placed under the command of the *Kommandant des Rückwärtigen Armeegebiet* (abbr.: *Korück*) [Army Rear Area Command] *3. Panzer-Armee*, *Generalleutnant* Denecke. While most of the unit was used at Neustrelitz to construct rear positions, volunteers from the *Grenadier-Regimenter* formed a *Batallion*-strength *Kampfgruppe*. Reinforced by a company of *SS-Fusilier-Batallion 15*, the *Kampfgruppe* was set in march by the *XI. SS-Panzer-Korps* to Herzfelde (north of Erkner). Against German orders, *Kampfgruppe Kommandeur Waffen-Standartenführer* Janums led his men (forty *Führer*, 126 *Unterführer* and 658 *Mannschaften* [other ranks]) northwest, past Berlin and into American captivity at Guterglück on the Elbe.

Only the *Kompanie* of *SS-Fusilier-Batallion 15* marched to Berlin and took part in the final battle there, in the end at the *Reichsluftfahrtsministerium* [Reich Air Ministry]. The remaining units of *15. Waffen-Grenadier-Division der SS* were ordered on April 28, 1945, to build more fortifications on Lake Malchin and on May 2, 1945, moved on into the Schwerin forest. Here they were taken prisoner by the Western Allies.

The troops still remaining on January 23, 1945 at *SS-Truppenübungsplatz Westpreußen* (three *Grenadier-Batallione* and an *Artillerie-Abteilung*) were at the end of February 1945, placed under command of *227. Infanterie-Division,* which was retreating to the sector of the *XXXXVI. Panzer-Korps (2. Armee)*. Without being involved in hostilities, the some 3,000 Latvians marched northeast to Kartuzy [German: Karthaus]. From there, moving on completely clogged roads, they reached the Sargosch-Wielki Kack [German: Groß-Katz] area on March 8, 1945, and were used to build fortifications. Already by March 12, 1945, the Red Army broke through the *HKL*. As the enemy advanced to the Baltic Sea, *VII. Panzer-Korps* took over command in the area declared the *Festung Gotenhafen* [Fortress Gdingen, now Polish Gdynia]. On March 20, 1945, the Latvians were divided among the German *Kampfgruppen* and deployed in the defense. Most of the men were taken prisoner by the Soviets. Only about 500 reached Swinoujscie [German: Swinemünde] in early April 1945 by ship and followed the rest to the Neustrelitz area. From here, the Latvians marched northwest to Malchin and were there taken prisoner by the British.

The beginning of the end overshadowed the organization of this *Division*. Production bottlenecks in the arms industry, and the lack of capable commanders denied any success to this formation, which was made up of men who, as they had in 1918, saw Germany as a lesser evil than the USSR. The underlying reason for this was, as after the First World War, their desire for national sovereignty. Therefore, these men would probably, although serving in the *Waffen-SS*, in the wake of any hypothetical victory over the Soviet Union, again as happened in 1919, would have taken an anti-German stance, for the sake of national sovereignty.

Kommandeure:

02/43 – 05/43	*SS-Brigadeführer* Hansen
05/43 – 02/44	*SS-Brigadeführer* Pückler-Burghaus
02/44 – 07/44	*SS-Oberführer* Heilmann
07/44 – 01/45	*SS-Oberführer* von Obwurzer
01/45 – 02/45	*SS-Oberführer* Ax
02/45 – 05/45	*SS-Oberführer* Burk

Feldpost numbers:

Divisionsstab	34 400
Waffen-Grenadier-Regiment der SS 32 (lettische Nr. 3)	32 595
I. Bataillon	34 636
II. Bataillon	35 532
III. Bataillon	36 426
Waffen-Grenadier-Regiment der SS 33 (lettische Nr. 4)	36 982
I. Bataillon	37 849
II. Bataillon	36 099
III. Bataillon	66 884
Waffen-Grenadier-Regiment der SS 34 (lettische Nr. 5)	39 875
I. Bataillon	33 171
II. Bataillon	32 883
III. Bataillon	37 168
Waffen-Artillerie-Regiment der SS 15	40 253
I. Abteilung	41 204
II. Abteilung	42 277
III. Abteilung	37 313
SS-Pionier-Bataillon 15	38 935
SS-Flak-Abteilung 15	57 966
SS-Panzerjäger-Abteilung 15	33 542
SS-Nachrichtentruppe 15	33 857
SS-Wirtschafts-Bataillon 15	37 617
SS-Nachschubtruppen 15	40 866

19. Waffen-Grenadier-Division der SS (*lettische Nr. 2*)

2. Lettische SS-Freiwilligen-Brigade

When Hitler ordered the formation of the *Lettische SS-Freiwilligen-Legion* in February 1943, the two *Schutzmannschafts-Bataillone 21* and *19* of the *Ordnungspolizei*, already deployed at Leningrad in the sector of the *2. SS-Infanterie-Brigade (mot.)*, formed the *I.* and *II./Lettische Legion*.

Because the desire on propagandistic grounds was to give the Latvians the illusion that they were serving in a national formation, initially only a *Lettische Legion* was discussed, with no reference to the *Waffen-SS*. Rank designations, however, were already converted to match the *Waffen-SS*, with the *"SS-"* replaced by *"Legion,"* (such as *Legions-Sturmmann* [Legion Private First Class]).

On March 29, 1943, *Schutzmannschafts-Bataillon 16* formed the *III./Lettische Legion* and was sent to Pulkovo for the Siege of Leningrad, where the other two *Bataillone* had already been deployed. As many new *Waffen-SS* formations were being organized, it was decided to transform the at that time multinational[10] *2. SS-Infanterie-Brigade (mot.)* into a uniformly Latvian formation. Therefore, in April 1943, initially the Latvian *Schutzmannschafts-Bataillone 18, 24* and *26* were used to establish the second *Grenadier-Regiment* near Krasnoje Selo. Primarily pulled together from remnants and elements of the *Schutzmannschafts-Bataillone 27, 28, 267, 268, 269, 272, 280, 281,* and *311*, the *Regimenter* were brought up to their authorized strength in the next few weeks and the combat support units and supply troops assembled for the *Brigade*.

Transferred at the end of April 1943 to the *XXXVIII. Armeee-Korps* on the Volkhov in the Kretschno area (northwest of Novgorod), on May 18, 1943, the command followed to rename the *2. SS-Infanterie-Brigade (mot.)* as the ***Lettische SS-Freiwilligen-Brigade***. Under the command of *SS-Brigadeführer* von Scholz, the formation was organized into:

Brigadestab [*Brigade* Staff]
Lettische SS-Freiwilligen-Regimenter 4 and *5 (I. – III. Bataillon)*
SS-Artillerie-Abteilung/Lett. SS-Freiw.-Brigade
SS-Flak-Abteilung/Lett. SS -Freiw. -Brigade
SS-Panzerjäger-Abteilung (1 Kompanie)/Lett. SS-Freiw.-Brigade
SS-Pionier-Kompanie/Lett. SS-Freiw. -Brigade
SS-Nachrichten-Kompanie/Lett. SS-Freiw. -Brigade
SS-Sanitäts-Kompanie/Lett. SS-Freiw.-Brigade
SS-Nachschub-Kompanie/Lett. SS-Freiw. -Brigade
SS-Feldersatz-Bataillon/Lett. SS-Freiw.-Brigade

[10] Dutch and Flemish soldiers served alongside Latvians in the *Brigade*.

Members of the later 2. Lettischen SS-Freiw.-Brigade were awarded the Eiserne Kreuz 2. Klasse. They still usually wore Latvian uniforms and badges as members of the Schutzmannschaft Batle, but German steel helmets and winter clothing.

A Serzants (Non-Commissioned Officer) observing the area before him through service binoculars.

The Schutzmannschafts-Bataillone not deployed at the front were normally issued Czech (pictured left) and also some Dutch steel helmets.

On February 25, 1943, Arbeitspficht [compulsory labor duty] was proclaimed in Latvia for those born in the years 1919-1924. Young men could also choose to enlist in the Lettischen SS-Freiwilligen-Legion.

Swearing-in before Latvian and German flags.

There was no large-scale fighting on this sector of the front until the summer of 1943. On September 4, 1943, *SS-Brigadeführer* Schuldt replaced the previous *Kommandeur*, *SS-Brigadeführer* von Scholz, who was commissioned with the leadership of the *SS-Freiwilligen-Panzergrenadier-Division "Nordland"* ["Northland"].

When the Red Army took the offensive in early September 1943, the *Brigade* alone suffered about 145 killed and 650 wounded in just a week. To compensate for these and other losses, about 1,000 soldiers of the *Lettische SS-Freiwilligen-Division* were ordered to Volkhov and placed under the *Brigade* command.

On October 22, 1943, the *Brigade* was given number 2 in the *Waffen-SS* serial numbering, so that it was now designated the ***2. Lettische SS-Freiwilligen-Brigade***. The two *Regimenter* were simultaneously led as *SS-Freiwilligen-Grenadier-Regiment 39 (lettische Nr. 1)* and *40 (lettische Nr. 2)*. They were named the *lettische Nr. 1* and *2* because these were the first two Latvian *Regimenter* to be deployed. The remaining units were given the number *52* (such as *SS-Feldersatz-Bataillon 52*).

Still deployed northwest of Lake Ilmen, on December 31, 1943, the *Brigade* reported a strength of:

Führer	***Unterführer***	***Männer***	**Total**
239	1,133	6,661	8,033
3.0%	14.1%	82.9%	100%

The units were therefore at their authorized strength and the *Brigade* had a basis that could rapidly be increased to *Division* strength.

19. Waffen-Grenadier-Division der SS (*lettische Nr. 2*)

When it became clear that the upcoming general mobilization in Latvia would make it possible to realize this increase strength, at least in terms of numbers, in the short term, Himmler ordered on January 7, 1944, the reclassification of the *Brigade* into the ***19. Lettischen SS-Freiwilligen-Division***. This was to be organized as follows:

Divisionsstab
SS-Freiwilligen-Grenadier-Regiment 42[11] *(lettische Nr. 1)*
SS-Freiwilligen-Grenadier-Regiment 43 (lettische Nr. 2)
SS-Freiwilligen-Grenadier-Regiment 44 (lettische Nr. 6)
SS-Freiwilligen-Grenadier-Regiment 19 (lettische Nr. 2)

[11] Due to the formation of new *SS-Divisionen*, the serial numbering was changed.

SS-Panzerjäger-Abteilung 19 (only *1 Kompanie*)
SS-Pionier-Bataillon 19
SS-Nachrichten-Abteilung 19
SS-Feldersatz-Bataillon 19
SS-Flak-Abteilung 19
SS-Füsilier-Bataillon 19
SS-Wirtschafts-Bataillon 19
SS-Sanitäts-Abteilung 19

However, because the unit could still not be deployed after its reclassification, the lacking troops were to be formed up at home and then later sent to the forces on the front.

The Soviet winter offensive began there on January 14, 1944. The Red Army succeeded in making a deep incursion into the *HKL* of the adjacent *1. Feld-Division (L)*. Under the leadership of *Legions-Standartenführer* Veiss, the *I. / SS-Freiwilligen-Grenadier-Regiment 39* and the *III./SS-Freiwilligen-Grenadier-Regiment 40* were able to save forty *Wehrmacht* units surrounded there from annihilation. In the following heavy defensive battles, *II.* and *III./SS-Freiwilligen-Grenadier-Regiment 39,* as well as *Kampfgruppe Veiss*, had to pull back while *I.* and *II./SS-Freiwilligen-Grenadier-Regiment 40* initially remained in the position. On January 21, 1944, these two *Bataillone* also gave up the *HKL*, and pulled back to cover the retreat of the entire *Brigade*, by way of Finyev Lug and Pristani towards Orodesch.

On February 2, 1944, the troops of the *2. Lettischen SS-Freiwilligen-Brigade* moved into positions on both sides of Orodesch and secured the retreat of the German units in the direction of Luga. Yielding to the tremendous pressure from the Red Army, the Latvian *Freiwilligen* reached Luga on February 12, 1944, and continued to retreat to Stinya (northwest of Dno) until February 22, 1944. Constantly covering the retreat, on February 26, 1944, they occupied the Panther position at Ostrov along the Velikaya. In the previous six weeks, the Latvian *Freiwilligen* had not only maintained cohesion and brought back the greater part of their equipment, but also inflicted heavy losses on the Soviet troops. On February 29, 1944, the *Wehrmachtbericht* made a special report:

> *"In the heavy defensive battles in the northern sector of the Ostfront, the 2. Lettische SS-Freiwilligen-Brigade, under the command of Eichenlaubträger [awarded the Oak Leaf Cluster] SS-Oberführer Schuldt and their Latvian Infanterie-Führer, Ritterkreuzträger [awarded the Knight's Cross] SS-Standartenführer Veiss, performed particularly well."*

The former *SS-Unterscharführer* Gerhard Nitzschke remembers his period of service in the *Division*:

Auskunftstelle für Kriegerverluste
der Waffen-SS
beim Hauptfürsorge- und -versorgungsamt-SS
Berlin-Siemensstadt

SS-Feldpost

~~Herrn~~

Frau

Anna Skrupskis

in Kr. Jékabpils, Gem. Sauka,

Ges. Klauži / Lettland

Vordruck 106

SS-Vordruckverlag W. F. Mayr, Miesbach 17956

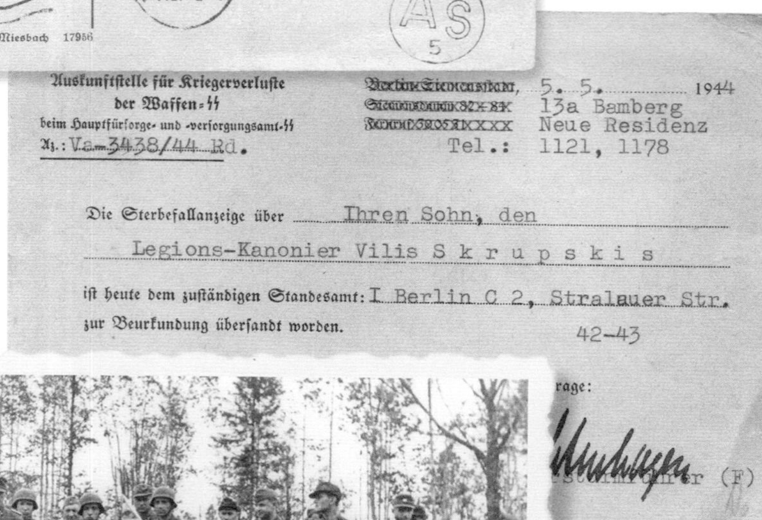

Auskunftstelle für Kriegerverluste
der Waffen-SS
beim Hauptfürsorge- und -versorgungsamt-SS
Az.: Va-3438/44 Rd.

5. 5. 1944
13a Bamberg
Neue Residenz
Tel.: 1121, 1178

Die Sterbefallanzeige über Ihren Sohn, den
Legions-Kanonier Vilis Skrupskis
ist heute dem zuständigen Standesamt: I Berlin C 2, Stralauer Str. 42-43
zur Beurkundung übersandt worden.

Some 3,000 members of the Latvian Waffen-SS were killed in World War II.

"After attending the Waffen-SS Verwaltungsschule [Administration School], beginning in August 1942, I became a member of the SS- und Polizeiführer [SS and Police Command] Kaukasus [Caucasus]. In May 1943, I was transferred to become Rechnungsführer [pay and accounting officer] in the new organization of the Lettischen SS-Freiwilligen-Brigade. The members of the Brigade, the later 19. Waffen-Grenadier-Division der SS, were generally good, and at times, fanatical fighters. As a Latvian Versorgungsunterführer [Supply NCO] told me, there were many victims of the events of 1940 in the men's families. The Versorgungsunterführer had been in Moscow at the outbreak of the Russian campaign, at a teachers' conference, and was drafted there immediately. In the first Kesselschlachten [encirclement battles], he was taken prisoner by the Germans and signed up voluntarily after discharge for a Schutzmannschafts-Bataillon, and then was deployed in the 2. SS-Infanterie-Brigade (mot.). Our later Kommandeur, Käpt'n Schuldt as we called him, once ordered that all Verwaltungsführer had to personally take coffee and supplies to the positions during the night. That earned him tremendous sympathy from the Grenadiere. At the beginning of the retreat in January 1944, the staff of our SS-Freiwilligen-Regiment 40 was sent back over the corduroy roads in horse-drawn carts. There were no more vehicles for some of the groups, or for the IV a [maintenance officers]. So we had to retreat along the so-called 'Volkhov narrow gauge railway' to Gluchaja-Karesty and get from there further to the rear. We waited at the station and no train came. Suddenly, a message came through the ranks, the Russians had broken through, and there would be no more trains. In a panic, we took our most important personal belongings and fled to the rear. With a few comrades, I organized a sledge with horses in the next village and got away fast. We unfortunately had no idea where the front ran and did not want to fall into the hands of the Russians.

In the supply depot, the brandy barrels were left open, so that the Russians would get totally drunk, this would delay their advance. In the hasty departure, we lost contact with other units and only rejoined the Regiment back at Ostrov."

The troops were reassembled in the Panther position with the *15. Lettischen SS-Freiwilligen-Division* and *12. Feld-Division (L)* under *VI. SS-Freiwilligen-Armee-Korps (lettisches)*. When the Red Army took the offensive in the plateau between Ostrov and Opochka in mid March 1944[12] (*SS-Brigadeführer* Schuldt was killed in the defensive fighting on March 15, 1944), it was able – although taking heavy losses – to reach its operational goal, the Velikaya River south of Pskov and establish a bridgehead. On April 10, 1944, the Soviet High Command

[12] In 1999, the Latvian Parliament declared March 16 "Soldiers' Day" in memory of the World War II veterans who fought against the Soviet Union.

halted the offensive for the time being. Since the unit, de facto still a part of the *2. Lettischen SS-Freiwilligen-Brigade*, had been very badly hit in the defensive fighting *Heeresgruppe Nord* ordered a speeded up refitting and refurbishment of the *Division* in the area southwest of Novorshev (about 75km southeast of Ostrov).

During the ongoing organization of the *19. Lettischen SS-Freiwilligen-Division der SS*, the third *Grenadier-Regiment* was formed of one *Bataillon* each from the first two *Grenadier-Regimenter*. The *III. Battalione* were new formations, which were now to be sent to the *Division* from Latvia. In addition during the nearly three months of rest and refurbishment, a *II. (leichte) Artillerie-Abteilung* arrived in the organizational area. Another *leichte* and a *schwere Artillerie-Abteilung* were still being organized in Vainode.

While formation training was speeded up and the front positions extended, it was renamed in June 1944 as the ***19. Waffen-Grenadier-Division der SS (lettische Nr. 2)*** and the *Regimenter* renamed *Waffen-Grenadier/Artillerie-Regimenter der SS*. With a strength of:

	Führer	*Unterführer*	*Männer*	**Total**
Actual	329	1,421	8,842	10,592
	3.1%	13.4%	83.5%	100%
Auhorized	473	2,587	11,615	14,675
	3.2%	17.6%	79.2%	100%

The formation was some 4,000 men short of its authorized strength. However, since some units were still being trained and organized in Latvia, it was ensured that it would eventually reach its authorized strength. *SS-Brigadeführer* Streckenbach became the new *Divisionskommandeur*, and he led the formation until the end of the war.

Exactly three years after the German attack on the Soviet Union, the Russian summer offensive was launched on June 22, 1944. On July 10, 1944, the Red Army began fighting in the area of the *VI. Waffen-Armee-Korps der SS (lettisches,* in the second phase of its offensive. Deployed on the left flank of the *16. Armee*, it had had almost ten weeks of rest and should have had good defense potential. Under the powerful enemy attacks, the *19. Waffen-Grenadier-Division der SS* was able to hold its lines; but the neighboring *15. Waffen-Grenadier-Division der SS* defense quickly collapsed.

When the *Kommandierende General* of *VI. Waffen-Armee-Korps der SS, SS-Gruppenführer* Treuenfeld, ordered the withdrawal to the Odenwald position, they lost contact with the *18. Armee*, positioned to the north. This created the so-called "Latvian gap." Instead of being able to resist the Soviet troops, the front was set in motion as a result. Strong enemy tank units pushed immediately into the retreat, and unleashed chaos among the German-Latvian troops. The units were no longer in enough order to carry out the defense. Instead, the Latvian

Freiwilligen crossed the Velikaya at Opochka on July 13, 1944. Since many swam over the Velikaya in their hopeless flight, large amounts of heavy equipment left on the east bank fell to enemy troops.

On July 16, 1944, the remnants of the *19. Waffen-Grenadier-Division der SS* reached their Latvian homeland and for a short time moved into defensive positions in the area of Karsava-Merdzene (about 20km north of Ludza). Here, the remaining troops were placed under command of their brother *Division*. Three days later, it was reclassified as *Divisionsgruppe Streckenbach*. Especially due to the desertion of hundreds of Latvian soldiers, three *Bataillon*-strength *Regimentsgruppen* were formed from the total of nine *Grenadier-Bataillone* of the three *Regimenter*. *Heeresgruppe Nord* described the *19. Waffen-Grenadie-Division der SS* on July 24, 1944 as *"shattered."* However, since it, unlike its brother unit, still had a *Division Kommandeur*, deployable elements of the *15. Waffen-Grenadier-Division der SS* (especially two *Artillerie-Abteilungen*, including personnel) were taken under command. Marching north from Rositten westwards, *Gruppe Streckenbach* moved into positions on sides of Lake Lubans (about 170km east of Riga).

On August 1, 1944, *SS-Feldersatz-Bataillon 19* had to be sent to reinforce the units on the front and was later renamed *SS-Fusilier-Battalion 19*. After fierce attacks by the Red Army, *Gruppe Streckenbach* pulled back on August 5, 1944, over the Aiviekste River towards Modohn-Cesvaine [German: Seswegen], about 18km north of Modohn. Under constant danger of being caught and crushed by Soviet troops, they succeeded temporarily in taking defensive positions in this area. The *Wehrmachtbericht* stated in a supplementary report on August 9, 1944:

> *"In the northern sector of the Ostfront, the north German 83. Infanterie-Division under Oberst [Colonel] Gölz with elements of the East Prussian 61. Infanterie-Division under its command and the 19. lettische SS-Division led by SS-Brigadeführer und Generalmajor der Waffen-SS Streckenbach proved its valor especially in attacks and defense."*

Up until August 21, 1944, there was heavy defensive fighting along the Modohn-Cesvaine line. After a few days of rest, the enemy renewed his attacks, and succeeded in taking Modohn and forcing *Gruppe Streckenbach* to pull back to the northwest by way of Gulbene [German: Schwanenburg] to Tirza. Nevertheless, the *Wehrmacht* announced on September 16, 1944:

> *"In the region of Bauska, Modohn, and Valka, the Soviets, supported by tanks and fighter-bomber squadrons, continued their violent attacks. Our Divisionen, in fierce fighting, side by side with the Latvian Freiwilligen units and with outstanding support from strong forces of the Luftwaffe, threw back all enemy attempts to break through."*

Inserted into the Segewold [Latvian: Sigulda] position (about 50km northeast of Riga), large numbers of replacements were integrated into the units, thus bringing the *Regimentsgruppen* again almost up to *Regiment* strength. On September 20, 1944, the *Division* therefore again had a strength of:[13]

	Führer	*Unterführer*	*Männer*	**Total**
Actual	414	1,974	10,119	12,507
	3.3%	15.8%	80.9%	100%
Auhorized	473	2,587	11,615	14,675
	3.2%	17.6%	79.2%	100%

As a result, *19. Waffen-Grenadier-Division der SS (lettische Nr. 2)* was a strong formation, at least in terms of numbers. In fact, a majority of the men had been assigned to the front from an *Ersatzdepot* [Replacement Depot] and had no combat experience. The unit's combat strength therefore was generally rather weak.

At the end of September 1944, fighting resumed at the Segewold position, in which the Latvians achieved numerous defensive successes. This was all the more surprising, since most of the men in the unit had no combat experience. The *Wehrmacht* announced in a supplement to their daily report on September 30, 1944:

> *"In the defensive battle in Latvia, the 19. Waffen-Grenadier-Division der SS (lettische Nr. 2) under the leadership of SS-Brigadeführer und Generalmajor der Waffen-SS Streckenbach fought outstandingly in the defense of the soil of their homeland."*

After Hitler had approved the withdrawal of German forces from Livonia and Latgale to Courland, *19. Waffen-Grenadier-Division der SS* was ordered on October 7, 1944 to abandon their lines in the Segewold position. The unit was briefly taken from the command of the *VI. Waffen-Armee-Korps der SS* and transferred to the vulnerable right flank of the *16. Armee* near Dobele (approx. 35km west of Jelgava). In this move, the newly formed *Waffen-Grenadier-Regimenter der SS 106 (lettische Nr. 7)*, was sent to the unit; this was initially placed under *Division* command as a *Korpstruppe* [Corps troop]. Fierce fighting with the Red Army followed, in the sector of *Korpsgruppe* [Corps Group] *Kleffel* on October 15, 1944 (the first battle of Courland). The Soviets used a huge deployment of materiel to try to win a quick victory at Courland. The *19. Waffen-Grenadier-Division der SS* was in the thick of the fighting. Suffering heavy losses, the lines had to fall back eastwards with the front. To reinforce the units, *Schutzmannschafts-F(ront)-*

[13] The *Division* had briefly received a large number of replacements. In addition to recruits, who had been drafted in spring 1944, a Latvian *Kampfgruppe* was integrated under the leadership of the *SD* [*Sicherheitsdienst* Security Service] member *SS-Hauptsturmführer* Fritz Ulrich. Two *Artillerie-Abteilungen* and *SS-Pionier-Bataillon 15* from the *15. Waffen-Grenadier-Division der SS* were in the formation.

Members of the 2. Lettischen SS-Freiwilligen-Brigade later of the 19. Lettischen SS-Freiwilligen-Division were supposed to wear the Latvian Ugunskrusts (fire cross/swastika), instead of Sigrunen [victory runes] on the right collar. In fact, they usually wore the SS runes. In the picture below, SS-Sturmbannführer Koop is wearing the special design for Führer.

From left to right:
SS-Sturmbannführer Koop (Ia of 19. Waffen-Grenadier-Division der SS (lett. No. 2)) Waffen-Standartenführer Skaistlaukis (Kdr. Waffen-Artillerie-Regiment der SS 15) SS-Gruppenführer Bangerskis (Inspekteur of the Lettischen SS-Freiwilligen-Legion) SS-Brigadeführer Streckenbach (Kdr. of 19. Waffen-Grenadier-Division der SS) Waffen-Oberführer Silgailis (Chef des Stabes [Chief of Staff]/Inspekteur of the Lett. SS-Freiw. Legion)

Bataillon 271 and others were transferred to *Waffen-Grenadier-Regiment der SS 43*.

The enemy therefore shifted its operational goal, and as a result things remained relatively quiet during the second battle of Courland (October 27-November 25, 1944) in the *Division* sector. After Hitler had already abandoned large parts of Latvia, fear spread among the population as well as the *Freiwilligen* that Germany would also withdraw rapidly from Courland. Therefore, many soldiers left their units (temporarily) and went to their families.

On December 23, 1944, during the third battle of Courland, heavy attacks were launched against the *VI. Waffen-Armee-Korps der SS*. This now led the:

93. Infanterie-Division
19. Waffen-Grenadier-Division der SS
Gruppe Barth [remainder from *21. Feld-Division (L)*] with its subordinate *Waffen-Grenadier-Regiment der SS 106 (lettische Nr. 7)*

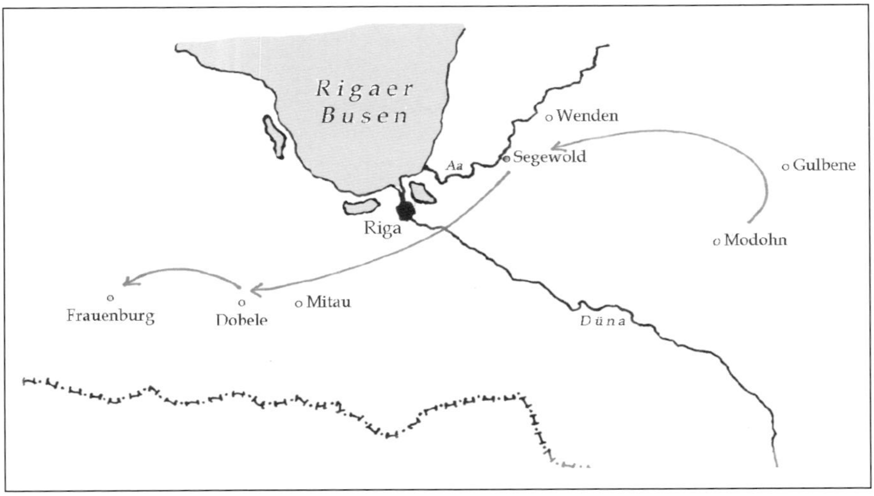

Area of operations of 19. Waffen-Grenadier-Division der SS (lett. Nr. 2) between October 1944 - May 1945.

After large-scale enemy breakthroughs near *Gruppe Barth*, the *HKL*, under the weight of the enemy offensive, had to be pulled back about four kilometers westwards, in front of Lestene (about 30km north of Dobele). As the momentum of the Soviet attack ran out, *VI. Waffen-Armee-Korps der SS (lettisches)* launched a counterattack on January 5-6, 1945, and was able to regain ground. When the *93. Infanterie-Division* was transferred to Germany in January 1945, the *19. Waffen-Grenadier-Division der SS* took over the positions of its right-hand neighbor. This meant that the *HKL* ran about 15km between Dzukste [German: Siuxt] to Jaunpils [German: Neuenburg].

To increase the Latvian *Freiwilligen*'s motivation and give visible recognition of their proven fighting power, on January 15, 1945, the *Waffen-Grenadier-Regiment der SS 42 (lettische Nr. 1*[14]) was awarded the name of the fallen first Latvian *Ritterkreuzträger* [Knight's Cross holder] Voldermars Veiss. The *Waffen-Grenadier-Regiment der SS 43 (lettische Nr. 2)* was honored with the name of the fallen *Kommandeur* of *2. Lettischen SS-Freiwilligen-Brigade* Hinrich Schuldt. It was, however, no longer possible to make the corresponding stripes to be worn on the left sleeve forearm.

Since the Red Army was unable to achieve any resounding success in this front sector, the focus of the fourth battle of Courland (January 23 - February 3, 1945) shifted to the Priekule area. The fifth Courland battle (February 12 - March 10, 1945) began in the same area a few days later. This swung to the east as it unfolded and led to violent attacks on *19. Waffen-Grenadier-Division der SS*. This meant primarily that the left wing near Irlava (about 15km northwest of Lestene) had to be retaken. The *SS-Fusilier-Bataillon 19*, along with *Waffen-Grenadier-Regiment der SS 106*, was placed under command of *Gruppe Barth*, because it no longer had any significant combat value.

Fighting broke out again a week later, when the Red Army launched a strike against Saldus (German: Frauenburg) in the sixth Courland battle (March 17 - April 4, 1945). When the enemy succeeded in breaking through the German positions at Blidene (about 15km northeast of Saldus), elements of *Waffen-Grenadier-Regiment der SS 43* were transferred to the hotly contested area about 20km to the west. *Waffen-Grenadier-Regiment der SS 42* units followed to the Kaulaci area (about 3km northwest of Blidene) and *Waffen-Grenadier-Regiment der SS 43* units to Saldus. Along with elements of the *24.* and *218. Infanterie-Divisionen*, they were at least able to contain the enemy breakthroughs. When the Red Army took the offensive at Jaunpils, the *Division*, then serving at the rear, had to form *Alarmeinheiten* [emergency units] to reinforce its weakened left flank. Despite heavy fighting, they were able to hold most of the positions. As this offensive dissipated, the battle of Courland ended.

On May 7, 1945, *19. Waffen-Grenadier-Division der SS* had an infantry strength of about 3,500 men. This represented about 60% of its authorized strength of 6,000 men in three *Grenadier-Regimenter*. If one assumes that the infantry strength was already largely being increased by transfers of men from the *Versorgungseinheiten* [supply units], on the day of capitulation, the *Division* had a few more than 8,500 men. In terms of heavy weapons, the unit still had:

- 6 *Panzerabwehrkanonen* 7.5cm
- 9 *leichte Artillerie-Batterien*
- 3 *schwere Artillerie-Batterien*

[14] The chronological serial numbering of the Latvian *Grenadier-Regimenter* was repeatedly changed, so that some *Regimenter* of the *15. SS-Division* came numerically before those of the *19. SS-Division*, and the first two deployed *Regimenter* of the Latvian *SS-Freiwilligen-Brigade* designated as *"lettische Nr. 1 und 2."* As of late summer 1944, the first two *Regimenter* of *19. Waffen-Grenadier-Division der SS* again were given the designation *"lettische Nr. 1 und 2."*

Only a part of the *Division* members laid down their arms on May 8, 1945. Most of them sought to escape capture, and went into the forests, where they continued to fight the Red Army or attempted to assume new identities. Those who were taken prisoners by the Soviets were deported to Siberia or Karelia in the 1950s. The last of so-called *"Waldbrüder,"* ["Forest Brothers"], who were often supported by the Latvian people, continued to operate in the forests against the re-established Communist regime, but ended their fight in the 1950s.

Then *SS-Untersturmführer* Grawe recalls his time in the *19. Waffen-Grenadier-Division der SS (lettische Nr. 2)*:

"Born on October 31, 1923, I joined the SS-Totenkopf-Infanterie-Ersatz-Bataillon I [SS Death's Head Infantry Replacement Battalion I] on February 1, 1941. In 1943 I was transferred to the Hauptamt SS-Gericht [SS Court] and from there in April 1943, as office manager of the Feldgericht [Military Court], to the staff of the 19. Lettischen SS-Freiwilligen-Division. When I arrived at the Division after travelling over muddy roads and trails, it was still engaged in heavy defensive fighting near Ostrov. There I learned to know Veiss and Schuldt. The latter was described to me as the father of the troops. He also gave that overall impression. Both unfortunately fell in battle a few weeks later.

Our staff section was quartered in one of the many typical villages. I think it was called Medvedevo. The residents were not openly hostile. Although we were often completely cut off by impassable roads, there were no problems with partisans. In a village I even once became the village judge. The village elders wanted me to settle quarrels between spouses and neighbors. Fortunatel, I was able to restore peace once again.

In July-August 1944, the big withdrawals and defensive battles began, which then ended in Courland. Up until October 1944, we were constantly on the move. Our staff section made its way back over the Daugava River in daily marches, sometimes entirely on our own. The Regimenter of the Division had it especially hard, since they still had to fend off the Russians pressing after us.

In early October 1944, the defensive struggle began in Courland. Our section was quartered in Irlava. We built Igelstellungen ['hedgehog,' all-round defense positions], and formed Alarmeinheiten that were often used to close up incursions.

At the last meeting with Division Kommandeur Streckenbach, he let us know that he had given the order for surrender negotiations, which some of the Latvian Kommandeure would not obey. The units would be allowed to break up and go their own way. We were also allowed to make our own decisions.

But in the end we were left no other way but to be captured. For me, this meant five years behind barbed wire. In December 1949, a war crimes

> *tribunal in Zhitomir sentenced me to twenty-five years hard labor, because of my affiliation with the 19. Waffen-Grenadier-Division der SS. Nevertheless, in May 1950 I was unexpectedly released."*

Formed from a former *Schutzmannschaften der Ordnungspolizei*, the *2. Lettischen SS-Freiwilligen-Brigade* and later *19. Waffen-Grenadier-Division der SS* (*lettische Nr. 2*) had a battle-ready cadre, which was reinforced by recruits. Its *Grenadier-Division* equipment was sufficient, since it was regularly deployed for defense. No other foreign national unit was awarded so many *Ritterkreuze des Eisernen Kreuze* as the *Lettische SS-Freiwilligen-Brigade* and *19. Waffen-Grenadier-Division der SS*. Although these awards were at times made for propaganda reasons, they nevertheless demonstrate how much the Latvians were motivated to fight the Red Army.

Former *Waffen-Obersturmführer* Teodors Kalnajs recalls the stages of his war deployment in a *Schutzmannschafts-Bataillon* up to the *19. Waffen-Grenadier-Division der SS* (*lettische Nr. 2*):

> *"Our Schutzmannschafts-Bataillon 24 moved directly into the front positions near Leningrad. An Estonian comrad told me that this is not the famous 'eiserne Ring' ['iron ring'], but more a 'rubber ring' ... We barricaded ourselves and built wooden bunkers, half buried in the ground and reinforced with sand on the outside. In November 1942, there were heavy storms. The waters of the nearby inlet overflowed its banks and flooded the plains. The light snowfall did the rest and our bunker was full of water. Finally, we sat on the tables – the water rose up to the table edge. The trenches were running full of water, and even the rats ran away ... In March-April 1943, two Regimenter were formed out of the six Bataillonen on the Leningrad front and transferred to the Volkhov. Here there was only swamp and marsh. It was impossible to dig in. The dead were strewn everywhere; the bodies thawed in the spring and the decay caused an unbearable stench. Up to September 1943, the front remained quiet. Then the Russian offensive broke loose and in a few days we had 700 killed and wounded! We were pulled out of the positions and were replaced. I was wounded and went to Riga. That way I got out of the total mess and then came the organization of the newly formed 3. Grenadier-Regiment for the 19. Lettischen SS-Freiwilligen-Division. The new recruits were barely trained and the Regiment, whose 8. Kompanie I led, was ordered to the front already on March 4, 1944. By March 16, 1944, we were engaged in heavy fighting. Since this was the only battle in which the 15. and 19. SS-Freiwilligen-Divisionen fought together against the Red Army, this day was later celebrated as the 'Day of the Legion.' With my Kompanie, I covered the withdrawal of the Regiment to the Segewold Position and was given an award for this ... We pulled back from there into the Dobele area and built good positions there. Our men went to church and used the sauna.*

On December 23, 1944, a big offensive broke out. On the first day it was still quiet for us, but then, with the breakthrough by the 21. Luftwaffen-Feld-Division, there was heavy fighting where we were. Then I became ordnance officer in the Regiment staff. Once a Grenadier brought in a Russian prisoner, maybe a defector. It turned out, that he was from Lettgalle [Latgale]. When we asked him if he wanted to keep fighting on our side, he said no, he never wanted to fire a weapon again. One day the phone rang, and our Division Kommandeur Streckenbach informed me that the war was over. I immediately woke up my Regiment Kommandeur Praulins and told him about the German surrender! I did not see any white flags among us; we withdrew. The Red Army soldiers got out of their firing trenches and advanced. We took what we could carry from the supply depots, and wanted to go into the forest. We thought that the Americans or English would come to protect Latvia from re-occupation. Think again! While many of us wanted to fight as partisans against the Red Army – what alternative did they have? – I met a friend who was able to provide me with "good" documents. But these did not help for very long, since I was arrested by Interior Ministry troops and they knew all about me. Finally I ended up in a labor camp in Vorkuta."

Kommandeure:

05/43 – 09/43	*SS-Brigadeführer* von Scholz
09/43 – 03/44	*SS-Brigadeführer* Schuldt
03/44 – 03/44	*SS-Oberführer* Bock
03/44 – 05/45	*SS-Gruppenführer* Streckenbach

Feldpost numbers:

Divisionsstab	43 500
Waffen-Grenadier-Regiment der SS 42 (lettische Nr. 1)	33 595
I. Bataillon	45 849
II. Bataillon	15 205
III. Bataillon	42 515
Waffen-Grenadier-Regiment der SS 43 (lettische Nr. 2)	34 300
I. Bataillon	35 118
II. Bataillon	36 164
III. Bataillon	47 278
Waffen-Grenadier-Regiment der SS 44 (lettische Nr. 6)	09 015
I. Bataillon	58 978
II. Bataillon	10 217
III. Bataillon	08 570

Waffen-Artillerie-Regiment der SS 19 (lettische Nr. 2)	02 280
I. Abteilung	57 958
II. Abteilung	12 451
III. Abteilung	11 861
IV Abteilung	06 462
SS-Pionier-Bataillon 19	05 818
SS-Flak-Abteilung 19	59 824
SS-Panzerjäger-Abteilung 19	58 680
SS-Nachrichtentruppe 19	00 577
SS-Füsilier-Bataillon 19	08 471

20. Waffen-Grenadier-Division der SS (*estnische Nr. 1*)

Estnische SS-Legion [Estonian SS Legion]

In Estonia, as in Latvia, *Freiwilligen* were already enlisting in the summer of 1941 to fight against the Soviet Union. Pulled together in the so-called *Ost-Bataillonen des Heeres* [Army Eastern Battalions] or *Schutzmannschafts-Bataillonen der Ordnungspolizei*, they were deployed by *Heeresgruppe Nord*. After it became apparent that most *Freiwilligen* would not extend their usually one-year service contracts, Hitler proposed in late summer 1942 that a separate, larger formation – the ***Estnischen SS-Legion*** – be organized.

Himmler was the initiator here, since many of the approximately one million Estonian people were considered to have a positive appearance. He wanted these *"racially valuable"* men to be taken into the *Waffen-SS*.

Organization of a *Regiment*-strength Legion began at *SS-Truppenübungsplatz* Debica in October 1942:

Legionsstab with Stabskompanie
I. Bataillon (1. – 4. Kompanie)
II. Bataillon (5. – 8. Kompanie)
III. Bataillon (9. – 12. Kompanie)
13. (Infanteriegeschütz) Kompanie
14. (Panzerabwehr) Kompanie
16. (Pionier) Kompanie[15]

However, the number of *Freiwilligen* for the SS-Legion remained well below expectations. After six months, the unit was only battalion strong:

Führer	***Unterführer***	***Männer***	**Total**
37	175	757	969
3.8%	18%	78.2%	100%

3. Estnische SS-Freiwilligen-Brigade

Only as a result of the imposition of compulsory service for those born between 1919-1924 in Estonia in spring 1943, did more *Freiwilligen* come forward for military service, because they did not want to work in the arms industry. Although at this time the Estonian *SS-Legion* had not even reached one-third of its authorized

[15] No *15. (Flak) Kompanie* was trained.

Heidelager 1943: Swearing-in of the Estnische SS-Legion.

strength, the *SS-FHA* already ordered on March 23, 1943, the formation of an ***Estnischen SS-Freiwilligen-Brigade*** organized as follows:

Estnisches SS-Freiwilligen-Regiment 1 (I. – III. Bataillon) Estnisches
SS-Freiwilligen-Regiment 2 (I. – III. Bataillon) Estnisches
SS-Panzerjäger-Abteilung/Estnische
SS-Freiwilligen-Brigade
SS-Artillerie-Abteilung/Estnische
SS-Freiwilligen-Brigade
SS-Flak-Abteilung/Estnische
SS-Freiwilligen-Brigade
SS-Feldersatz-Bataillon/Estnische
SS-Freiwilligen-Brigade
SS-Pionier-Kompanie/Estnische
SS-Freiwilligen-Brigade
SS-Nachrichten-Kompanie/Estnische
SS-Freiwilligen-Brigade

As the men from Estonia gradually arrived at *SS-Truppenübungsplatz* Heidelager, the until, then barely 1,000 members of the Estonian *SS-Legion,* were inducted into *SS-Panzergrenadier-Bataillon "Narwa"* ["Narva"] and placed under command of *SS-Panzergrenadier-Division "Wiking"* ["Viking"]. There they were to at least temporarily serve as replacements for *SS-Panzergrenadier-Regiment "Nordland,"* which was being pulled out.

Leo Sipelgas volunteered for the *Waffen-SS* at the age of seventeen:

"I was born on January 14, 1926, in Pärnu, the son of an Estonian and a Baltic-German mother, and entered the Estnische SS-Legion on April 23, 1943, as a seventeen-year-old. In addition to my love of adventure, my hatred of the Russians was my main motivation – my parents had been deported to Siberia by the Soviets. My father died in 1940 – my mother in 1949. SS-Truppenübungsplatz Heidelager was a former training camp for the Polish cavalry and consisted of four so-called rings. We were in the fourth ring. Around each ring were six troops barracks and two canteens. Inside the rings were the parade ground and two motor vehicle pools.

During our time, the approximately twenty hectare-large Truppenübungsplatz was guarded by Romanians – there were, incidentally, members of the Galizischen SS-Freiwilligen-Division on the third ring. In addition to Polish civilian personnel (hairdressers, shoemakers, photographers and even a House of Pleasure with the telling name 'Waldeslust' ['Love of the Forest'], run by a fifty-year-old woman from Hamburg), there was a small labor camp at the Kochanówka train station, where Jews and Poles were imprisoned. The

Estonian Freiwilligen. Left: a Freiwilliger Unterscharführer. Center: members of SS-Panzergrenadier-Bataillon Narwa in 1943. Bottom: members at the time of an Ost-Bataillon in summer 1944.

> *Jewish men wore a Star of David, repaired the roads, picked up the garbage, cleaned the toilets, and otherwise had to do a lot of dirty work. After four months, however, they were all taken away. The officers' families were housed outside the Heidelager.*
>
> *The daily routine was as follows: wake up at 6:00 o'clock, breakfast at 6:30, and exercise between 7:00 and 11:45. From 12:00 to 12:30 we had lunch, followed by rest until 13:00. Then there was ideological instruction until 14:00 and between 14-15:00 we were often at the shooting range outside. Up to 17:00 we practiced in the field and then after cleaning our weapons were generally off duty. Twice a week, night exercises were scheduled. The training was pretty tough."*

On October 22, 1943, Waffen-SS troops were given serial numbers. The two *SS-Freiwilligen-Regimenter* received numbers 42 and 43, the *Brigade* was designated "***3.***" from then on. The remaining units were assigned the number 53 (e.g. *SS-Flak-Abteilung 53*).

At the end of the month, the unit was transported by rail to *Heeresgruppe Nord* and put under the commanding *General der Sicherungstruppen* and *Kommander* of *Heeresgebiet Nord* [Army Sector North]. From Riga, they took part in *Unternehmen Heinrich* [Operation Henry] in early October 1943, which was intended to wipe out the so-called Rassony Partisan Republic in the Polotsk-Krassnopolje-Pustoschka-Idriza-Sebesh region.

The later *Waffen-Unterscharführer* Leo Sipelgas recalls:

> *"I remember about the fighting with the partisans in the Rassony region; we captured a large guerrilla camp. With five killed of our own, we took twenty prisoners and captured ten horses, some peasant carts, many pigs, cows, a few barrels of vodka, Machorka cigarettes, a radio station, a medic station and a print shop. In the latter, we discovered thousands of newspapers and a lot of German-Russian dictionaries. We also found sacks full of rubles. During the fighting, many guerrillas fled into the surrounding woods, and yet this was the first time I saw so many dead. We took some naked Russians prisoner in their sauna!*
>
> *Our mood was fantastic – it was our first victory and all wanted to continue storming forward. We were all young guys and thought that the victory was waiting for us to win it."*

When powerful Soviet forces broke through the front near Nevel at that same time, *Unternehmen Heinrich* ended early and many units were thrown into the front as part of *Polizei-Kampfgruppe Jeckeln*. Thus, Estonian *SS-Freiwilligen* was deployed at the front on November 11, 1943, in the area between Lakes Nesherda and Meschno.

Through the reclassification of the older *SS* units, as of November 12, 1943, the numbers of the two *SS-Freiwilligen-Regimenter* were changed from 42 and 43 to 45 and 46. A week later, in the Polizei-Kampfgruppe Jeckeln sector, they were put under command of the *VIII. Armee-Korps* and counterattacked at Pustoschka. When the attack failed, it was called off on December 8, 1943 and the *HKL* pulled back. At the end of the month, the *Brigade* reported a strength of:

Führer	***Unterführer***	***Männer***	**Total**
178	864	4,057	5,099
3.5%	17%	79.5%	100%

With over 20% of *Führer* and *Unterführer* positions filled, this ensured adequate leadership for the approximately 4,000 men for a frontline deployment at any time.

20. Waffen-Grenadier-Division der SS (*estnische Nr. 1*)

After those Estonian men born between 1915 and 1918 and up to 1925, had been registered and drafted for military service in November 1943, and subsequently, a general mobilization was declared in Estonia in spring 1944, the order was issued on January 24, 1944, that the *3. Estnische SS-Freiwilligen-Brigade* be used to expand the ***20. Estnischen SS-Freiwilligen-Division.*** The then-director of the Estonian *Selbstverwaltung* [Self-Administration], Dr. Mae, recalled the mobilization that drafted approximately 40,000 men born between 1904-1923:

> *"In autumn 1943 I received a telephone call from Generalkommissar [Commissioner General] Litzmann, who told me that Himmler had arrived and wished to speak to me. In the Generalkommissar's presence, Himmler told me, in a very friendly way, that they had worked out a very broad autonomy for Estonia and submitted this to Hitler for his signature; it would be just a matter of days until it's made public. However, Hitler expected a reciprocal service from the Estonian side for this concession, as a sign of goodwill.*
>
> *I asked, what sign? Himmler replied verbatim: We are in the fifth year of the war; now, numbers alone are decisive. You have many Freiwillige at the front, but the Legion is very weak in numbers. This way, it's not possible to build up a larger formation to secure your future at the end of the war. You must take the step of introducing Wehrpflicht [conscription] – this is certainly part of your sovereignty, in which you can take pride. He said that nothing stood in the way of this step from the German side. I said that I would be happy if our imminent autonomy would give us this right, because it is indeed a state's right.*

Oberst Soodla, Generalinspekteur der Estnischen Legion, carried out the mobilization under orders signed by me; he was authorized to issue the necessary orders, with the approval of the Generalkommissar. At about the same time, Himmler appointed Soodla head of the Ersatzkommando [Replacement Command] der Waffen-SS in Estonia. In January 1944, the German front at Leningrad collapsed. German troops fled in panic. The Estonian people were terrified, because it was winter, the lake was frozen, and there was no way to escape. I was invited, in a telephone call from Höhere SS- und Polizeiführer [Higher SS and Police Leading Officer] Jeckeln in Riga, to participate that same evening in a meeting in that city. Soodla got the same. When we arrived in Riga, we also met the Estonian Generalkommissar. The meeting was attended by General Bangerskis and another gentleman from the Latvian side. In attendance were several senior German officers and representatives of the higher-ranking staffs. Höhere SS- und Polizeiführer Jeckeln presided and gave us a speech. Since he was obviously drunk, the only thing you could understand from his confused statements, that there was nothing to secure the front anymore and no help could be expected. Other men gave sober overview of the situation.

Then Jeckeln and Litzmann directed a question to myself and Bangerski, on whether we could help them with our own national units, since the lives of our people were at stake. I requested a break and spoke with Soodla, while the Latvian men spoke among themselves; then, we conferred with the Latvians. It was clear to us that the situation was catastrophic for our homelands and we considered it would be better to take over the front ourselves, if possible. If we had enough weapons and more forces than the Germans, for a favorable moment we were in a position to take power ourselves, to disarm the Germans and take independent foreign policy measures to protect ourselves. Therefore, I and General Bangerski stated when the meeting resumed, that we would of course make every effort to protect our homeland and asked them to tell us how much materiel and weapons they could make available to us. Several of the deputies stated what they had available, and that was how the meeting ended."

Not only six *SS-Grenzschutz-Regimenter* [Border Guard] were organized – at least in terms of personnel – through the general mobilization, but also the *20. Estnische SS-Freiwilligen-Division* was formed in the following organization:

Divisionsstab
SS-Freiwilligen-Grenadier-Regiment 45 (estnische Nr. 1)
SS-Freiwilligen-Grenadier-Regiment 46 (estnische Nr. 2)
SS-Freiwilligen-Grenadier-Regiment 47 (estnische Nr. 3)
SS-Freiwilligen-Artillerie-Regiment 20 (estnische Nr. 1)

SS-Panzerjäger-Abteilung 20
SS-Pionier-Bataillon 20
SS-Nachrichten-Abteilung 20
SS-Feldersatz-Bataillon 20
SS-Flak-Abteilung 20
SS-Füsilier-Bataillon 20
SS-Wirtschafts-Bataillon 20
SS-Sanitäts-Abteilung 20

On February 8, 1944, the former *3. Estnischen SS-Freiwilligen-Brigade* was sent to the Narva front. Moving by way of Opochka-Tartu [German: Dorpat], the units were transferred from the Sebesh area to the *III. (germanischen) SS-Panzer-Korps* in their homeland. During this transfer, *I./SS-Freiwilligen-Grenadier-Regiment 45* was unloaded at Tartu and placed under command of the *207. Sicherungs-Division* for deployment against the Red Army. On February 19, 1944, the unit, by now as a *Division*, followed the *Bataillon* to the Narva front.

It had already replaced what remained of the *9.* and *10. Feld-Division (L)* along the coast up to the town of Narva. In its first successful deployment, it was able, fighting alongside elements of the *11. SS-Freiwilligen-Panzergrenadier-Division Nordland,* to force back the enemy forces whc had crossed the Narva at Vepsküla. The *Wehrmachtbericht* reported here:

> *"[At] Narva, our counterattacks have gained more ground against stubborn enemy resistance. In several days of attacks, the 3. estnische SS-Brigade led by SS-Oberführer Augsberger, together with German Freiwillige from an SS-Panzer-Korps, shattered both enemy Narva bridgeheads and inflicted heavy and bloody losses on the enemy. Renewed Soviet attacks were repulsed after the destruction of fourteen enemy tanks."*

In mid-March 1944, the Red Army again attempted to establish bridgeheads across the Narva. In heavy defensive fighting, the Estonian *SS-Freiwilligen* succeeded in preventing this. After the fighting subsided, the Narva front remained relatively quiet until the summer of 1944. On April 17, 1944, the *Division* – still organized as a *Brigade* – reported a strength of:

	Führer	***Unterführer***	***Männer***	**Total**
Actual	245	952	6,563	7,760
	3.2%	12.3%	84.5%	100%
Authorized	495	2,743	12,895	16,133
	3%	17%	80%	100%

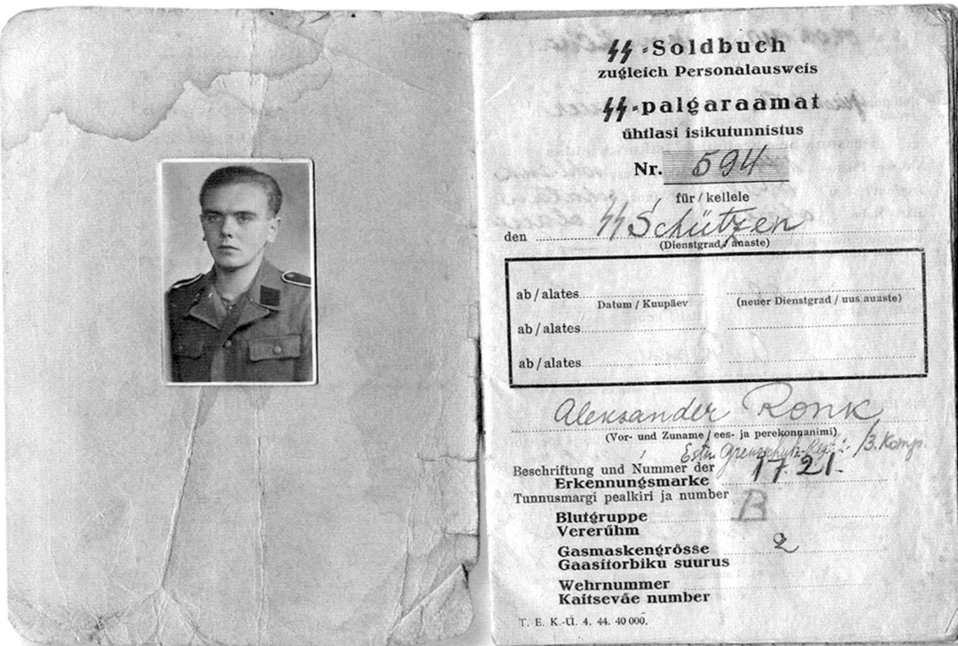

ϟϟ-Soldbuch
zugleich Personalausweis
ϟϟ-palgaraamat
ühtlasi isikutunnistus
Nr. 594
für / kellele
den ϟϟ-Schütze
(Dienstgrad / auaste)

ab / alates .... Datum / Kuupäev .... (neuer Dienstgrad / uus auaste)
ab / alates
ab / alates

Aleksander Ronk
(Vor- und Zuname / ees- ja perekonnanimi)

Beschriftung und Nummer der Erkennungsmarke
Tunnusmargi pealkiri ja number Estn. Grenzschutz-Regt. 1/3. Komp. 1721.
Blutgruppe
Vererühm B
Gasmaskengrösse
Gaasitorbiku suurus 2
Wehrnummer
Kaitseväe number
T. E. K.-Ü. 4. 44. 40 000.

Dual-language Soldbuch [military pay book] for SS-Schütze Aleksander Ronk (SS-Grenzschutz-Regiment 2).

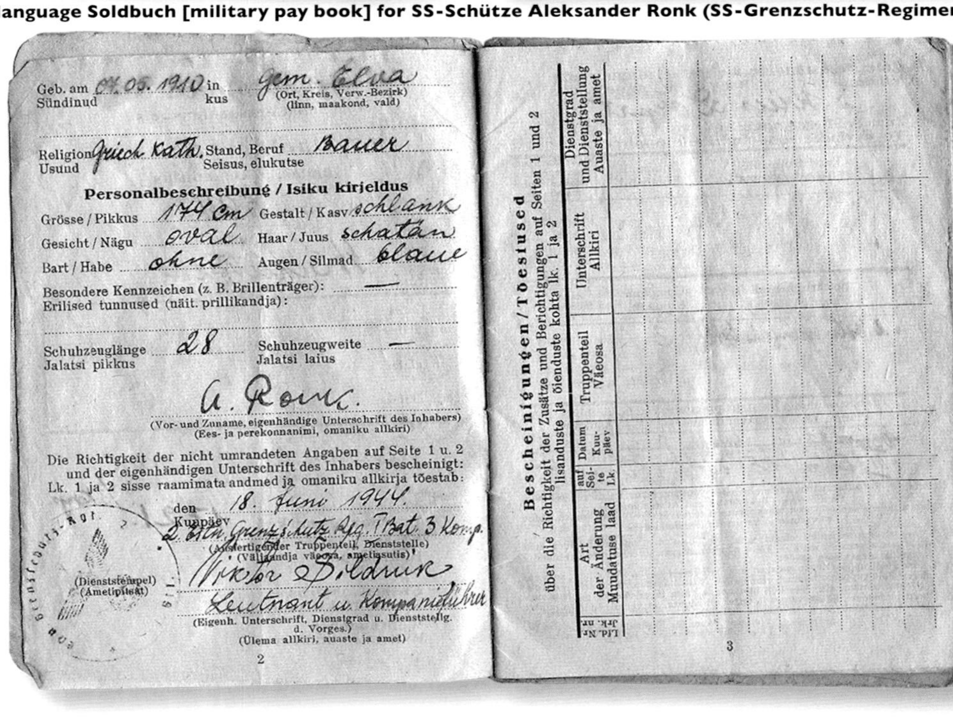

Geb. am 07.05.1910 in Gem. Elva
Sündinud kus (Ort, Kreis, Verw.-Bezirk) (linn, maakond, vald)

Religion Griech. Kath. Stand, Beruf Bauer
Usund Seisus, elukutse

Personalbeschreibung / Isiku kirjeldus
Grösse / Pikkus 174 cm Gestalt / Kasv schlank
Gesicht / Nägu oval Haar / Juus schatan
Bart / Habe ohne Augen / Silmad blaue
Besondere Kennzeichen (z. B. Brillenträger): —
Erilised tunnused (näit. prillikandja):

Schuhzeuglänge 28 Schuhzeugweite —
Jalatsi pikkus Jalatsi laius

A. Ronk.
(Vor- und Zuname, eigenhändige Unterschrift des Inhabers)
(Ees- ja perekonnanimi, omaniku allkiri)

Die Richtigkeit der nicht umrandeten Angaben auf Seite 1 u. 2 und der eigenhändigen Unterschrift des Inhabers bescheinigt:
Lk. 1 ja 2 sisse raamimata andmed ja omaniku allkirja tõestab:

den 18. Juni 1944.
Kuupäev
2. Estn. Grenzschutz Reg. I Bat. 3 Komp.
(Ausfertigender Truppenteil, Dienststelle)
(Väljaandja väeosa, ametiasutis)
(Dienststempel)
(Ametipitsat)
Viktor Sildnik
Leutnant u. Kompanieführer
(Eigenh. Unterschrift, Dienstgrad u. Dienststellg. d. Vorges.)
(Ülema allkiri, auaste ja amet)

2

Bescheinigungen / Tõestused
über die Richtigkeit der Zusätze und Berichtigungen auf Seiten 1 und 2
lisanduste ja õienduste kohta lk. 1 ja 2

Lfd. Nr. Jrk. nr.	Art der Änderung Muudatuse laad	auf Seite Lk.	Datum Kuupäev	Truppenteil Väeosa	Unterschrift Allkiri	Dienstgrad und Dienststellung Auaste ja amet

3

The *SS-Freiwilligen-Grenadier-Regiment 47* was formed at the end of April 1944 in Kehra, by taking command of the two Estonian *Wehrmach Ost-Bataillone, 658* and *659. Ost-Bataillon 660* was taken over as *III./SS-Freiwilligen-Grenadier-Regiment 46*, while the *III./SS-Freiwilligen-Grenadier-Regiment 45* was also being organized in Kehra using newly inducted Estonians. Thus, the *Division* attained a strength of around 10,000 men in May 1944.

In the general categorization of the *Waffen-SS* carried out in June 1944, the formation was renamed the ***20. Waffen-Grenadier-Division der SS (estnische Nr. 1)***. At the same time, the newly formed *Regimenter*, now designated *Waffen-Grenadier-Regiment der SS 47* and *III. Waffen-Grenadier-Regiment der SS 45,* reached the *HKL*.

Plans to form up a second *Waffen-Grenadier-Division der SS* as well as a *Waffen-Armee-Korps der SS (estnisches),* using the members of the Estonian *SS-Grenzschutz-Regiment* which had been ordered organized in spring 1944, failed because there was no way to supply the men with uniforms, weapons, and equipment.

During the Soviet summer offensive launched on July 25, 1944, against *Armee-Abteilung Narwa*, the *III. SS-Panzer-Korps* yielded their positions on the Narva and fell back to the Tannenberg position. Some of the heaviest fighting for the strategically important Blue Mountains occurred here in early August 1944.

When the German front between Ostrov and the southern end of Lake Pskov collapsed, *Kampfgruppe Wagner* was pulled together from elements of the *III. (germanischen) SS-Panzer-Korps* and transferred south. Four *Grenadier-Bataillone* of the *20. Waffen-Grenadier-Division der SS* were integrated into this almost *Division*-strength formation, organized out of *Heer* and *Waffen-SS* units.

Deployed in front of Tartu, it engaged in heavy defensive fighting that began on August 21, 1944. Although the Red Army succeeded in breaking into Tartu three days later, they were still able to stabilize the front between Lake Vortsjärv and Lake Peipus. Things remained quiet in the positions along the Emajogi River until September 17, 1944. As the Soviets expanded their offensive to the northwest, the deployed elements of *20. Waffen-Grenadier-Division der SS* were ordered to assemble with what remained of the *Division*, which had also pulled out of the Tannenberg position on September 18, 1944, in the Rakke-Koeru area.

On September 20, 1944, the *Division* reported a strength of:

	Führer	***Unterführer***	***Männer***	**Total**
Actual	439	1,978	12,965	15,382
	2.8%	12.9%	84.3%	100%
Authorized	474	2,590	11,634	14,698
	3.2%	17.6%	79.2%	100%

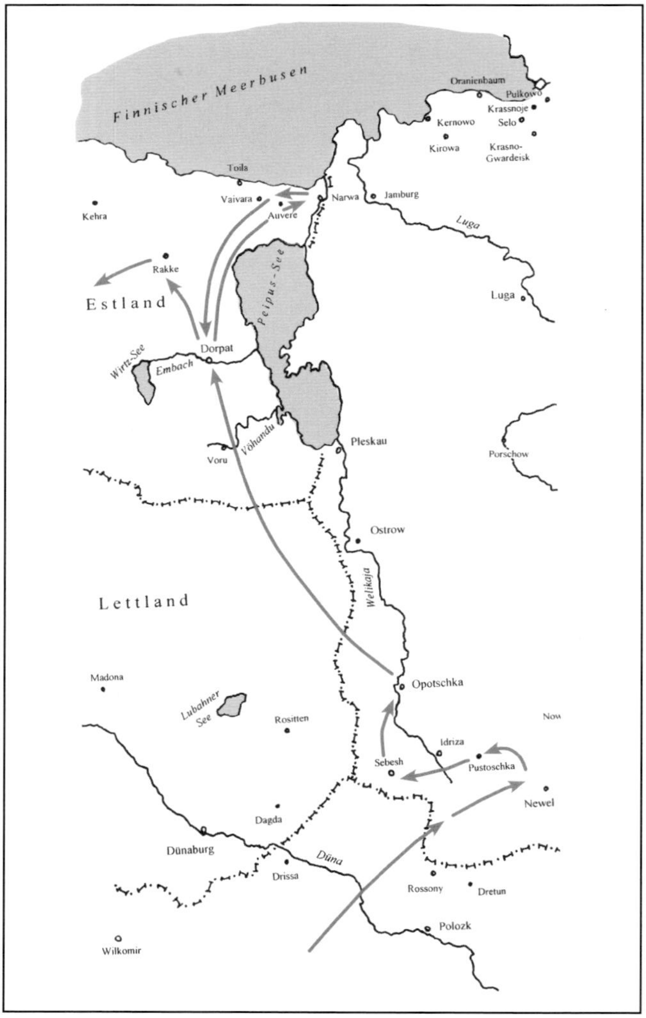

The Ostfront operational area (October 1943 - September 1944).

Numerous desertions occurred, due to the looming evacuation of Estonia and relocation of the Estonian *Division* to Germany. Some 5,000 Estonians left their units, some to take part in the partisan struggle against the Red Army as the so-called "Forest Brothers." It is interesting that *Divisionkommandeur SS-Brigadeführer* Augsberger gave the instruction that the men should not be coerced or kept in the units under force of arms and evacuated to Germany. This behavior earned him great sympathy among the veterans, long after the war.

What remained of the unit pulled back without fighting, to Latvia, by way of Suure-Jaani and Kilingi-Nomme. The removal of *20. Waffen-Grenadier-Division der SS* from Riga to *SS-Truppenübungsplatz* Neuhammer began on September 26, 1944. While most of the units were sent by ship to Germany, the heavy units were tranported by road, southwest through Lithuania to Germany. The then-*Waffen-Unterscharführer* Valtin recalls:

"We reached a camp at Frauenburg [Saldus], east of Libau [Liepaja]. The transports let us off, and we remained with our weapons, alone at first. After a week, we gave our guns up to a Wehrmacht unit that had remained in Courland, while we were transferred to Memel [Klaipeda]. We moved through the deserted city towards Ostpreußen [East Prussia]. Memel was the first German city to be 'temporarily' evacuated. All the house doors stood open, and behind them were scrupulously clean and tidy apartments. I still remember how we stood in front of a large display window and wondered at the display of countless women's shoes, something we had not seen for over four years. At noon, the column halted; the Russians had reached the Baltic at Heydekrug [Silute] and so cut off the way to Ostpreußen for us. In the evening we were back in Memel and moving towards the port. There, they began to use small boats to ferry us to the Curonian Spit. First the refugees, then the military. Meanwhile, Soviet long-distance artillery was firing indiscriminately into the city. I waited with about fifty men in a yard about sixty meters from the loading dock. At about 23:00 o'clock, a grenade hit the quay and wounded our Regimentkommandeur, Waffen-Obersturmbannführer Sobolev, the Kommandeur of the I. Abteilung, Waffen-Sturmbannführer Vöhma, and some of the men. Sobolev died about a week later in a field hospital.

In the morning, it was our turn, and we were set off in a boat over the approximately three kilometer wide lagoon. Then we marched on foot along the 96km long Curonian Spit to Königsberg [Kaliningrad]. We managed this in two and a half days. We stayed a few days at the Labiau manor. Then we marched to the train station area and reached SS-Truppenübungsplatz Neuhammer on October 30, 1944."

The *Truppenübungsplatz* served as an assembly area for all Estonian formations – including the so-called *Selbstschutz* [self-defense]. This led to clashes between *SS-Brigadeführer* Augsberger and *Selbstschutzkommandeur Oberst* Sinka, who refused to allow his men to be classified as part of the *Waffen-SS*. Himmler then decided that especially the younger men and the *Selbstschutz Führer* and *Unterführer*, had to be integrated into the *Division*. The *SS-FHA* commanded it to be ready for operations by May 30, 1945. This eight-month period was to allow for complete reorganization of the formation. In fact, however, it was only given infantry training. It was barely supplied with any heavy weapons.

When the Red Army pushed forward to the Oder in mid-January 1945, the *20. Waffen-Grenadier-Division der SS* was put on alert after a good three months of refitting and retraining, and was assigned to the *17. Armee* as a *Kampfgruppe*. It comprised mainly the:

Waffen-Grenadier-Regiment der SS 45 (2 Bataillone)
Waffen-Grenadier-Regiment der SS 46 (2 Bataillone)
SS-Panzerjäger-Abteilung 20[16]
Elements of *Waffen-Artillerie-Regiment der SS 20*[17]

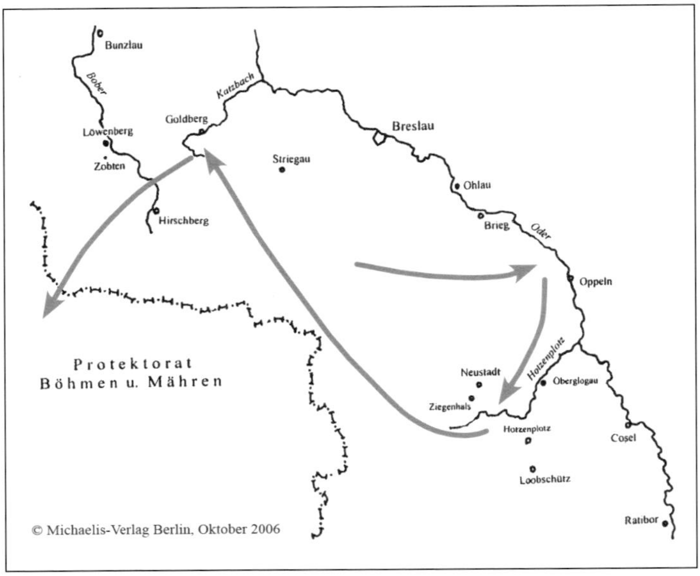

Deployment of the Kampfgruppe/20. Waffen-Grenadier-Division der SS in Silesia [German: Schlesien].

[16] The *Abteilung* had gotten 12 *Panzerabwehrkanonen* from *Heeres-Panzerjäger-Abteilungen 653* and *663* as well as many *Jagdpanzer Hetzer* ["agitator" hunting tanks] from *Panzerjäger-Kompanie 1384* and *Panzerjäger-Abteilung 248*.

[17] The *Regiment* had taken over in total thirty-three guns from different *Heeres-Artillerie-Abteilungen*.

Im Namen
des
Führers
und
Obersten Befehlshabers der Wehrmacht
verleihe ich
~~dem~~
der

Schwester Elies-Aino T o o m l a
20. Waffen-Gren.Div. der SS (estn.Nr.1)

das

Kriegsverdienstkreuz 2. Klasse
mit Schwertern

K. H. Qu., den 20. April 1945

Gen. Kdo. VIII. A. K.
Dienstsiegel

Dienstgrad und Dienststellung
General der Artillerie
u. Kommandierender General

6180. W.B.A., II. 43. 180. K/0732

A rare award of the Kriegsverdienstkreuzes [War Merit Cross] 2. Klasse mit Schwertern [2nd Class with swords] to Estonian Red Cross nurse Elies-Aino Toomla on April 20, 1945.

Placed under command of the *VII. Armee-Korps* as of February 10, 1945, it immediately occupied positions in the area northwest of Opole [German: Oppeln]. On February 24, 1945, *Korpsgruppe Schlesien* took command in this region. When the Red Army offensive encircled most of *Korpsgruppe Schlesien* and the *XI. Armee-Korps* southwest of Opole on March 17, 1945, the troops attempted to break out to the southwest, towards Prudnik [German: Neustadt] and Osoblaha [German: Hotzenplotz]. *Kampfgruppe/20. Waffen-Grenadier-Division der SS* was shattered in the heavy fighting and constant bombardment by enemy air force, tanks and artillery. In addition to the *Divisionkommandeur*, countless *Division* members were either killed or taken prisoner by the Soviets.

On March 23, 1945, the *Kriegstagebuch des Generalstabs des Heeres* [Army General Staff War Diary] indicated that the *Kampfgruppe* still had the following strength:

> *"A combined Grenadier-Regiment with 500-600 men and fifty Machinengewehre as well as 200 Artillerie without weapons. In addition, a Pionierkompanie with thirty men and a Jagdpanzer."*

This shows that it had lost almost all its heavy weapons (*Artilleriegeschütze, Panzerabwehrkanonen* and *Jagdpanzer*). The *Division* elements initially left at *SS-Truppenübungsplatz* Neuhammer – especially *Waffen-Grenadier-Regiment der SS 47* – were put on alert in February 1945, when the Red Army was able to break out of the Steinau bridgehead to the west. A *Bataillon*-strength *Kampfgruppe* was trained and ordered to the front along the Bobr at Kittlitzstreben. Placed under command of the *Regimentsgruppe* of *Oberst* Hoffmann, in the sector of *Korpsgruppe Friedrich (4. Panzer Armee)*, *SS-Kampfgruppe* Rehfeldt continued fighting in the area in front of Swietoszow [German: Neuhammer] in mid-February 1945 and was finally disbanded at end of the month at Rothenburg, on the Neisse River.

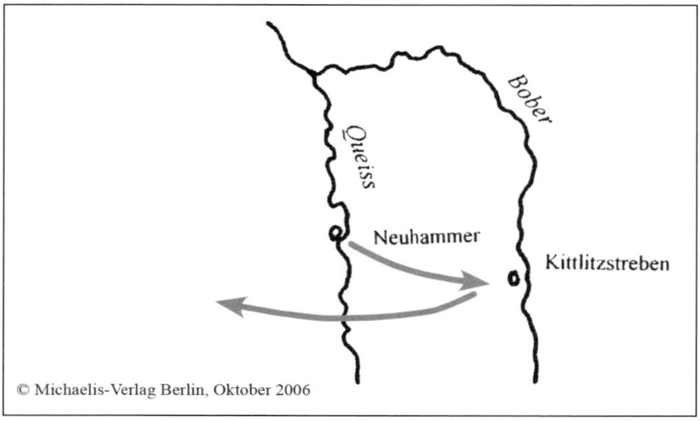

Combat-ready elements followed the *Divisionskampfgruppe* to the front, while others were marched to the *Waffen-Grenadier-Ausbildungs- und Ersatz-Regiment der SS 20* at Odense (Denmark). A former German *Führer* recalls the battles east of the *Truppenübungsplatz*:

> *"Put on alert, we marched along the highway up to the Zumm forester's lodge, then left the highway, going northwards. We were to work our way forward through this wooded terrain to the positions on the Bober [Bobr] and replace the Polizei stationed there. However, we didn't get to these positions first, but we kept running right into the Russians in these woods. With all the firing around us and our poorly trained and armed men, they started immediately escaping to the rear, and they even swept us Führer along. We were only able to bring the men to a halt after a few hundred meters, by holding our weapons in front of us, but quite a number had already disappeared, never to be seen again.*
>
> *Our unit was led by a Heer Hauptmann [Captain], who served in the 20. Waffen-Grenadier-Division der SS. We heard what this Hauptmann said over the Truppenübungsplatz telephone line, which was still working, to SS-Obersturmbannführer Rehfeldt: Obersturmbannführer, I'm not able to hold the positions; the men are fleeing in droves. Reply: I could care less; you are responsible for your men, that's why you're an officer. Then he threatened him with court-martial. We moved into new positions in the woods, but only as strong points; you couldn't speak of any real continuous line. We tried to launch an attack from these positions, or, more like it, we tried to attack, but it came to nothing. Now I was faced with the Volkssturm ['Peoples militia'] for the first time, which meant that I was supposed to put a weak line of sick old men and children in the positions. Later I sent some of the them back on my own responsibility, which could easily have cost me my head."*

At the end of March 1945, *SS-Oberführer* Maack took over what remained of the *Division*. Reinforced with elements of *Waffen-Grenadier-Regiments der SS 47*, the units were sent to the *VIII. Armee-Korps* in the area south of Goldberg. There was no more significant fighting; instead, the news of the surrender started the troops marching by way of Liberec [German: Reichenberg] in the *Protektorat Böhmen und Mähren* towards Turnov [German: Turnau]. In Czechia, partisans repeatedly attacked the units, causing many losses. Near Melnik, the units crossed the Elbe and marched towards Annaberg. Here, they capitulated to the Red Army.

The *20. Waffen-Grenadier-Division der SS (estnische Nr. 1)* was initially organized as a result of the introduction of compulsory service and later through the general mobilization. The fear of renewed occupation led to fierce defensive battles at the Narva and the Blue Mountains. After it was encircled in Silesia in 1945, only a *Kampfgruppe* was still operational by the end of the war.

Kommandeure:
03/43 – 03/45 *SS-Brigadeführer* Augsberger
03/45 – 05/45 *SS-Oberführer* Maack

Feldpost numbers:

Divisionsstab	59 340
Waffen-Grenadier-Regiment der SS 45 (estnische Nr. 1)	48 001
I. Bataillon	56 475
II. Bataillon	48 958
III. Bataillon	13 803
Waffen-Grenadier-Regiment der SS 46 (estnische Nr.2)	36 341
I. Bataillon	39 340
II. Bataillon	38 304
III. Bataillon	15 973
Waffen-Grenadier-Regiment der SS 47 (estnische Nr. 3)	22 166
I. Bataillon	16 836
II. Bataillon	25 712
III. Bataillon	24 586
Waffen-Artillerie-Regiment der SS 20 (estnische Nr. 1)	48 052
I. Abteilung	09 046
II. Abteilung	27 051
III. Abteilung	18 194
IV Abteilung	28 668
SS-Pionier-Bataillon 20	23 417
SS-Flak-Abteilung 20	01 199
SS-Panzerjäger-Abteilung 20	48 886
SS-Nachrichtentruppe 20	17 403
SS-Füsilier-Bataillon 20	48 314
SS-Nachschubtruppen 20	19 766
SS-Feldersatz-Bataillon 20	38 087

25. Waffen-Grenadier-Division der SS "Hunyadi" (*ungarische Nr. 1*)

After the shift in Hungary's political direction in October 1944, the new Prime Minister Szálasi ordered the reorganization of the Hungarian Armed Forces. This was to bring about closer German-Hungarian cooperation. Four of the eight *Divisionen* to be newly reorganized were to be trained under the *Waffen-SS*. While Hungary was primarily to provide the required personnel, Germany was responsible for training and equipment: a paradox, considering the German *Reich* was no longer able to equip its own forces.

On November 2, 1944, the *SS-FHA* announced its order for formation of the ***25. Waffen-Grenadier-Division der SS "Hunyadi" (ungarische Nr. 1)***. János Hunyadi, after whom the *Division* was named, was a Hungarian general who was appointed regent in 1444 and died in 1456.

Hungarian daily newspapers reported the organization of *Panzergrenadier Division Hunyadi* on November 3, 1944. Hungarian Prime Minister Szálasi called on Hungarian youth to come forward to *"again dispel the enemy from our homeland."* All Hungarian men born between 1914-1927 (17 to 30 years old) could and should register, if they were not yet serving in the military, as well as those born between 1902-1921 (23 to 42 years old) who had already had military training. All professional soldiers were also called on to register, whatever their age.

The men were to report to the recruiting offices located in many cities by November 20, 1944 – for the duration of the war – although those *Freiwilligen* born in 1927 needed the consent of their parents if they were not yet eighteen years old.

The *Freiwilligen* were to reach the front as rapidly as possible, wearing Hungarian uniforms and with the latest German weaponry and equipment. Hungarian youth especially were called on to defend *"their homeland [with] pride and heart."*

However, discussion of forming a *Panzergrenadier Division* ended, in terms of practical planning. Instead, the authorized composition of the formation was the same as an *SS-Grenadier-Division*:

Waffen-Grenadier-Regiment der SS 61 (ungarische Nr. 1)
Waffen-Grenadier-Regiment der SS 62 (ungarische Nr. 2)
Waffen-Grenadier-Regiment der SS 63 (ungarische Nr. 3)
Waffen-Artillerie-Regiment der SS 25 (ungarische Nr. 1)
SS-Füsilier-Bataillon 25

SS-Pionier-Bataillon 25
SS-Panzerjäger-Abteilung 25
SS-Nachrichten-Abteilung 25
SS-Versorgungs-Regiment 25
SS-Veterinär-Kompanie 25
SS-Sanitäts-Kompanie 25
SS-Feldersatz-Bataillon 25

Some 16,700 Hungarians had been assembled for the *Division* by November 18, 1944. Transfer of the men by train started two days later at the Zala Egerszeg assembly point (about 30km west of Lake Balaton), to *SS-Truppenübungsplatz* Neuhammer. On December 10, 1944, the *Divisionskommando* reported a strength of 20,567 *Führer* and *sonstige Dienstgrade* [other ranks].

In Silesia, the shortcomings of what had been announced about equipping the *Freiwilligen* became apparent. While the former *Honvéd* [Hungarian Army] soldiers kept their uniforms, the newly inducted *Freiwilligen* were increasingly issued (German) uniforms. In fact, Szálasis' avowal that the unit would wear Hungarian uniforms was just as untrue as the assertion that it would be a *Panzergrenadier-Division*.

Weapons were delivered for the first time on December 19, 1944. These included:

2,000	*Gewehre 98k* [98k rifles]
1,000	*Pistolen 08*
100	*Maschinenpistolen 40*
50	*Maschinengewehre 42*
5	*Granatwerfer* [mortars] 8.14cm

Ten days later arrived:

100	*Maschinenpistolen 40*
50	*Maschinengewehre 42*
25	*Granatwerfer* 8.14cm
5	*Panzerabwehrkanonen* 7.5cm
3,000	*Panzerfäuste*
1,600	bicycles

Also issued were:

5	saddle horses
7	motorcycles
5	*Personenkraftwagen* [personnel cars]
27	trucks

Since the actual strength of *Infanterie-Division 44* (authorized strength: 12,700 men) was much too high, at the new year, some 8,000 recruits were commandeered to form the *26. Waffen-Grenadier-Division der SS "Hungaria" (ungarische Nr. 2)*.

On February 7, 1945, *Divisionskommandeur Waffen-Brigadeführer* vitéz Grassy made it known that – about three months after the organization order – all *Freiwilligen* at least, would from now on be issued uniforms. The continued lack of equipment had made it impossible both to train the recruits and give unit training to the already trained former *Honvéd* members.

As the Red Army approached *SS-Truppenübungsplatz* Neuhammer, the unit was given a transfer order to *Truppenübungsplatz* Grafenwöhr. A reinforced *Regiment* (four *Bataillone* with a total of 2,600 men) was formed using the combat-ready men, led by the *Kommandeur* of *Waffen-Grenadier-Regiments der SS 63 (ungarische Nr. 3), Waffen-Standartenführer* vitéz Peinlich. It was outfitted with what weapons were available and transferred to *XXXXVIII. Armee-Korps*. South of Szprotawa [German: Sprottau], the *Bataillone* occupied positions along the Bobr.

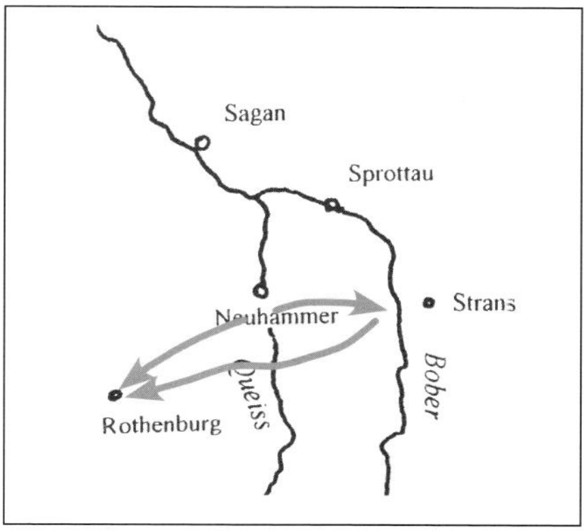

February 8, 1945 saw the first battles with advancing enemy troops. Without the support of heavy weapons, it was impossible for the Hungarians to halt the Red Army advance. Very heavy fighting, including much hand-to-hand combat, started at Strans on February 10, 1945.

At times encircled and suffering from severe lack of ammunition, *Waffen-Standartenführer* vitéz Peinlich ordered a breakout to the west. On February 14, 1945, the remaining combat-ready troops pulled out of the *HKL* and marched to Czerwieńsk, 30km distant. From there, the remaining approximately 1,500 men tried to reach the new quarters of the *25. Waffen-Grenadier-Division der SS (ungarische Nr. 1)* between Zwickau and Chemnitz, about 200km distant.

The majority of the formation was marched out of *SS-Truppenübungsplatz* Neuhammer towards southern Germany, starting on February 7, 1945, and reached the area of Saxony in mid-February 1945. On February 22, 1945, they marched

Soldbuch of Hungarian Freiwilligen Sandor Bors (born April 20, 1926).

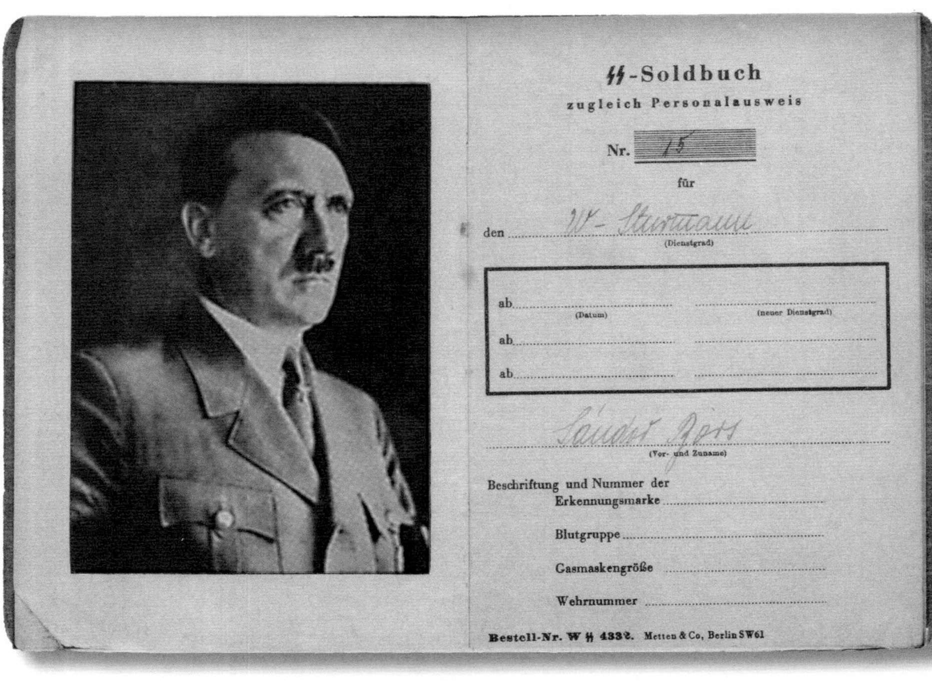

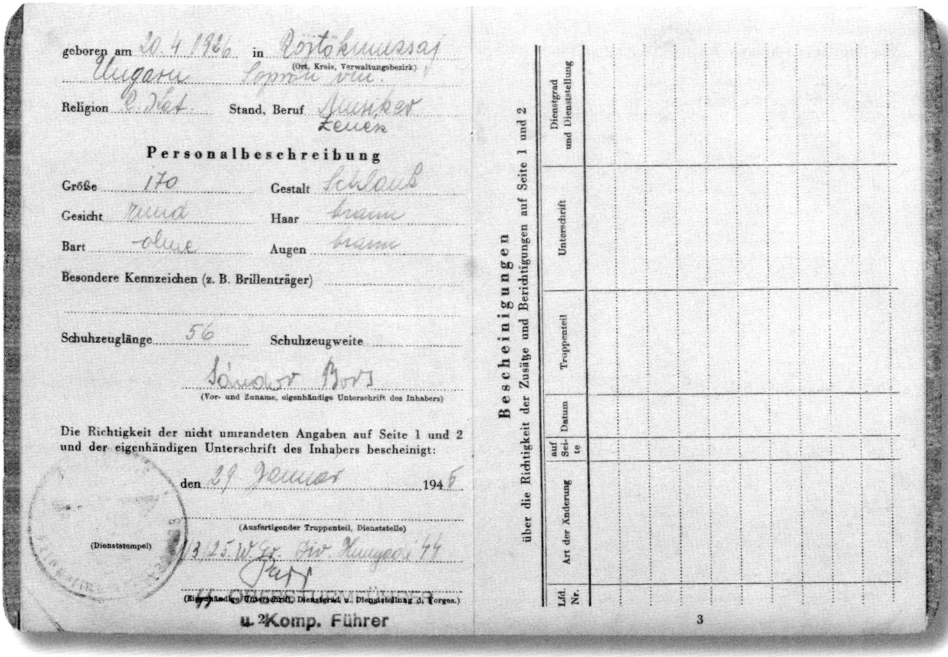

geboren am 20.4.1926 in Rőjtőkmuzsaj
(Ort, Kreis, Verwaltungsbezirk)
Ungarn Sopron vm.

Religion r. Kat. Stand, Beruf Musiker Lernen

Personalbeschreibung

Größe 170 Gestalt schlank

Gesicht rund Haar braun

Bart ohne Augen braun

Besondere Kennzeichen (z. B. Brillenträger)

Schuhzeuglänge 56 Schuhzeugweite

Sándor Bors
(Vor- und Zuname, eigenhändige Unterschrift des Inhabers)

Die Richtigkeit der nicht umrandeten Angaben auf Seite 1 und 2 und der eigenhändigen Unterschrift des Inhabers bescheinigt:

den 29. Januar 1945

(Ausfertigender Truppenteil, Dienststelle)

(Dienststempel) 13/25. W. Gr. Div. Hunyadi 44

Papp

(Eigenhändige Unterschrift, Dienstgrad u. Dienststellung d. Vorges.)

u. 2Komp. Führer

Bescheinigungen
über die Richtigkeit der Zusätze und Berichtigungen auf Seite 1 und 2

Lfd. Nr.	Art der Änderung	auf Seite	Datum	Truppenteil	Unterschrift	Dienstgrad und Dienststellung

3

Bors was a member of 8. Kp. [Co.] of the 25. Waffen-Grenadier-Division der SS.

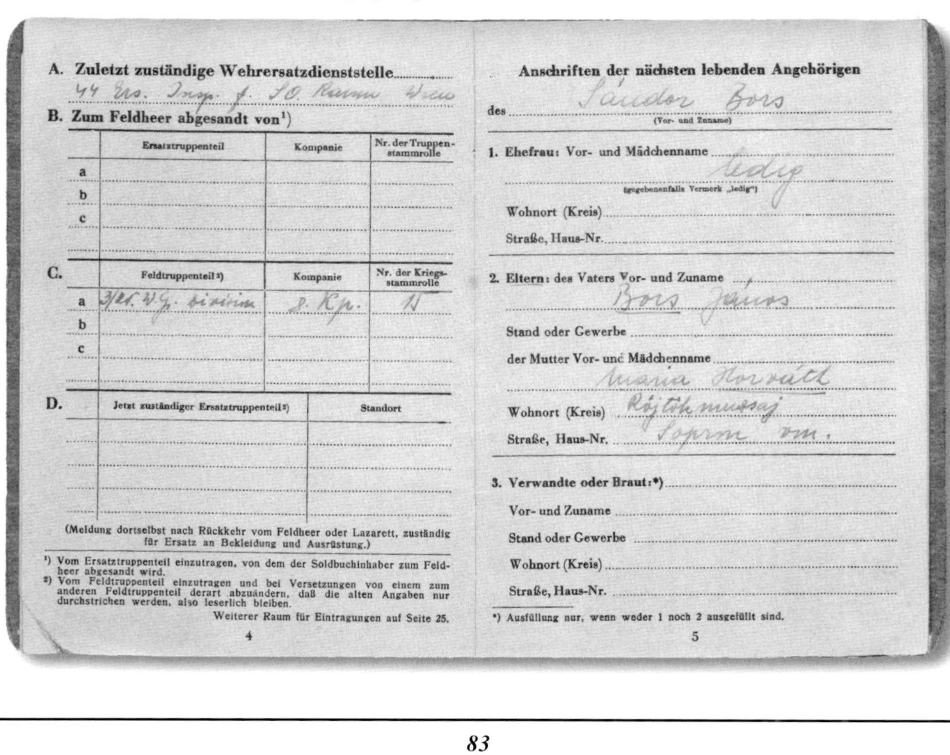

A. Zuletzt zuständige Wehrersatzdienststelle
44 Ers. Insp. f. S.O. Raum Wien

B. Zum Feldheer abgesandt von[1])

	Ersatztruppenteil	Kompanie	Nr. der Truppenstammrolle
a			
b			
c			

C.

	Feldtruppenteil[2])	Kompanie	Nr. der Kriegsstammrolle
a	3/25. W.G. division	8. Kp.	11
b			
c			

D.

Jetzt zuständiger Ersatztruppenteil[2])	Standort

(Meldung dortselbst nach Rückkehr vom Feldheer oder Lazarett, zuständig für Ersatz an Bekleidung und Ausrüstung.)

[1]) Vom Ersatztruppenteil einzutragen, von dem der Soldbuchinhaber zum Feldheer abgesandt wird.
[2]) Vom Feldtruppenteil einzutragen und bei Versetzungen von einem zum anderen Feldtruppenteil derart abzuändern, daß die alten Angaben nur durchstrichen werden, also leserlich bleiben.

Weiterer Raum für Eintragungen auf Seite 25.

4

Anschriften der nächsten lebenden Angehörigen

des Sándor Bors
(Vor- und Zuname)

1. Ehefrau: Vor- und Mädchenname
ledig
(gegebenenfalls Vermerk „ledig")
Wohnort (Kreis)
Straße, Haus-Nr.

2. Eltern: des Vaters Vor- und Zuname
Bors János
Stand oder Gewerbe
der Mutter Vor- und Mädchenname
Maria Horváth
Wohnort (Kreis) Rőjtőkmuzsaj
Straße, Haus-Nr. Sopron vm.

3. Verwandte oder Braut:*)
Vor- und Zuname
Stand oder Gewerbe
Wohnort (Kreis)
Straße, Haus-Nr.

*) Ausfüllung nur, wenn weder 1 noch 2 ausgefüllt sind.

5

to the area south of Nuremberg (Spalt-Roth-Hilpoltstein) and were placed under command of the *Wehrkreisbefehlshaber* [military district command] *XIII*. Here the Hungarians were issued more weapons and equipment:[18]

5,000	*Gewehre 98k*
300	*Maschinenpistolen 40*
100	*Maschinengewehre 42*
50	*Granatwerfer* 8.14cm
3,000	*Panzerfäuste*
12	*leichte Feldhaubitzen* 10.5cm

A discussion was held March 17, 1945, in which the *SS-FHA* explained that the *Waffen-SS* could only organize two instead of the previously promised four Hungarian *Divisionen*. Six days later, Hungarian *Honvédminister* [Defense Minister] *Generaloberst* [full General] Beregfy, together with the Chief of the general *Heeresamt* [Army Office], *General der Artillerie* Keiner, and chief of the *SS-Führungshauptamt, SS-Obergruppenführer* Jüttner, inspected the Hungarian units of the *Waffen-SS* at Hilpoltstein.

When U.S. troops reached Nuremberg from the north on April 11, 1945, the Hungarians marched southwards. *25. Waffen-Grenadier-Division der SS "Hunyadi"* crossed the Danube on April 20, 1945, near Neustadt and was put under command of the *LXXXII. Armee-Korps*. Since the units, under the agreements, were only to be deployed in Hungary, they were not involved in any more fighting. However, *25. Waffen-Grenadier-Division der SS* handed over their *leichte Artillerie-Abteilung*, with twelve *Haubitzen* and 1,000 *Gewehre 98k* and 100 *Panzerfäuste*, to the *Generalkommando LXXXII. Armee-Korps*.

Moving by way of Landshut, the unit reached Salzburg on May 2, 1945, and marched on to Attersee. They were still involved in some skirmishes with advancing U.S. troops two days later, in which they destroyed some tanks with *Panzerfäusten*. Finally, the units of the two Hungarian *Waffen-SS* formations were collected and taken into American captivity.

This ended the history of the *25. Waffen-Grenadier-Division der SS "Hunyadi."* The catastrophic lack of armaments made it impossible to train and equip the formation, which was intended to fight against the Red Army and was to be deployed by April 30, 1945. As a result, the units were only able to constantly fall back before the Red Army or U.S. troops, and wait for the end of the war.

Then-*SS-Untersturmführer* Wamser recalls his time in *19. Waffen-Grenadier-Division der SS "Hunyadi"*:

> *"I was born on May 11, 1912. After serving in 3. SS-Panzergrenadier-Division Totenkopf, I was ordered to the SS-Führerschule [Officers' School]*

[18] The weapons were divided between the *25.* and *26. Waffen-Grenadier-Division der SS (ungarische Nr. 1* and *2)*.

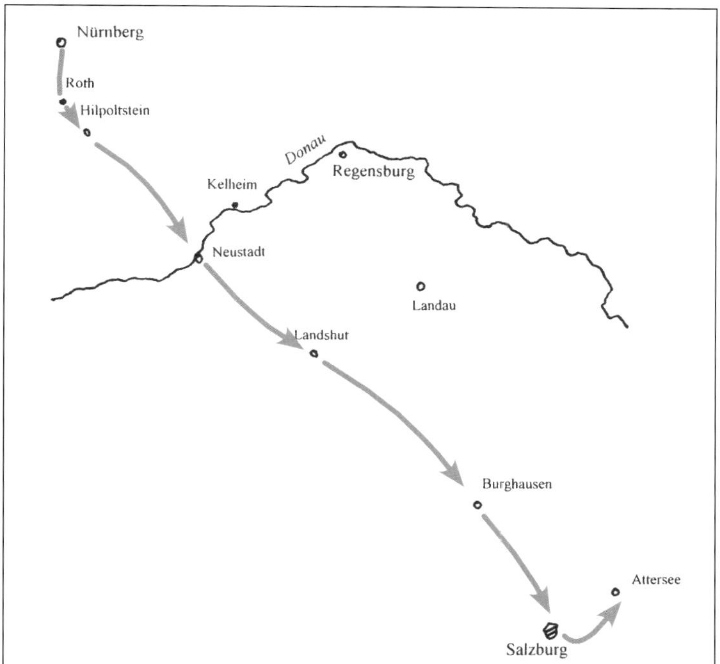

of the Verwaltungsdienst [Administrative and Supply Service] Arolsen. In 1944, I first joined SS-Panzergrenadier-Ausbildungs- und Ersatz-Bataillon 3. as an SS-Untersturmführer. From there, in mid-December 1944, I was transferred as an Rechnungsführer [Accounting officer] to IV. /Waffen-Artillerie-Regiment der SS 25 at SS-Truppenübungsplatz Neuhammer. In early February 1945, we marched on foot through the Sudetenland to Bohemia. Our packs and forage were loaded onto horse-drawn wagons, which we found on the Truppenübungsplatz. Since there were no horses, the men were harnessed to them. And so it went on until we were loaded onto trains near Tetschen [Czech: Decin], going to Roth near Nuremberg. I can only keep remembering the terrible cold, and that we were in a place where we could watch the bombing of Dresden on February 13-14, 1945. From Roth, we were able to reach Spalt by foot or by bicycle.

Strict order and discipline prevailed among the soldiers, as well as absolute obedience. But there was no more military service as we knew it. The Hungarians' morale was good; tremendous camaraderie. The Hungarian officers even believed in an ultimate victory until the very end, even if they did not display any particular enthusiasm for the war.

Our Artillerie-Abteilung had neither artillery nor other weapons, no motorized vehicles, only four horses, some harnesses, and a few bicycles. The men drilled on the street in front of the Bayrischen Hof [Bavarian Tavern]. The Führer and Unterführer were quartered in private houses; the men in the school building. Since there was nothing to administer in our Artillerie-Abteilung due to our lack of equipment, except the pay every ten days, the days we spent in Spalt were very fine.

Just before we were set off to march to Attersee, we passed through St. Georgen. We walked past the church when the pastor was hanging out the Austrian flag from the church tower. A young Wehrmacht Leutnant standing next to me, immediately shouted up to him, he should pull the flag in again. When the priest did not respond, he drew his pistol and shot up at the church tower several times. When I asked him what that was about, since everything was certainly over, he fired again, after which the flag was lowered. He got his satisfaction and we moved on.

On May 10, 1945, the Führerkorps of Waffen-SS-Artillerie-Regiment der SS 25 gathered at a farm in Attersee. We German Führer then disappeared into the mountains, on the advice of Regimentsadjutant Turner. Since we had no food, we gave ourselves up as Hungarians to the Americans in mid June 1945."

Kommandeure:
11/44 – 05/45 *Waffen-Brigadeführer* vitéz Grassy

Feldpost numbers:

Divisionsstab	00 020
Waffen-Grenadier-Regiment der SS 61 (ungarische Nr. 1)	08 104
I. Bataillon	39 881
II. Bataillon	00 706
Waffen-Grenadier-Regiment der SS 62 (ungarische Nr. 2)	01 121
I. Bataillon	17 380
II. Bataillon	01 817
Waffen-Grenadier-Regiment der SS 63 (ungarische Nr. 3)	20 689
I. Bataillon	02 110
II. Bataillon	39 933

Waffen-Artillerie-Regiment der SS 25 (ungarische Nr. 1)	41 777
I. Abteilung	64 266
II. Abteilung	42 525
III. Abteilung	65 614
IV. Abteilung	03 527
SS-Füsilier-Bataillon 25	02 629
SS-Pionier-Bataillon 25	44 395
SS-Panzerjäger-Abteilung 25	03 307
SS-Nachrichten-Abteilung 25	38 732
SS-Versorgungs-Regiment 25	03 872
SS-Veterinär-Kompanie 25	43 330
SS-Sanitäts-Kompanie 25	31 293
SS-Feldersatz-Bataillon 25	34 545

26. Waffen-Grenadier-Division der SS "Hungaria" (*ungarische Nr. 2*)

As part of the announced reorganization of the Hungarian Army, *Honvédminister Generaloberst* Beregfy let it be known on December 23, 1944, that a second Hungarian *Freiwilligen-Division* would be organized. It was to be ready for combat by April 30, 1945. Since the infantry traditionally did not have a high reputation in Hungary, they called for enlistments in a *Panzergrenadier-Division,* just as had been done for *25. Waffen-Grenadier-Division der SS "Hunyadi."*

A few days later, 8,100 Hungarians were ordered from the Rajka collection point for Hungarian *Freiwilligen* to *SS-Truppenübungsplatz* Neuhammer. They were reinforced there with the approximately 8,000 extra men of *25. Waffen-Grenadier-Division der SS (ungarische Nr. 1),* so that by the end of December 1944, the formation had the following strength:

	Führer	***Unterführer***	***Männer***	**Total**
Actual	351	1,270	15,140	16,761
	2.10%	7.57%	90.33%	100%
Authorized	333	2,164	10,204	12,701
	2.62%	17.04%	80.34%	100%

Conditions at the *Truppenübungsplatz* were chaotic for the newly enlisted 30,000 Hungarians, due to the lack of supplies, food, and the overburdened sanitary facilities. To relieve the situation, the second *Division* being organized was transferred to *Truppenübungsplatz* Schieratz, about 240km further east on the Warta River at the turn of the year 1944-45.

Besides the overall lack of matching uniforms, weapons were available for only about 25% of the soldiers. At the beginning of January 1945, the newly formed unit had only:

2,711	*Gewehre 98k*
50	*Gewehre 98k mit Zielfernrohr*
792	*Gewehre Mannlicher* [Mannlicher rifles]
450	*Pistolen 08*
271	*Pistolen 09* (Hungarian)
300	*Maschinenpistolen* (Italian)
50	*leichte Maschinengewehre 42*
10	*schwere Maschinengewehre 42*
10	*Granatwerfer* 8.14cm
10	*Granatwerfer* 12cm

10	*Panzerabwehrkanonen* 7.5cm
10	*leichte Feldhaubitzen* 10.5cm
10	*schwere Feldhaubitzen* 15cm
50	*Panzerschreck* [literally "tank scarer," anti-tank weapon]
500	*Panzerfäuste*
1,000	*Handgranaten* [hand grenades]
10	motorcycles
3	cars
2	trucks
500	bicycles

This materiel corresponded to that of three *Grenadier-Bataillone*, two *Artillerie-Abteilungen* and *Panzerjäger* [anti-tank "hunters"]-*Kompanie*. Some 12,000 Hungarians had no weapons and often still wore civilian clothes at the *Truppenübungsplatz*. The materiel situation got even worse on January 14, 1945, when almost all weapons and equipment had to be given over to the hard-pressed *9. Armee*. The *Division* retained only about 1,500 rifles, 100 *Maschinenpistolen* and some *Maschinengewehre* and *Panzerfäuste*. With this it was possible to improvise equipping two *Grenadier-Bataillone*.

This was the worst possible situation for the ***26. Waffen-Grenadier-Division der SS (ungarische Nr. 2)***, which the *SS-FHA* ordered should be formed as of January 29, 1945. It was possible to organize the planned units in terms of personnel:

Waffen-Grenadier-Regiment der SS 64 (ung. Nr. 4) (I. – III. Bataillon)
Waffen-Grenadier-Regiment der SS 65 (ung. Nr. 5) (I. – III. Bataillon)
Waffen-Grenadier-Regiment der SS 85 (ung. Nr. 6) (I. – III. Bataillon)
Waffen-Artillerie-Regiment der SS 26 (ung. Nr. 2) (I. – IV. Abteilung)
SS-Füsilier-Bataillon 26
SS-Pionier-Bataillon 26
SS-Panzerjäger-Abteilung 26
SS-Nachrichten-Abteilung 26
SS-Versorgungs-Regiment 26
SS-Veterinär-Kompanie 26
SS-Sanitäts-Kompanie 26
SS-Feldersatz-Bataillon 26

As the Red Army approached *Truppenübungsplatz* Schieratz on January 17, 1945, *Divisionskommandeur Waffen-Oberführer* vitéz Pisky ordered a night retreat march towards Kalisz [German: Kalisch]. The troops had only been in the area for two weeks. A *Kampfgruppe* of around 300 men, led by *Waffen-Hauptsturmführer* Krasznay, covered the withdrawal of *26. Waffen-Grenadier-Division der SS*.

On January 21, 1945, the formation divided into two groups: one, led by the *Divisionskommandeur*, moved toward Jarocin [German: Jarotschin], while the other marched southwest to Ostrowo. Two days later, *Waffen-Oberführer* vitéz Pisky was killed in a battle with Soviet units. *SS-Oberführer* Maack was given command of the *Division*.

The two marching groups met on January 24, 1945, at Leszno [German: Lissa]. By then, they had covered – in deep sub-zero temperatures and falling snow – some 150km within a week.

When all the troops, including the remnants of *SS-Kampfgruppe Krasznay* (190 men) had assembled in Leszno, the *26. Waffen-Grenadier-Division der SS* marched further on January 27, 1945, to Wschowa [German: Fraustadt], about 20km to the west. The next day, the *SS-FHA* ordered that the unit should finally be deployed to *SS-Truppenübungsplatz* Neuhammer.

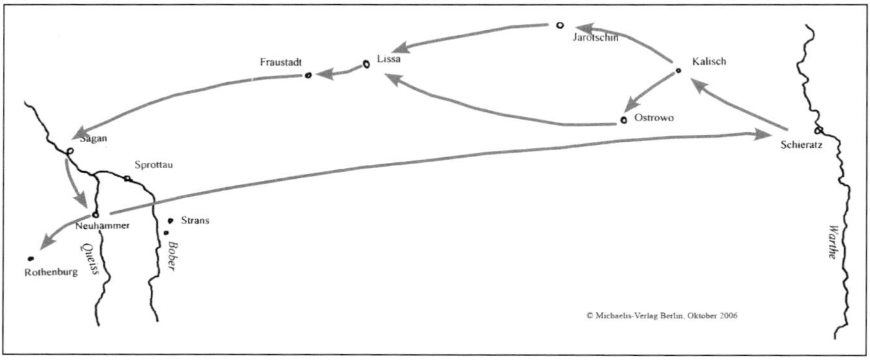

Route of 26. Waffen-Grenadier-Division der SS (end of December 1944 - February 1945).

The units reached the some 70km distant *Truppenübungsplatz* at the beginning of February 1945, moving by way of Zagan [German: Sagan] and briefly moved into the empty barracks of the *20. Waffen-Grenadier-Division der SS (estnische Nr. 1)*, which had been marched off to the front. They were issued any available articles of clothing from the depot, so that on February 7, 1945, it could be reported to the *SS*-FHA that the unit was now fully uniformed. At the same time the *Divisionskommando* reported their stock of weapons and equipment as:

810	*Gewehre 98k*
17	*Gewehre k43*
610	*Gewehre Mannlicher*
171	*Gewehre Tokarev* (Soviet)
507	*Pistolen 08* and *09* (Hungarian)
73	*Maschinenpistolen* (Italian)
11	*leichte Maschinengewehre 42*
3	*schwere Maschinengewehre 42*

SS-Füsilier-Bataillon 25	65 940
SS-Pionier-Bataillon 25	66 211
SS-Panzerjäger-Abteilung 25	39 037
SS-Nachrichten-Abteilung 25	66 843
SS-Versorgungs-Regiment 25	67 241

27. *SS*-Freiwilligen-Grenadier-Division der SS "Langemarck" (*flämische Nr. 1*)

Freiwilligen-Legion "Flandern"[19]

In May 1940, the *Waffen-SS* began to recruit *Freiwilligen* in Belgium among the just under five million Flemish population, for *SS-Standarte* [*SS* Regiment] *"Westland."* With an enlistment period of at least two years, and extraordinarily high physical standards, their success, however, was very moderate. By September 1940, not even fifty Flemings had joined the *Standarte* of *SS-Division "Wiking."*

Since they wanted to utilize any *Freiwilligen* who would not qualify for serving in the *SS*, organization of SS-Freiwilligen-Verband *"Nordwest"* began on April 10, 1941, in Hamburg-Langenhorn. By lowering the physical standards, it would be possible to form two *Standarden*, one each of Flemish and Dutch men. While a candidate for *SS*-Standarte Westland was supposed to be between 17 and 25 years old and at least 1.74m tall, the age limit for *SS-Freiwilligen-Verband "Nordwest"* was raised to forty and height requirement reduced to at least 1.65m.

The first men left Belgium already by April 14, 1941. Since the number of enlistments again fell short of expectations, what had been planned as a two *Regimenter* formation – stationed since the end of July 1941 at *SS-Truppenübungsplatz* Debica[20] – was renamed the *SS-Freiwilligen-Standarte "Nordwest"* on August 6, 1941. In this unit, the Flemish were to form one *Sturmbann* (*SS-Bataillon*) and the Dutch two. In September 1941, the *Standarte* moved to *Truppenübungsplatz* Arys in Ostpreußen. The Flemish *Sturmbann* had at this time a strength of:

Führer	*Unterführer*	*Männer*	**Total**
25	78	1,009	1,112
2.25%	7%	90.75%	100%

In addition to the 162-man German *Rahmenpersonal* [cadre staff], there were 950 Flemish in the units. The fact, however, that of more than 100 *Führer* and *Unterführer*, only fifteen were Felmish, soon led to resentment among the *Freiwilligen*. It made matters worse that the German *Rahmenpersonal* displayed no tact whatever towards them. The leader of the *Vlaamsch Nationaal Verbond*, Staf de Clercq, expressed his indignation to Himmler in March 1942 about this treatment of his countrymen:

[19] In Flemish and Dutch, it was designated: *Vrijwilligers-Legioen Vlaanderen*.

[20] The *Truppenübungsplatz* was renamed *SS-Truppenübungsplatz* Heidelager on March 15, 1943.

Members of the Freiwilligen-Legion “Flandern” wore a special cufftitle and a national badge displaying the Flemish lion.

"In the 1. Kompanie, the Kompanieführer makes no secret of his contempt for the Flemish. In his unjust view, only the Spieß [slang for First Sergeant] outranks him. The boys are abused for the slightest little thing in the crudest words, and even caned [...]

Some 140 soldiers [were] recruited at that time among the schaffenden Arbeitern [productive workers] in northern France, who had been promised that they would be employed in the German labor force and earn more [...] I am even more outraged by what the officers of the Flemish Legion say about our people. 'In the 1. Kompanie, for example, the Flemish are regularly denounced as 'grubby people,' 'dirty people,' 'stupid people,' 'gypsy-folk' etc. And to the Flemish officers: "Translate that into your Russian language.' Worse, these insults are used in the presence of people from the occupied territories. When the 1. Kompanie was billeted in Zapol, the Legion men were summoned to a local place where they were called 'gypsy folk' in front of 100 Latvians, 'that they were wrong if they thought that they had come there to fatten themselves up, because they had to work for their pay.' Afterwards, the Latvians came to us and asked if we were really mercenaries who are paid to fight. The boys' morale has been destroyed ..."

By November 6, 1941, *SS-Freiwilligen-Standarte "Nordwest"* was disbanded and its soldiers used to form the *Freiwilligen-Legionen "Flandern"* and *"Niederlande."* This move corresponded somewhat more to the wishes of the foreign nationals, who basically wanted to participate in an independent, national troop in the fight against communism. A former member recalls:

"When the Vlaams Legioen was set up very shortly after the outbreak of war with the Soviet Union, it was believed in Flanders that the Legion was a kind of Freikorps [irregular militia], that it likely was part of the Waffen-SS, but would be very much based on the VNV [Vlaams Nationaal Verbond: Flemish National Union]. The Vlaams Nationaal Verbond had been a political party before the war and had pursued its Flemish-nationalist ideas after May 28, 1940, with the good will of the Germans. The VNV was pro-German, because you knew that its fate depended upon Germany. When war broke out with the Soviet Union, the leader of the VNV wanted a Flemish Legion to be able to fight on the Ostfront. Since you wanted to show some independence, there were no SS runes on the collar patches, but a three-spoke sun rune. The majority of the Legion Freiwilligen came from VNV circles or the NSJV [Nationaal-Socialistische Jeugd Verbond: National-Socialist Youth Union]."

For Germany, the independent legions primarily provided propaganda benefits, representing the participation of Western European countries in the *"ideological war."* On November 6, 1941, Himmler announced:

> *"The Führer has approved the participation of foreign-national Freiwilligen in the fight against Bolshevism. However, they are to participate in cohesive units under their own leadership. Foreign Freiwilligen of related blood types – Danes, Flemish, Dutch and Norwegians – will be, as far as they enlist in sufficient strength, formed into Freiwilligen-Legionen by the SS-FHA and organized into the Waffen-SS."*

This affiliation did not mean direct membership. Therefore, *"SS"* was deliberately omitted from the unit designations. The foreign soldiers were given *SS Soldbücher* and ranks, but the form differed, so that instead of *"SS-"* the rank was designated as *"Legion"*; e.g., *Legions-Untersturmführer.*

In any case, on November 6, 1941, after a good six months of training, Himmler put the *Freiwilligen-Legion "Flandern"* under the command of the *2. SS-Infanterie-Brigade (mot.)* Four days later, the *Legion*, transported by way of Jelgava-Taurage [German: Tauroggen] -Riga-Valga-Tatu [German: Dorpat], reached the Tosno-Adrianova area. Together with a Latvian *Schutzmannschafts-Bataillon* which arrived at the same time, the *Legion* replaced the departing *SS-Infanterie-Regiment 4 (mot.).* Initially used in anti-partisan operations, on December 3, 1941, it was transferred to the front. The Flemish were deployed for a week under the leadership of *Legions-Kommandeur SS-Obersturmbannführer* Lippert, in the region of Maluksa (between Mga and Kirishi), and were then transferred by way of Tosno-Lugo-Pskov-Riga to Kandava [German: Kandau] and moved into winter quarters in the Curonian "Switzerland" area.

After about four weeks of rest, on January 10, 1942, the troops were given marching orders to the Novogorod region, in anticipation of the expected large-scale Soviet offensive on the Volkhov. Here the *Legion* formed *SS-Kampfgruppe* Debes, together with the *Begleit-Bataillon* [Escort Battalion] *Reichsführer-SS* and *SS-Flak Abteilung Ost.* Fighting started in the sector of *XXXVIII. Armee-Korps* near Podberesyje (about 20km northwest of Novgorod) on January 19, 1942. Fighting at times at minus 50 degrees C, the troops tried to cut off the far-advanced Soviet 2 Shock Army from its rear support west of the Volkhov. The severe offensive and defensive fighting led the *Wehrmachtbericht* to report on February 10, 1942:

> *"In the successful defense against the enemy's heaviest mass attacks, the Württemberg 25. motorisierte Infanterie-Division and the SS-Legion Flandern distinguished themselves."*

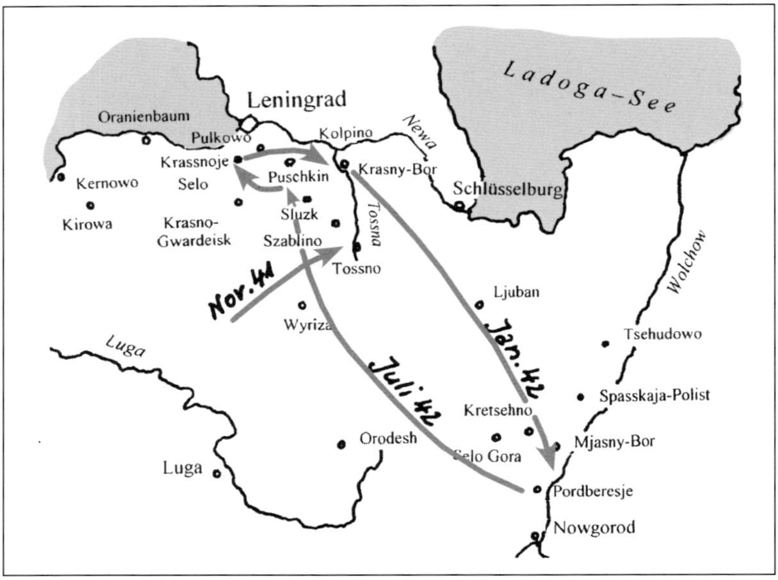

Operational area of Freiwilligen-Legion "Flandern" (November 1941 - May 1943).

The Flemings were again mentioned on March 4, 1942:

> *"At various positions in the central and northern front sector, enemy attacks remained unsuccessful. In their own local attack operations, the enemy was thrown out of their positions. The SS-Legion Flandern took twenty-five enemy bunkers in fierce hand-to-hand combat."*

On March 24, 1942, *Freiwilligen-Legion "Flandern"* announced their current losses in action on the Russian front as 517 killed and wounded. This means that it had lost about 50% of its original strength especially in the fighting from January 19, 1942.

After a few days of rest, the Flemish *Freiwilligen* again took part in the back-and-forth battles to smash the Volkhov pocket. Here, *Freiwilligen-Legion "Flandern"* was placed under command of *Kampfgruppe* Hoppe and was to push through the pocket to the north. This was to establish contact with the German troops advancing from Krechno. After this successfully fought operation, which resulted in heavy losses, the encircled Soviet 2. Shock Army was destroyed by the end of June 1942. The Flemings were pulled out of the front by the end of June 1942 and transferred to the rest area near the front at Osiya (southeast of Selo-Gora). Here *SS-Hauptsturmführer* Schellong took command of the *Freiwilligen-Legion*, and its badly thinned ranks were simultaneously replenished with replacements.

As part of the *2. SS-Infanterie-Brigade (mot.),* it was transferred four weeks later to the Leningrad front. Under command of the *I. Armee-Korps*, the unit marched to the area south of Pulkovo (17km south of Leningrad), to the west of Pushkin. Stationed in a front sector about four kilometers long, which ran like a spike into the Soviet main line of combat, the Flemings held this exposed position for almost six months, despite severe enemy attacks.

At the end of January 1943, *Freiwilligen-Legion "Flandern"* was relieved by elements of the *SS-Polizei-Division* and moved to the area west of Krasny-Bor. It remained here in rest quarters for about three weeks, as a *Korpsreserve*. Due to the Soviet winter offensive, the Flemings were placed under command of the hard-pressed *SS-Polizei-Division*. Starting February 25, 1943, there were fierce defensive battles in the Neva river bend north of Krasny Bor, with the Red Army repeatedly trying to get across the frozen Neva. In mid-March 1943, it was again transferred as a reserve to Szablino (about 10km south of Krasny Bor), and was again engaged in renewed, extremely heavy defensive fighting on March 22, 1943, near Krasny Bor. The *Legion* was almost bled to death after one week. Of the 500 men deployed, only a *Zug* [platoon] of barely fifty soldiers remained! All the others had been killed or wounded. On April 1, 1943, the remnants of the *Legion* were assembled in Szablino and again reinforced with 250 replacements. On May 13, 1943, *Freiwilligen-Legion "Flandern"* was transferred to *SS-Truppenübungsplatz* Heidelager, to be reinforced there as *SS-Freiwilligen-Sturmbrigade "Langemarck."*

A former member recalls:

> *"I was born on January 15, 1925, in Flanders and signed up for the Vlaams Legioen at the age of 17. On July 23, 1942, I was in the town hall of Kortrijk for the physicals for Flemish volunteers for Freiwilligen-Legion 'Flandern.'*
>
> *The volunteers were also examined for the Waffen-SS (SS-Regiment Westland). All kinds of information was collected: height, weight, chest circumference, visual acuity, etc. I had seen with concern that most of those ahead of me were not considered very good. These guys were all bigger than me, with my 165cm. It surprised me all the more when an SS-Führer asked me if I wanted to report directly to the Waffen-SS, although there the minimum height was 168cm. I kept to my wish to join the Vlaams Legioen. On August 10, 1942, I was already moved to Antwerp. Wearing black dyed Belgian uniforms, we got our first training here, with the result that some were sent back home again. In September 1942, we were transferred to SS-Ausbildungslager [training camp] Sennheim in Alsace. Here we got the field-gray Waffen-SS uniforms with the SS collar patches. The replacements for all Flemish Ostfrontfreiwilligen were in Sennheim. Also for the Waffen-SS (in particular for SS-Regiment 'Westland').*

In October 1942, the SS volunteers were sent to Klagenfurt and transferred to Graz as the Leion Ersatz-Bataillon. After the infantry basic training, I went to Nuremberg for communications training. In May 1943, I found myself again in Graz. Here we, the Flemish members of the Bataillon, one day had to buckle on our equipment and report for duty on the parade ground wearing Stahlhelm [German steel helmets]. The Kommandeur came and announced to us, after the usual report and greeting, a Führerbefehl [order from the Führer], that went something like this: The Führer pays tribute to the mission and dedication of the Flemish in the fight against our common enemy. Now a new, strong unit will be trained that will bear the honorable name Langemarck. SS-Sturmbannführer Schellong will continue in command.

Thus, the Flemish Legion was no more. The name 'Flanders' disappeared and in exchange we got the name of a small Flemish town – we could not understand why? Some of us thought that we knew that many German soldiers had been killed there in the First World War, and a large and beautiful cemetery remained as witness for this.

The mood among most of us was very depressed; we had volunteered for the Flemish Legion, which embodied a treasured idea for us, and not the Waffen-SS!

We were still wearing the three-spoke sun wheel on our collar patches, which should now be replaced by SS runes. There were comrades who publicly expressed their opposition to this new situation. An acquaintance of mine, Cyriel Peleman, even refused to wear the SS collar patch. Most, however, accepted the new situation – including me. In practice, things were not so different. But it left a very bad taste!"

6. SS-Freiwilligen-Sturmbrigade "Langemarck"

As part of the effort to compensate for the losses at Stalingrad and Tunis, an attempt was made to expand the existing *Freiwilligen* formation at least to the two *Bataillone* of a *Sturmbrigade neuer Art* [new model], by using new enlistees in Belgium as well as by Flemish arms industry workers in Germany. As had been seen since 1940, calls for enlistment had never brought in the desired numbers, so the idea became to recruit the Flemish de facto by force. To this end, Himmler planned to introduce *Arbeitsdienstpflicht* [compulsory labor service] for entire cohorts of men by birth year, as had been done in the Baltic States. The men would be able to choose whether they wanted to work in the arms industry or join the *Waffen-SS* or *Polizei*. Since this kind of human rights violations would likely have led to widespread unrest and strikes, the plan was ultimately abandoned.

Left: Jan de Vriese.

Remy Schrijnen was awarded the Ritterkreuz on September 21, 1944.

Collar patch for Flemish SS-Freiwilligen: the three-spoke sun.

In the course of various reclassifications and new formations of the *Waffen-SS*, the *Freiwilligen-Legion "Flandern"* was finally dissolved as of May 31, 1943. The some 700 Legion members gradually assembled at *SS-Truppenübungsplatz* Heidelager were initally commandeered as *Ersatz* troops for *SS-Grenadier-Ausbildungs-Bataillon Ost* and sent to Zhitomir. Here they took part in the anti-partisan operations Vistula I and II in the Pripet Marshes. On July 8, 1943, the Flemings were transferred back to *SS-Truppenübungsplatz* Heidelager.

For the formation of *SS-Freiwilligen-Sturmbrigade "Langemarck"* which had been ordered, the units were transferred to *SS-Truppenübungsplatz* Böhmen. As *Freiwilligen* enlistment, as already expected, remained far below the hoped-for level, physical standards were further relaxed. Entry age was raised to forty-five years, among other things. At the end of July 1943, about 300 new recruits from Gent arrived at Milovice [German: Milowitz]. In August 1943, another 400 Flemings arrived at Milovice, near Prague, from the previous *Legion Ersatz-Bataillon* in Graz, by way of *SS-Grenadier-Ersatz-Bataillon Ost* in Wroclaw [German: Breslau].

Organized as a *Sturmbrigade n.A.* [*neuer Art*: new model], the unit was to form a motorized *Grenadier-Bataillon* and a *schwere Bataillon*. Effective as of October 22, 1943, the formation was designated, within *Waffen-SS* serial numbering, as *6. SS-Freiwilligen-Sturmbrigade "Langemarck."*[21]

Following some six months of training, the organization process was considered completed by the beginning of December 1943, and was finished off with a parade in Prague. Formation strength corresponded to that of a reinforced *Regiment* and amounted to:

Führer	***Unterführer***	***Männer***	**Total**
40	202	1,774	2,016
2%	10%	88%	100%

As was the situation for most (newly) formed units, it lacked cadre and officer personnel, in this case, about twenty *Führer* and 150 *Unterführer*. The *Brigade* was therefore understrength to face the upcoming large-scale combat.

By the end of 1943, the Red Army succeeded in breaking through about 30km of the *4. Panzer-Armee* (on the northern flank of *Heeresgruppe Süd*) *HKL* along the Kiev-Zhitomir highway. *Heeresgruppe Süd* then moved the *1. Panzer-Armee* to the threatened area, to encircle the advancing Soviet troops, using flanking attacks together with the *4. Panzer-Armee*. To strengthen the formations

[21] An interesting fact was that the Flemish unit was given a name that marked a place in Flanders, but had no historical reference for the Flemish. Rather, it was the place where on November 10, 1914, the German *XXIII. Reserve-Korps* (usually *Freiwilligen* who had not seen service and reservists) stormed the Franco-Belgian troops in the first Battle of Ypres, suffering extraordinarily high losses. Later, there was an attempt to create a German heroic epic here. However, there was a reference in that the *Freiwilligen-Legion Flandern* had also suffered very high losses in this battle. These were substantially higher for the same period than those of the *SS-Freiwilligen* in *SS-Division "Wiking."*

6. SS-Freiwilligen-Sturmbrigade "Langemarck" cufftitle.

Conrad Schellong was born on February 7, 1910 in Dresden. As an SS-Hauptsturmführer, he took over command of Freiwilligen-Legion "Flandern" on July 10, 1942. After his appointment as SS-Sturmbannführer, he commanded SS-Freiwilligen-Sturmbrigade "Langemarck" from spring 1943. As SS-Obersturmbannführer, and Deutschen Kreuz [German Cross] in Gold and Ritterkreuz recipient, he then led SS-Freiwilligen-Grenadier-Regiments 66.

for this operation, *6. SS-Freiwilligen-Sturmbrigade "Langemarck"* was among those given movement orders on December 26, 1943. Transported by rail, the Flemish reached the *HKL* four days later at Chudnov (southwest of Zhitomir). As soon as they got off the trains, they were plunged into the fighting to free the cut-off *Kampfgruppe/2. SS-Panzergrenadier-Division "Das Reich"* as part of the *XXXXVIII. Panzer-Korps*.

The formation was used in offensive fighting near Zhitomir up until January 5, 1944. At that point, however, the Soviet pressure was so great that the units – under command of *SS-Kampfgruppe "Das Reich"* – had to retreat to Severinovka by January 11, 1944. When the enemy shifted the focus of their attack, it was possible to hold the ground (now in the sector of the *1. Panzer-Armee*) until mid-February 1944. On February 17, 1944, the *Sturmbrigade* was ordered to the approximately 70km northwest left flank of *1. Panzer-Armee* near Shepetovka.

The first skirmishes with advancing enemy troops occurred five days later, and then another few days later the unit was given a movement order to Yampol, about 60km southwest on the Horyn River. Replacements from Wrocklow [German: Breslau] arrived to reinforce the decimated *Brigade* on February 28, 1944, which constituted the left wing of the *1. Panzer-Armee* in the forefield of the *Generalgouvernement*. After violent bombardment, *SS-Sturmbannführer* Schellong, who was shortly afterwards wounded, ordered a withdrawal on March 3, 1944. The units were encircled when Soviet troops to their west broke through southwards and swung to the east. Repeatedly embattled by enemy troops, only some 50% of the original unit manpower reached Starokostiantyniv on March 19, 1944.

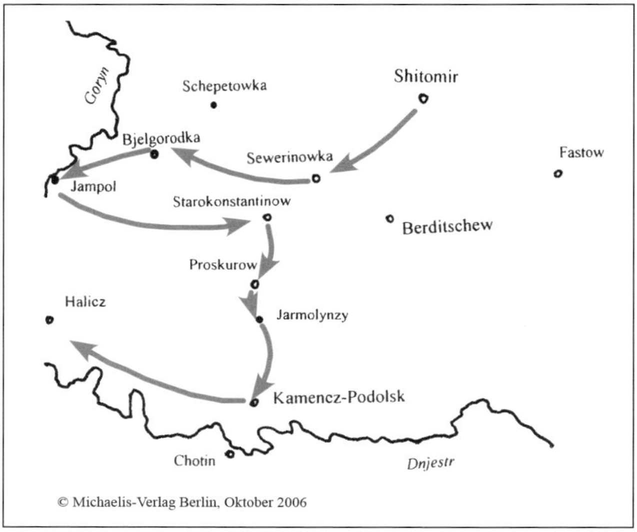

Deployment of the 6. SS-Freiwilligen-Sturmbrigade "Langemarck" in Ukraine.

Under command of the *LIX. Panzer-Korps*, the unit was ordered to occupy positions at Khmelnytskyi [formerly Proskurov], about 40km to the south. The plan was for the *1. Panzer-Armee,* effectively trapped by the Dniester to its rear, would cross the Zubruch River to the west and break through the Soviet lines, and then link up with the *4. Panzer-Armee*. For this operation, the remaining Flemish *Freiwilligen* were placed under command of *Korpsgruppe Breith* on March 26, 1944. On March 28, 1944, they fell in for the attack on enemy-occupied Kamenetz-Podolsk. Fighting constantly, the men reached the bridgehead position at Chotin on the Dniester. While the northern sections of *1. Panzer-Armee* were able to make contact with the elements of *4. Panzer-Armee* pushing towards them, in the first week of April 1944, the Flemish troops crossed the Dniester under heavy enemy fire – sometimes swimming across. The last vehicles and heavy weapons were left on the northeast bank. First transferred to the *Generalgouvernement*, on April 27, 1944, they got the command at Jaslo to assemble the men at *SS-Truppenübungsplatz* Böhmen.

The remaining *Freiwilligen* reached *SS-Truppenübungsplatz* Böhmen by rail on May 3, 1944. As part of the *Sturmbrigade* refitting the order arrived on June 28, 1944, to form a second *Grenadier-Battalion (mot.)* and reorganize the *Sturmgeschütz-Batterie* [assault gun battery] into *SS-Sturmgeschütz-Abteilung 56* with three batteries.[22] Since they had lost all artillery in the previous operations, the *SS-Führungshauptamt* ordered that the eight-gun *Sturmgeschütz-Batterie* planned for the *19. Waffen-Grenadier-Division der SS (lettische Nr. 2)* be diverted to the *6. SS-Freiwilligen-Sturmbrigade*. However, it was as impossible to realize an actual expansion into an *Abteilung* as it had been to form a second *Grenadier-Battalion*.

On June 30, 1944, the *6. SS-Freiwilligen-Sturmbrigade "Langemarck"* reported a strength of:

	Führer	***Unterführer***	***Männer***	**Total**
Actual	47	262	1,422	1,731
	2.72%	15.14%	82.14%	100%
Authorized	63	497	1,995	2,555
	2.47%	19.45%	78.08%	100%

The authorized strength had been increased by about 700 men due to the ordered formation of a second *Grenadier-Bataillon*. Although it was not possible initially to reach this number, at least it was possible to compensate for the losses incurred in the previous four months by enlisting new *Freiwilligen*. In fact, the formation required approximately six months of training and refitting to become combat ready for a frontline deployment.

[22] The number 56 came from the general designation of the *Brigade* units with a 5, with an additional special *Brigade* number. In this case 6, thus, 56.

Nevertheless, the formation was already ordered by mid-July 1944 to organize a *Kampfgruppe*, which was sent to the badly hit *III. (germanischen) SS-Panzer-Korps* in Estonia. On July 19, 1944, 245 men under the command of *SS-Hauptsturmführer Rehmann* left the *Protektorat Böhmen und Mähren*. As the *III. SS Panzer-Korps* withdrew to the Tannenberg position, the two Flemish *Kompanien* reached the Toila area on July 25, 1944. The men were immediately sent in action and occupied positions, together with Estonians of the *I. /Waffen-Grenadier-Regiments der SS 47 (estnische Nr. 3)* on the so-called *Kinderheimhöhe* [Estonian: *Lastekodumägi*, Orphanage Hill]. Already the next day, three *Führer* were killed by grenade strikes during a situational briefing. *SS-Hauptsturmführer* Rehmann was wounded in the hand, and went to a field hospital. This destroyed his reputation among the Flemish *Freiwilligen*, who thought he had left out of cowardice. *SS-Untersturmführer* D'Haese then took over leadership of the *Kampfgruppe*. On July 28, 1944, Soviet troops overran the hill and immediately attacked the so-called *Grenadierhöhe* [Grenadier heights]. During these days, *SS-Sturmmann* Schrijnen, deployed as a *Richtschütze* [gunner] on a *schwere Panzerabwehrkanone*, shot down – ultimately, completely on his own – ten Soviet T-34 tanks and three Soviet "Joseph Stalin" heavy tanks. For this, he was awarded the *Ritterkreuz des Eisernen Kreuzes* on September 21, 1944. He recalls:

> *"Since I was too short for the Waffen-SS, I volunteered in 1942, as a worker in the German armaments industry in Kempten, Allgäu, for the Gebirgsjäger [Mountain Troops]. Before I could anyway be integrated there, in November 1942, I got an enlistment order for the Freiwilligen-Legion 'Flandern.' After training, I was initially deployed as a messenger, and later as a Richtschütze in the Panzerjäger-Kompanie of SS-Sturmbrigade Langemarck.*
>
> *In Ukraine on December 31, 1943, we were ordered directly into action from the loading ramp. Here I was able to shoot up my first three T-34s. In spring 1944, when we got into the 1. Panzer-Armee pocket, I also fought enemy field gunners who were trying to prevent our retreat. In March 1944, I was wounded and taken to a field hospital. In June 1944, I got four weeks convalescent leave after discharge from the hospital. I did not take it, but instead drove to my troop, which was now at Truppenübungsplatz Milowitz near Prague. In mid-July 1944, I reached the Narva bridgehead in a Kampfgruppe. Our losses were extraordinary. Our guns and operations kept breaking down under the Soviet Trommelfeuer [heavy barrage]. Finally, only mine was left, and I fired it alone! For this, I was awarded the Ritterkreuz zum Eisernen Kreuz. At the end of September 1944, the remnants of our Kampfgruppe were taken to Pommerania with the Gotland."*

Deployment of Kampfgruppe Rehmann in Estonia.

As the positions were contested in brutal see-saw battles, the Red Army shifted their attacks to the area west of Pskov [German: Pleskau]. On August 10, 1944, the Soviet 3. Baltic Front attacked the *XXVIII.*

The *Armee-Korps* on the left wing of the *18. Armee, Armee-Abteilung Narwa*, charged with defending the ground between Lakes Peipus and Wirz, ordered the Kommandeur of *4. SS-Freiwilligen-Grenadier-Brigade "Nederland," SS-Brigadeführer* Wagner, to organize a *Kampfgruppe* on August 14, 1944, which was to re-establish contact with the *XXVIII. Armee-Korps* which had been pushed back. For this operation, the remnants of *SS-Kampfgruppe Rehmann*, now only *Kompanie*-strength were put under command of *Kampfgruppe/5. SS-Freiwilligen-Sturmbrigade "Wallonien."* In the sector of the *Division*-strength *Gruppe Wagner*, they were able to restore contact to the neighboring *Korps* and establish a reasonably stable front along the Emajõgi River [German: Embach]. Nevertheless, the Red Army was able to establish a bridgehead across the river between Lakes Wirz and Peipus at Tartu.

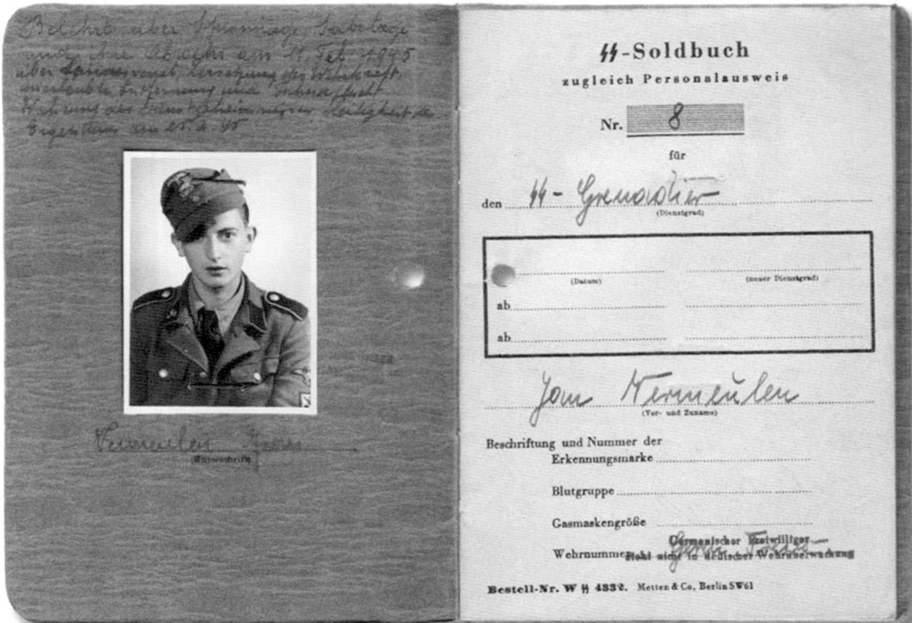

ϟϟ-Soldbuch
zugleich Personalausweis
Nr. 8
für
den ϟϟ-Grenadier
(Dienstgrad)
(Datum) (neuer Dienstgrad)
ab
ab
Jan Verneulen
(Vor- und Zuname)
Beschriftung und Nummer der Erkennungsmarke
Blutgruppe
Gasmaskengröße
Wehrnummer ~~Germanischer Freiwilliger — Steht nicht in deutscher Wehrüberwachung~~
Bestell-Nr. W ϟϟ 4332. Metten & Co, Berlin SW61

Jan Verneulen joined 27. SS-Freiwilligen-Grenadier-Division "Langemarck" in 1944, and finally served in SS-Freiwilligen-Grenadier-Regiment 66.

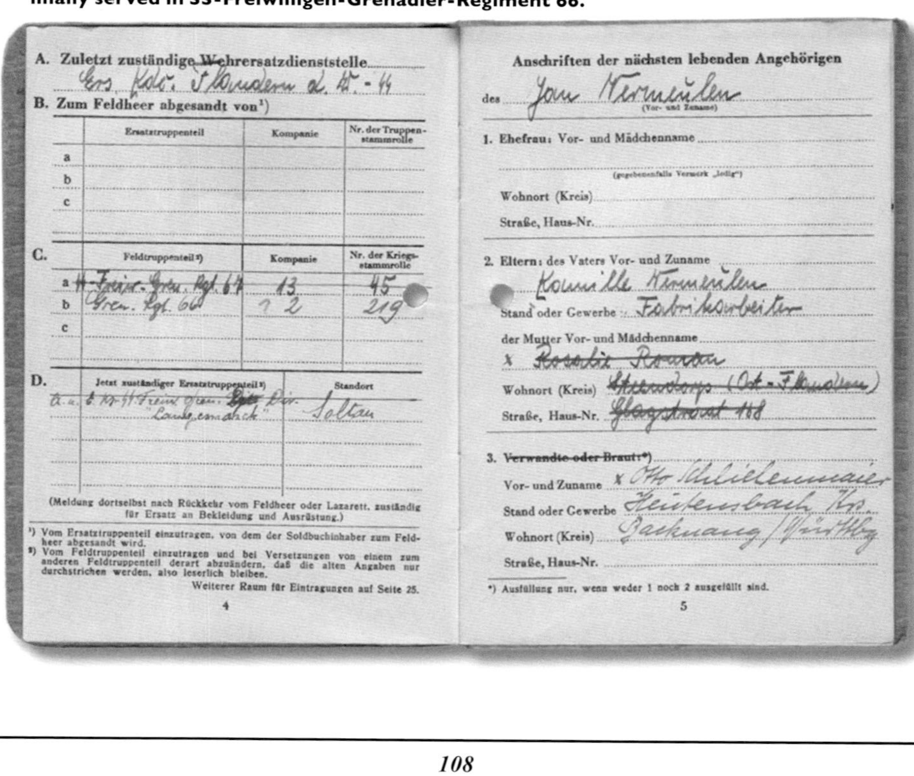

A. Zuletzt zuständige Wehrersatzdienststelle
Ers. Kdo. Flandern d. W.-ϟϟ
B. Zum Feldheer abgesandt von¹)

	Ersatztruppenteil	Kompanie	Nr. der Truppenstammrolle
a			
b			
c			

C.

	Feldtruppenteil²)	Kompanie	Nr. der Kriegsstammrolle
a	~~ϟϟ-Freiw.-Gren. Rgt. 67~~	~~13~~	~~45~~
b	Gren. Rgt. 66	12	219
c			

D.

Jetzt zuständiger Ersatztruppenteil²)	Standort
A. u. E. Btl. ϟϟ-Freiw. Gren. Div. "Langemarck"	Soltau

(Meldung dortselbst nach Rückkehr vom Feldheer oder Lazarett, zuständig für Ersatz an Bekleidung und Ausrüstung.)

¹) Vom Ersatztruppenteil einzutragen, von dem der Soldbuchinhaber zum Feldheer abgesandt wird.
²) Vom Feldtruppenteil einzutragen und bei Versetzungen von einem zum anderen Feldtruppenteil derart abzuändern, daß die alten Angaben nur durchstrichen werden, also leserlich bleiben.
Weiterer Raum für Eintragungen auf Seite 25.
4

Anschriften der nächsten lebenden Angehörigen
des Jan Verneulen
(Vor- und Zuname)
1. Ehefrau: Vor- und Mädchenname
(gegebenenfalls Vermerk „ledig")
Wohnort (Kreis)
Straße, Haus-Nr.
2. Eltern: des Vaters Vor- und Zuname
Kamille Verneulen
Stand oder Gewerbe: Fabrikarbeiter
der Mutter Vor- und Mädchenname
x ~~Rosalie [illegible]~~
Wohnort (Kreis) ~~[illegible] (Ost-Flandern)~~
Straße, Haus-Nr. ~~[illegible] 118~~
3. ~~Verwandte oder Braut~~*)
Vor- und Zuname x Otto [illegible]
Stand oder Gewerbe [illegible]
Wohnort (Kreis) Backnang/Württbg.
Straße, Haus-Nr.
*) Ausfüllung nur, wenn weder 1 noch 2 ausgefüllt sind.
5

In September 1944, Hitler decided to evacuate Estonia. For the Flemish *Freiwilligen*, this initially meant a retreat march to Tallinn. Here they embarked on the ship *Gotland* on September 19, 1944, and arrived in Swinoujscie [German: Swinemünde] on September 25, 1944. From there, those who remained marched to *Truppenübungsplatz* Hammerstein (west of Chojnice). On November 1, 1944, *SS-Kampfgruppe Rehmann* was finally loaded up there and transported to the Lüneburger Heide [Heath], to form up the *27. SS-Freiwilligen-Grenadier-Division "Langemarck."*

27. SS-Freiwilligen-Grenadier-Division "Langemarck" (*flämische Nr. 1*)

Himmler issued the order on September 18, 1944, that: *"A SS-Freiwilligen-Grenadier-Division would be trained from the former SS-Freiwilligen-Sturmbrigade "Langemarck," because of the large number of volunteer enlistments."* Since there were no such *"large number of volunteer enlistments"* at that time, nor were ever to be expected, the question arises, why Himmler made such a declaration. Goebbels once referred to him as a *"Realpolitiker,"* so one can assume that he initiated this farce possibly to deceive the German skeptics in politics and in the *Wehrmacht*, as well as to deceive enemy reconnaissance.

Belgium had already been taken by the Western Allies, which meant that in any case, it would only be possible to recruit primarily from among the approximately 19,000 Flemish collaborators who had been evacuated (including their families) and armaments workers. Any interest in experiencing the end of the war – or possibly not experiencing it – in the *Waffen-SS*, was very limited. Besides Flemish youth, who were assembled in a separate *Bataillon* and came forward out of enthusiasm, the *Infanterie-Division 44* that was to be newly organized could count only on adding a few more members. On September 20, 1944, it reported the following strength to the *SS-FHA*:

	Führer	***Unterführer***	***Männer***	**Total**
Actual	46	236	1,659	1,941
	2.37%	12.16%	85.47%	100%
Authorized	433	2,262	9,926	12,621
	3.4%	17.9%	78.7%	100%

This was some 10,000 men short of its authorized strength, making it impossible to carry out the organization of an *Infanterie-Division*! Former *Kommandeur* of *SS-Panzergrenadier-Regiments 20*, *SS-Standartenführer* Müller, was given the command.

During October 1944, the *Division*, at times touted as the *Volks-Grenadier-Division "Langemarck"* [Peoples' Infantry Division], was supplied with recruits. After some ten weeks of training, a swearing-in ceremony was held in mid-December 1944. However, it was not possible to organize most of the units, such as *SS-Freiwilligen-Grenadier-Regiment 68* or *SS-Divisions-Füsilier-Bataillon 27*, due to lack of personnel.

Shortly before Christmas 1944, a *Regiment*-strength *Kampfgruppe* was formed led by the *Kommandeur* of *SS-Freiwilligen-Grenadier-Regiments 66, SS-Obersturmbannführer* Schellong, comprising:

I. /SS-Freiwilligen-Grenadier-Bataillon 66
I. /SS-Freiwilligen-Grenadier-Bataillon 67
SS-Panzerjäger-Abteilung 27[23]

About 2,000 men reached Cologne-Wahn by rail transport on December 24, 1944. From here, the units marched into the *Urftalsperre* [Urftal valley barrier] (the fore-Eifel). Especially since it had only been intended for deployment on the *Ostfront, SS-Kampfgruppe Schellong* was given the primary task of securing the area and thereby freeing up German troops. This was certainly also to deceive enemy defense operations.

Since it was far from able to do this, and also only capable of approximating its authorized strength, the order came on January 18, 1945, to reclassify it as an *Infanterie-Division 45*. Although the actual strength had now increased by some 2,000 men, to about 4,000 men, the unit, even in its new, truncated form, still lacked about 5,000 men.

In the meantime, the Red Army had launched a large-scale offensive on January 12, 1945, causing a collapse of the German *Ostfront* within a few days. Since Hitler forbade relocating the *6. SS-Panzer-Armee* from the west or the *Heeresgruppe* fighting in Courland to Pomerania, *Heeresgruppe Weichsel* [Vistula] was organized in great haste starting January 21, 1945. *Reichsführer-SS* Himmler was appointed *Oberbefehlshaber* four days later and was to close the about 150km wide breach in the front between *9. Armee* and the to be newly formed *11. Armee* (*Heeresgruppe Weichsel*) between Glogau and Elbing. This made a man become an *Oberbefehlshaber* of a *Heeresgruppe* who had never attended an officers' training school or completed any course on higher troop command.

In the course of reinforcing *11. Armee* as well as preparing for their own offensive, at the end of January 1945, *SS-Kampfgruppe Schellong* was among the units taken from *Oberbefehlshaber West*, and sent from the Vor-Eifel to Pomerania. In early February 1945, supplied to the *III. (germanischen) SS-Panzer-Korps* it reached the area west of Ravenstein. The intention was, starting February 16,

[23] The *Abteilung* was formed using the existing *schwere Bataillon* or *Brigade* units.

1945, to cause the Red Army, which had broken through over the Oder, to falter by simultaneous attacks from Himmler in Pomerania and *Generaloberst* Schörner in Silesia.

Without any *Luftwaffe* support and with no appropriate artillery preparation, there was no way this offensive could develop. The troops were stationed on muddy ground and lay exposed to the Soviet tanks, anti-tank guns, and artillery positions. The Flemish *SS-Freiwillige* joined with elements of the *11.* and *23. SS-Freiwilligen-Panzergrenadier-Division* in the encircled town of Choszczno [German: Arnswalde] and secured the right flank of the *Stoßkeile* [spearhead] near Piecnik-Ziemomysl [German: Petznick-Schönwerder] (about 12km northwest of Choszczno).

Even after seven tanks and an armored personnel carrier had penetrated directly into the city on February 16, 1945, especially *11. SS-Freiwilligen-Panzergrenadier-Division "Nordland"* pushed through two days later to the northern edge of Choszczno and was able to hold a one- to one-and-a-half kilometer wide corridor. On the evening of February 19, 1945, the evacuation of some 7,000 civilians began on foot through the corridor. Unnoticed by the Red Army, on the evening of February 21, 1945, the remnants of the *Kampfgruppe*, under *Generalmajor* Voigt, followed.

Since the other units of *11. Armee* there were barely able to win any ground and the Soviet defense was being constantly reinforced, *Unternehmen Sonnenwende* [Opertion Solstice] was halted. When the Red Army in turn took the offensive a few days later on March 1, 1945, extremely heavy fighting followed up to March 9, 1945, near Stargard-Suchań [German: Zachan]. By way of Seefeld (about 5km northwest of Stargard), *Kampfgruppe "Langemarck"* moved into the area, around Dąbie [German: Altdamm], which was envisaged as a bridgehead. Here they were put under command of what remained of the *Walloon SS-Kampfgruppe* of the *XXXII. Armee-Korps* at Hökendorf. After a few days of rest, the Red Army attacked the bridgehead position on March 15, 1945, with heavy tank and artillery bombardment. Four days later, Hitler approved the surrender of the area, which originally had been intended as a base for a German offensive towards Gdańsk [German: Danzig]. On March 20, 1945, the last German troops left the bridgehead.

What remained of *Kampfgruppe "Langemarck"* then moved back towards Prenzlau. Since well over half of the men deployed in the last six weeks had been killed or wounded, there were only some 600 men in the new quarters. At the same time *SS-Standartenführer* Müller received in Soltau the command to pull those elements of the *Division* not yet in action out of the Lüneburger Heide in front of the advancing Allies and move them to the Prenzlau area. On April 6, 1945, the unit reported a strength of 4,102 men. After half a year, it was impossible to compensate for the lack of around 4,000 men needed to reach the authorized strength of an *ID 45* [*Infanterie-Division 45*]. The newly enlisted *Freiwilligen* only made up for the losses of the dead and seriously wounded.

The *Oberbefehlshaber* of *3. Panzer-Armee*, *General der Panzertruppen* von Manteuffel evaluated the Flemish *SS* formation at this time: *"The Division is only a Regimentsgruppe with two strong Bataillone with schwere Infanteriegeschützen and three schwere Panzerabwehrkanonen. The Division has good men, but poor officers. Not appropriate for offensive operations, but only for defense, in this case required Artillerie support."*

The *27. SS-Freiwilligen-Grenadier-Division "Langemarck"* itself reported at this time:

120	*leichte Maschinengewehre*
20	*schwere Maschinengewehre*
4	*mittlere Granatwerfer* 8.14cm
4	*leichte-* and 2 *schwere Infanteriegeschütze*
6	*leichte-* and 2 *schwere Feldhaubitzen*
41	field kitchens
22	motorcycles
26	cars
41	trucks
2	*Zugmaschinen* [prime movers]
300	horses

This meant that the combat troops at least, could be considered sufficiently armed. After assembling his units, *SS-Standartenführer* Müller received the order on April 15, 1945, from the *3. Panzer-Armee* to take command of a mixed-Belgian *Divisionsgruppe*. This was to comprise elements of the *27.* and *28. SS-Freiwilligen-Grenadier-Division* and be reinforced from *Panzerjäger-Abteilung 6* and the *Sturm-Bataillon* of the *3. Panzer-Armee*. Put under command of the *Oder-Korps* of *SS-Obergruppenführer* von dem Bach, the *Divisionsgruppe* was assembled for a counterattack near Damitzow-Hohenholz-Pomellen.

The Soviet 2nd Byelorussian Front took the offensive in the *Oder-Korps* sector on April 20, 1945. When the Soviets established a bridgehead south of Szczecin, the Belgian *SS-Freiwillige* were pulled into fighting in the area Kołbaskowo [Kolbitzow] Schillersdorf-Tantow. As a result, the Flemings had to withdraw to Prenzlau by way of Penkun. The Wotan position, running along the Randow breach, was of no importance for the defense. Because there were no more combat-ready units in the front sector, the Belgians were also drawn into the rapidly developing signs of disintegration.

Detached from the *Oder-Korps* staff and put under command of the *XXXXVI. Panzer-Korps*, *SS-Kampfgruppe "Langemarck"* was engaged in the preliminary fighting east of Prenzlau starting on April 25, 1945. Reinforcement by additional units of the *27. SS-Freiwilligen-Grenadier-Division* only made it possible to stabilize the situation somewhat. The additional troops could not prevent the Red Army from taking Prenzlau by April 27, 1945.

The *Oberbefehlshaber* of *3. Panzer-Armee, General der Panzertruppen* Manteuffel, described the situation on that same day very vividly:

> *"Complete breakup of formations 'Langemarck,' 'Wallonien,' 1. Marine-Division and the entire Flak-Abteilungen, to the extent that they, with or without fault, have lost their weapons. I never even saw such images as today in 1918. For Division 'Langemarck' and 1. Marine Division, [there are] only still the bravest Kommandeure and some men, as far as they can command with voice and heart ..."*

The next day, *XXXXVI. Panzer-Korps* moved into the lake-strewn region between the Strasburg and Lychen positions. The Flemish *SS-Freiwilligen* were deployed near Feldberg and retreated to Neustrelitz by the next day. By way of Waren, which they reached on April 30, 1945, they marched via Karow on May 2, 1945 into the Western Allies' captivity. First, assembled in the Fallingbostel camp, by the end of 1946, the Flemings had been handed over to the Belgian authorities in several batches. This ended their war deployment on the German side.

The *Freiwilligen* from Flanders, the majority of whom did not want to serve in the *SS*, were always deployed in especially hard-fought focal points along the *Ostfront*. This meant that, in relative terms, they suffered far greater losses than other units of the *Waffen-SS* or *Wehrmacht*. Fighting out of conviction in the battle against communism, this part of the Belgian population, almost insignificant in terms of numbers, did not disappoint the German leadership. Their disintegration at the end of April 1945 may have been all the more pronounced, since they faced a more uncertain future than the German troops did.

Kommandeure:
01/44 – 05/45 *SS-Standartenführer* Müller

Feldpost numbers:

Divisionsstab	44 853
SS-Freiwilligen-Grenadier-Regiment 66 (flämische Nr. 1)	04 206
SS-Freiwilligen-Grenadier-Regiment 67 (flämische Nr. 2)	05 294
SS-Freiwilligen-Grenadier-Regiment 68 (flämische Nr. 3)	64 712
SS-Freiwilligen-Artillerie-Regiment 27(flämische Nr. 1)	05 814
SS-Divisions-Füsilier-Bataillon 27	05 150
SS-Panzerjäger-Abteilung 27	21 836
SS-Pionier-Bataillon 27	66 467
SS-Nachrichtentruppe 27	44 853
SS-Feldersatz-Bataillon 27	65 597
SS-Versorgungstruppen 27	66 752

28. SS-Freiwilligen-Grenadier-Division der SS "Wallonien" (*wallonische Nr. 1*)

5. SS-Freiwilligen-Sturmbrigade "Wallonien"

The head of the *Hauptamt, SS-Gruppenführer* Berger, and the Wallonian politician Degrelle, who served as a *Leutnant* [Lieutenant] in the German *Wehrmacht*[24] held an initial discussion in December 1942. This sudden interest of the *Waffen-SS* was mainly due to Degrelle's capacity as leader of the Wallonian Rexists. Plans for the New Order in Europe meant that they also resorted to using the nationalist forces of this not insignificant movement.

After the talks, Degrelle informed the surprised visitors that at his political rally in January 1943 in the Brussels sports amphitheater, the Wallonian were thoroughly Germanic. A first propagandistic step had been taken for enlisting Wallonian *Freiwilligen* in the *Waffen-SS*.

He also promoted this propaganda line at the Berlin Sportpalast on January 31, 1943, before thousands of Belgian and French armaments workers. Finally, there were discussions with Himmler about the *Waffen-SS* assuming command of *Wallonischen Infanterie-Bataillon 373*. It is interesting that the negotiations were not carried out by the *Kommandeur* of *Wallonischen Infanterie-Bataillons 373*, *Hauptmann* Lippert, but with *Leutnant* Degrelle, regarded as the Walloon *Volksführer* [national peoples' leader].

After completing the two-day talks, the *Reichsführer-SS* inspected the Walloon war *Freiwilligen* on May 24, 1943, in Meseritz. Himmler remarked afterwards:

> *"After consultation with the OKW [Oberkommando der Wehrmacht: Supreme Armed Forces Command] and with the agreement of General Zeitzler, chief of the Heer Gernalstab [Army General Staff], I decided to include the wallonische Legion as a Germanic Freiwilligen-Legion in the Waffen-SS.*
>
> *The political path that challenged Rexist leader Leon Degrelle was one he pursued logically over years and correctly. He has chosen each of the forms that are undoubtedly the right ones for his Wallonian people, to build positive forces in a regenerative way. I have tended in the whole past year, as the designated 'Pan-German' and also internally appointed Reichsleiter*

[24] In 1941, Belgian military *Freiwilligen* were trained for the *Wallonische Infanterie-Bataillon 373* as part of the *Heer*, at *Truppenübungsplatz* Meseritz. As of January 1942, the unit was in action in the southern sector of the *Ostfront*. On December 12, 1942, the Walloons again reached *Truppenübungsplatz* Meseritz and were initially granted leave in their homeland.

Above: SS-Brigadeführer Vahl, Inspekteur SS-Panzertruppen; to his left, SS-Obersturmführer Reich; right, Hauptmann Lippert, Kdr of Legion "Wallonie."

Inspection of Legion "Wallonie" on May 24, 1943.

of the Nazi Party, held back from contacting Degrelle and his party. I would have only hindered the man in his movement, which then was not so far advanced. In 1941, when the Legion was organized, I therefore rejected its transfer to the Waffen-SS.

After the very decent fight which the Legion has been fighting on the Russian front, and due to the respect this gained from German soldiers, also in contrast to the past of the Belgian Army's reputation, this front experience has created the right point in time, at which he, in his great speech at the beginning of the year, could express the avowal that the Walloons are a Germanic people in their history and origin, which was Romanized in language and culture. Once this step had been taken on the part of Rexistenführer[25] Degrelle and his movement, it was up to me, commissioned by the Führer with appreciation of all Germanic questions, to recognize the Legion as a Germanic military troop unit and the movement in Wallonia as the revival movement of a at its core Germanic people."

The approximately 700 members of *Wallonischen Infanterie-Bataillon 373* formed the cadre. In Belgium, Degrelle launched a major propaganda campaign – this included the party newspaper *L'Avenir* calling on men to enlist in the ***SS-Freiwilligen-Sturmbrigade "Wallonien."*** All men between 17-40 years old, who were at least 1.65m tall, could join up. Since registering for service was for the duration of the war, the *Freiwilligen* naturally mostly came from the collaborationist organizations.

Overall, the propaganda campaign in Belgium recruited about 900 *Freiwilligen* for the *Waffen-SS*. With about three million Walloons in Belgium, this number speaks for the population's lack of interest! This was not changed even by the indication that the initial organizational order of July 3, 1943, was for formation of a very modern *SS-Freiwilligen-Sturmbrigade*.

Since membership could only be expected to reach about 1,600 men, the formation was to be organized as a so-called *Sturmbrigade neuer Art*. This meant organizing a *Brigade* staff, as well as a *Grenadier-Bataillon (mot.)* and a *schwere Bataillon (mot.)*. Thus, a troop that nominally was not even regimental strength, received the high-sounding name of a *SS-Freiwilligen-Sturmbrigade*.

Promoted to *SS-Sturmbannführer*, former *Bataillonsführer* Lippert was responsible for training the units at *Truppenübungsplatz Wildflecken*. Training the heavy units was carried out at respective schools.

After the Red Army launched a major offensive on the Dnieper on October 17, 1943, the majority of *SS-Freiwilligen-Sturmbrigade "Wallonien"* was alerted in early November 1943, and transferred to the *Ostfront* even before training

[25] In 1918 in Belgium, a renewal movement emerged whose members called themselves "Rexists," derived from *Christus Rex*. Its goal was a corporatist-structured authoritarian state, which had similarities with Nazism. In the 1936 elections, the party won 11.5% of votes.

Training SS-Freiwilligen-Sturmbrigade "Wallonien" at Wildflecken.

was completed. The formation, with over 300 vehicles and fully equipped for winter fighting, reached the area west of Cherkassy by rail transport, and was placed under command of the *5. SS-Panzer-Division "Wiking."* While most of the *Brigade* was lined up in the *HKL* from November 20, 1943, about 300 *Wallonischen SS Freiwilligen*, who had only four months of training behind them, scoured through the Irdyn area seeking partisans and Red Army stragglers. In this operation, suspected partisans were also shot.

On January 1, 1944, the *Brigade* reported a strength of:

Führer	***Unterführer***	***Männer***	**Total**
26	226	1,596	1,848
1.41%	12.23%	86.36%	100%

Of these, approximately 1,600 were in the front lines. The remaining about 250 recently recruited *Freiwilligen* were still being trained at Wildflecken.

More rear-area anti-partisan operations followed in early January 1944. When the Red Army again took the offensive on January 25, 1944, it succeeded three days later in encircling the *XI.* and *XXXXII. Armee-Korps*, a total of some 56,000 men, west of Cherkassy. These included the *5. SS-Panzer-Division "Wiking,"* which meanwhile had been incorporated in the *XI. Armee-Korps*, which meant as well the Belgian *SS-Formation*, designated since October 22, 1943, as the ***5. SS-Freiwilligen-Sturmbrigade "Wallonien."***

Attempts to relieve the 250km wide pocket from the outside on February 4, 1944, failed. Instead, the Red Army was able to compressi the pocket into the Shanderovka area. As a result, on February 16, 1944, Hitler approved that the troops would make a breakout. The breakout operation began on the night of February 17, 1944, in which the still fresh and well-equipped *5. SS-Freiwilligen-Sturmbrigade "Wallonien"* secured the Novo Buda sector. Partly by swimming

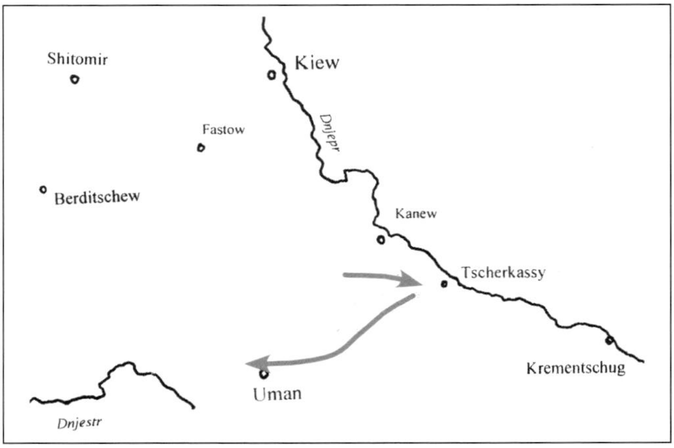

On April 1, 1944, the 5. SS-Freiwilligen-Sturmbrigade "Wallonien" returned to Belgium after the fighting at Cherkassy, to great propaganda fanfare. It was received in Charleroi by SS-Gruppenführer Jungclaus, the Bevollmächtigter des Reichsführers-SS [authorized representative of the Reichsführer-SS] in Belgium and northern France, and also welcomed by SS-Obergruppenführer Dittrich.

Freiwilligen-Sturmbannführer Leon Degrelle

the Tikich, where ice floes were still floating, about 35,000 soldiers were able to reach the positions of the *III. Panzer-Korps*. Of the approximately 1,600 Walloons, however, only 632 men reached the assembly area west of Uman by February 26, 1944.

Former *Freiwilliger Unterscharführer* Fernand Kaisergruber recalls:

> *"I was born on January 18, 1923, in Antwerp, and because I wanted to stand up for a new European order without Bolshevism, on November 3, 1941, I joined the Walloon Guard. From there, I signed up in early 1942 with some other comrades for the Wallonischen Infanterie-Bataillon 373. In June 1943 came the automatic transfer to the Waffen-SS. Our breakout from the Cherkassy pocket was dramatic. We ran, with practically only what we wore on our backs, towards the west! There was no order – at times, the breakout was like a Götterdämmerung. Maybe you can describe it like the apocalypse. On February 17, 1944, I was seriously wounded. My recovery took over a year – I only got back to Pomerania fit for duty on March 22, 1945."*

At the beginning of March 1944, the remaining Walloon *SS Freiwilligen* were moved back to *Truppenübungsplatz Wildflecken*. To exploit the *5. SS-Freiwilligen-Sturmbrigade "Wallonien"* deployment as propaganda and at the same time show that the German forces had escaped the Cherkassy pocket without major losses, Hitler approved a three-week furlough for the *Freiwilligen*. This was orchestrated very publicly by the current *Brigade* leader, *SS-Sturmbannführer* Degrelle. On March 28, 1944, the Walloons from Wildflecken reached Belgian *Truppenübungsplatz* Beverloo (about 25km southwest of Neerpelt). Here they obtained *Schützenpanzerwagen* in particular from the *12. SS-Panzer-Division "Hitlerjugend"* for the planned parade through Brussels, about 70km away, on April 2, 1944.

The furlough was over by the end of April 1944. The *Wallonischen SS Freiwilligen* were ordered to *SS-Truppenübungsplatz Heidelager*, near Debica, for reorganization of *5. SS-Freiwilligen-Sturmbrigade "Wallonien."*

Degrelle's demagogic appearances at German armament factories and other places up until summer 1944, made it possible to recruit a total of 800 new Walloon *Freiwilligen* for the *Waffen-SS*. After the necessary induction period, the *Brigade* could initially only report on June 30, 1944, a strength of:

	Führer	***Unterführer***	***Männer***	**Total**
Actual	53	232	903	1,188
	4.46%	19.53%	76.01%	100%
Authorized	64	497	1,996	2,557
	2.5%	19.44%	78.06%	100%

If you add to the 250 Walloons remaining in Germany, and about 630 returning from deployment, it is clear that by the end of June 1944, they were only able to induct about 300 new recruits.

At the beginning of August 1944, the *Brigade* was given orders to pull together a *Bataillon*-strength *Kampfgruppe*, which was to be supplied to *Armee-Abteilung Narwa* in Estonia.

When *Kampfgruppe/SS-Freiwilligen-Sturmbrigade "Wallonien"* arrived at Vaivara, it came under the command of *Division*-strength *SS-Kampfgruppe Wagner*. They also took command of the Flemish *SS Freiwilligen* (cf. previous chapter). After occupying temporary intermediate positions along the Ahja River, the units moved into the Embach position around Dorpat. The *Wehrmachtbericht* announced on August 22, 1944:

> *"West of Lake Pskov, a Kampfgruppe of SS-Sturmbrigade "Wallonien" stood the test, under the leadership of SS-Sturmbannführer Leon Degrelle, especially by its toughness and enthusiasm for attack."*

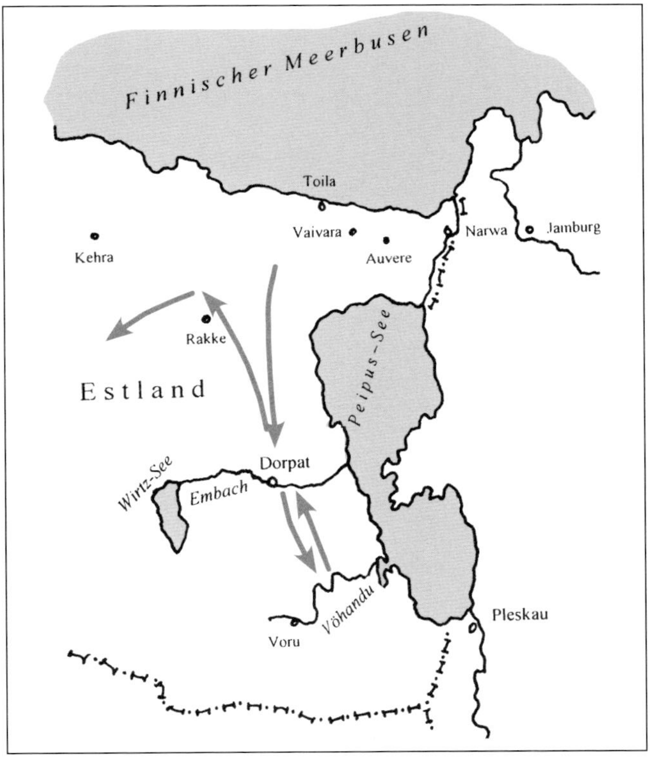

Note that the Unterscharführer in the front are only wearing plain black collar patches. Actually, a special collar patch with the Burgundy Cross was to have been introduced after the unit was organized. Later, in fact, they only wore patches with Sigrunen. Degrelle presented each of the newly formed elements of SS-Freiwilligen-Sturmbrigade "Wallonien" with a banner of the Wallonian resistance movement.

However, after fierce fighting, the Red Army was able to occupy Dorpat and establish a bridgehead over the Embach already by August 24, 1944. The enemy was initially satisfied with this, and called off the offensive, not least due to its own high losses.

The Wallonian *SS-Kampfgruppe* itself got 200 replacements from Debica. In mid-September 1944, amidst the general retreat from Estonia, the men were ordered back to Debica to form *SS-Freiwilligen-Grenadier-Division "Wallonien."*

28. SS-Freiwilligen-Grenadier-Division "Wallonien" (*wallonische Nr. 1*)

Himmler was so far out of reality, that he decreed, out of nothing more than wishful thinking, with effect from September 18, 1944, his desire to set up a Walloon *SS-Freiwilligen-Division "based on the many Freiwilligen registrations,"* from the former *SS-Freiwilligen-Sturmbrigade "Wallonien,"* organized as follows:

Divisionsstab
SS-Freiwilligen-Grenadier-Regiment 69 (wallon. Nr. 1) with *I. – II. Bataillon*
SS-Freiwilligen-Grenadier-Regiment 70 (wallon. Nr. 2) with *I. – II. Bataillon*
SS-Freiwilligen-Grenadier-Regiment 71 (wallon. Nr. 3) with *I. – II. Bataillon*
SS-Divisions-Füsilier-Bataillon 28 (as *Aufklärungs-Abt.*)
SS-Panzerjäger-Abteilung 28
SS-Freiwilligen-Artillerie-Abteilung 28
SS-Pionier-Bataillon 28
SS-Nachrichtentruppe 28
SS-Feldersatz-Kompanie 28
SS-Versorgungstruppen 28

SS-Oberführer Burk was appointed *Divisionskommandeur*. The earlier large-scale propaganda campaigns of 1943-44 only brought in a few hundred *Freiwilligen* from Belgium, but now, it was impossible even to launch any such campaign: Belgium had been occupied by the Western Allies on September 3, 1944.

The Germans now only had access to the approximately 15,000 Walloon refugees who had left the country with the German troops, or were still working in the arms industry in Germany. However, since it was anyway obvious that it would have been impossible to recruit 11,000 *Freiwilligen*, *SS-Sturmbannführer* Degrelle proposed that the French militia and Spanish *Freiwilligen* stationed in Wildflecken – and not especially popular with the German side – should be integrated into his formation.

In Estonia, Kampfgruppe/ SS-Freiw.-Sturmbrigade "Wallonien" was placed under the command of Divisionsgruppe Wagner. SS-Brigadeführer Wagner (above, at left) was Kommandeur of the 4. SS-Freiwilligen-Panzergrenadier-Brigade "Nederland."

Since the *SS-FHA* harbored reservations about mixing French and Wallonian soldiers, only a Spanish *SS-Kompanie* (the remnants of the Spanish Legion) was ordered to join the *28. SS-Freiwilligen-Grenadier-Division "Wallonien."*

With this addition, the unit strength on September 30, 1944, was only:

	Führer	***Unterführer***	***Männer***	**Total**
Actual	70	265	1,230	1,565
	4.47%	16.93%	78.60%	100%
		of these, were German:		
	10	19	15	44
Authorized	433	2,262	9,926	12,621
	3.4%	17.9%	78.7%	100%

On October 18, 1944, the unit got its transfer order to Gronau, south of Hannover. The *SS-FHA* issued a completely unrealistic command, that it be ready for action by March 31, 1945. A *Division* was to be formed within barely six months – but which had at this time a mere 12% of its authorized strength.

Because of the German Rundstedt Offensive, however, *SS-Freiwilligen-Grenadier-Regiment 69* was ordered to the Cologne-Reydt-Rommerskirchen-Liblar-Bliesheim-Lechenich region on December 20, 1944. Since it had been organized only for deployment on the *Ostfront* in the fight against Bolshevism, the *Regiment*'s primary function was to simulate German forces, in order to confuse enemy reconnaissance. For this purpose, *SS-Obersturmbannführer* Degrelle marched with his soldiers into the Limerlé area (about 25km southwest of St. Vith).

When the Ardennes Offensive was ended, the two *Bataillone* were ordered back to Gronau. They received the order on January 19, 1945, to reclassify the unit as an *Infanterie-Division 1945*. A decree that existed only on paper – the nominal *Division* was manned at this time by just over 3,000 men – the manpower of a reinforced *Regiment*.

On January 30, 1945, the formation was given the order to set up a *Regiment*-strength *Kampfgruppe*, which was to be transferred to Pomerania. Besides the two *Bataillone* of *SS-Freiwilligen-Grenadier-Regiment 69*, was the *I./SS-Freiwilligen-Bataillon 70* was sent by rail to the newly reorganized *11. Armee*. Here, it formed out of a number of *Alarm-Einheiten* [Emergency Units] the *Divisionsgruppe Munzel* in the sector of the *XXXIX. Panzer-Korps*.

The three *Bataillone* initially occupied positions in the Krępcewo [German: Kremzow] -Repplin area. Here, the Walloons were to hold back the Red Army advance by February 6, 1945, until the *10. SS-Panzer-Division "Frundsberg"* had been brought forward. Three days later, the *Kampfgruppe* was deployed to push through to Lindenberg. It was next engaged in heavy fighting to retake Krüssow.

On February 16, 1945, the Germans launched their Pomerania offensive, which was to take on the northern flank of the enemy forces, already on the Oder. The results were such as so often occur with great intentions. The approximately 80,000 *11. Armee* troops in *Offensive Sonnenwende* [solstice] could scarcely win any ground. This meant for the Walloon *SS-Kampfgruppe*, no longer motorized, deployed on the right flank of the *10. SS-Panzer-Division "Frundsberg,"* was to advance to Moskorzyn [German: Muscherin]. By February 17-18, 1945, most of the troops had already been pressed back on the defensive by strong Soviet counterattacks. The German Pomeranian Offensive was halted after three days and the troops pulled back across the Ihna. What remained of the Walloon *SS-Kampfgruppe* first occupied positions near Kolin-Strzebielewo [German: Collin-Strebelow] and were then transferred to Krępcewo.

After the *XXXIX. Panzer-Korps* was withdrawn from action by February 23, 1945, the Walloon *SS-Kampfgruppe* came under the command of the *III. (germanischen) SS-Panzer-Korps*. The *Wehrmachtbericht* reported on February 27, 1945 about the earlier fighting:

> *"In Pomerania, the Kampfgruppe der SS-Freiwilligen-Grenadier-Division 'Wallonien,' deployed to protect the flank under the leadership of SS-Obersturmführer Capelle struck with exemplary steadfastness and a fanatical will to fight."*

When the Red Army took the offensive in Pomerania on March 1, 1945, it was able to force the entire front into motion in just a few hours. The Soviet armored units rapidly succeeded in pushing through gaps, including between the *III. SS-Panzer-Korps* and *X. SS-Armee-Korps* to the north. This at least doubled the length of the front for left flank of *III. SS-Panzer-Korps*.

The Walloon *SS Freiwilligen* fought near Szczeciński [German: Stargard] starting March 3, 1945. Mentally and physically exhausted, the men, after they lost most of their equipment, were barely able to put up any resistance. They waged desperate battles against large numbers of Soviet tanks on March 6, 1945, in the Lubow-Zachodniopomorskie [German: Saarow] -Bruchhausen area. By way of Ziębice [German: Münsterberg] and Augustenwalde (about 12km east of Szczecin), the men reached Dąbie above the next day. Here the front remained quiet, at least for a brief period.

SS-Obersturmbannführer Degrelle marched with the remnats of his unit to Scheune (west of Stettin) and here was given a week of rest, under command of the *XXXII. Armee-Korps*. Degrelle released the survivors from any further service with the combat troops. About eighty Walloons took advantage of this. A new *Kampfgruppe* was formed from whoever remained of the former unit, and, with twenty-three officers and 650 other ranks, it marched on March 16, 1945, to the Dąbie [Altdamm] bridgehead in front of Zdroje [German: Finkenwalde].

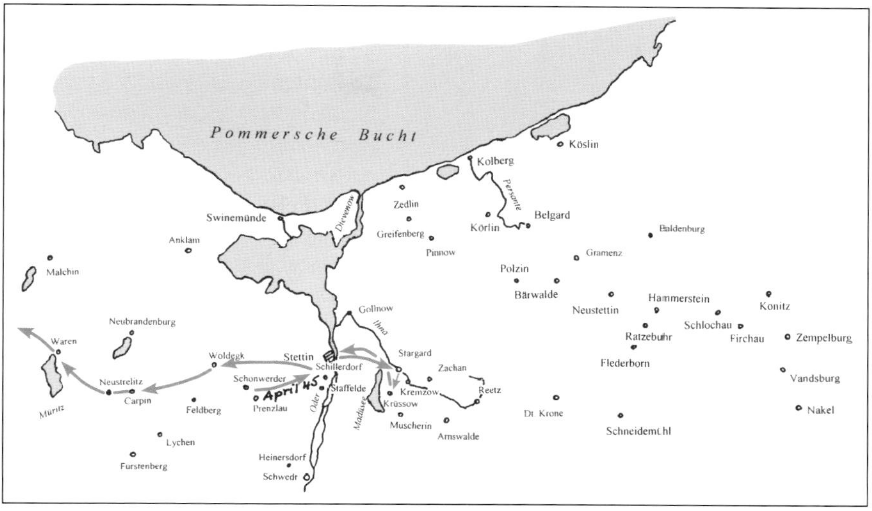

Operational area of the 28. SS-Freiwilligen-Grenadier-Division Wallonien, February-May 1945.

While the *Bataillon*, ultimately called *I. /SS-Freiwilligen-Grenadier-Regiment 6*, engaged in the fighting at Altamm, where losses were extremely heavy, the *SS-FHA* issued an order on March 9, 1945 to form another *Kampfgruppe* for deployment on the Oder front.

Since the men had had nothing but *Panzerfäusten* to resist the massed enemy tank attacks during the past weeks, two German *Panzer IV* supported the Wallonians' defense in the fiercely contested fighting at Finkenwalde. On March 20, 1945, the bridgehead was evacuated. Around 200 Walloons retreated over the Oder near Szczecin. This ended the fighting near Szczecin for around four weeks. In four days, about 450 men had been killed, wounded or taken prisoner.

The *Oberbefehlshaber* of *3. Panzer-Armee, General der Panzertruppen* von Manteuffel, assessed the Walloon *SS-Einheiten* on March 26, 1945:

> *"Division is only a Regiments-Gruppe, currently, there is a deployment-strength Grenadier-Bataillon, another of medium strength in preparation. The soldiers have lower capacity to stand fast than the members of Langemarck and urgently require, after the setbacks, a period of rest and refitting. Low-level rigor with weapons, Kampfgruppe not suitable for attacking, but only for defense."*

Simultaneously, *SS-Obersturmbannführer* Degrelle went to Gronau, to organize the formation of the second *Kampfgruppe* there. Meanwhile, the some 900 men who had been ordered to go to Prague for specialized training (*Artillerie* and

Pioniere) were brought back here. Some 200 young recruits had been mobilized by the *Wehrmacht* to fight with *Panzerfäusten*, to stop the American tank advance at Holzminden. Since the Walloons could only be deployed against the Red Army, they were eventually sent back. Aware of the agony of the German *Reich*, Degrelle demobilized the Wallonian convalescents who were in the barracks at Gronau.

While the *SS-FHA* had ordered the training of a *Kampfgruppe* of *Grenadier-Regiment* strength, as well as a *Panzerjäger-Abteilung*, ultimately, Degrelle only led one *Bataillon* of about 950 men to Szczecin. On April 6, 1945, the men reached the *3. Panzer-Armee* by railway transport. Here, he gave another 200 men the opportunity to leave the combat units. From those who remained, he re-formed the *II./SS-Freiwilligen-Grenadier-Regiment 69*.

In view of the expected major Soviet offensive, the *Kommandeur* of the *27. SS-Freiwilligen-Grenadier-Division "Langemarck"* – which in reality only existed on paper – *SS-Standartenführer* Müller, was ordered on April 15, 1945, by *3. Panzer-Armee* to set up a combined *Divisionsgruppe*. This was to comprise elements of the *27.* and *28. SS-Freiwilligen-Grenadier-Division* and be reinforced by *Heerestruppen* – under command of the *Oder-Korps* – to act as an *Eingreifreserve* [tactical reserve detachment] in the Hohenholz area (east of the *Randow-Bruch* [Randow marshes crossing]). It was organized into the:

SS-Kampfgruppe "Langemarck"
SS-Freiwilligen-Grenadier-Regiment 66
I. /SS-Freiwilligen-Artillerie-Regiment 27
SS-Kampfgruppe "Wallonien"
I. /SS-Freiwilligen-Grenadier-Regiment 69
Sturm-Bataillon/3. Panzer-Armee
Panzerjagd-Abteilung 6
Sturmgeschütz-Brigade 210

Although the units were, also in accordance with orders, combined into *SS-Divisionsgruppe Müller*, they fought separately in the difficult operations that followed. In addition to the fact that the approximately 5,000 soldiers were not trained as a formation, they also lacked the vital heavy units, such as *Flak-Artillerie*.

When the Red Army had succeeded in establishing a bridgehead in the area of the *Oder-Korps*, *SS-Standartenführer* Müller put the majority of his *Kampfgruppe* into the action at Schillersdorf on April 20, 1945, and was able to drive the enemy back to the Oder. The next day already, however, enemy advances forced the men back to the lines of the *II. /SS-Freiwilligen-Grenadier-Regiment 69* at Staffelde.

By April 25-26, 1945, the Red Army overran the so-called Wotan position along the *Randow-Bruch*. The Walloon units fought here, again separated from the others at Brüssow. The *Oberbefehlshaber* of *3. Panzer-Armee, General der Panzertruppen* Manteuffel, described the situation on April 27, 1945, very vividly:

> *"Complete disintegration of formations 'Langemarck,' 'Wallonien,' 1. Marine-Division and the entire Flak-Abteilungen, as far as they, with or without fault, have lost their weapons. I never even saw such images as today in 1918 ..."*

After the enemy broke through the so-called Uecker immediately, just as they had at the Wotan position, Manteuffel commanded the same day the occupation of the so-called Feldberg position. Here he intended to get the defense back in order. *SS-Divisionsgruppe Müller* had meanwhile again been disbanded and the Flemings and Walloons separately deployed in the *XLVI. Panzer-Korps*.

SS-Freiwilligen-Grenadier-Regiment 69 pulled back by way of Schönwerder, to Woldegk. At Carpin, they met about 500 members of the *33. Waffen-Grenadier-Division der SS "Charlemagne"* and marched together to Neustrelitz. Along with columns of civilians, *Wehrmacht* and prisoners from the Sachsenhausen concentration camp, they reached Waren.

On April 30, 1945, *SS-Obersturmbannführer* Degrelle met with *SS-Standartenführer* Müller in Nossentiner Hütte. Together they wanted to reach the Lübeck area with their units and either continue the struggle in Denmark or be taken prisoner by the Western Allies.

From the German side, they were ordered to march from Lübeck towards Bad Segeberg and to move into quarters there. These commands were overtaken by the advance of the Allied troops. Lübeck and Bad Segeberg were both taken almost without a fight. As of May 2, 1945, most of the remaining members of *28. SS-Freiwilligen-Grenadier-Division "Wallonien"* marched into captivity of the Western Allies as prisoners of war.

First assembled in the Fallingbostel camp, by the end of 1946, the Wallonians had been handed over to the Belgian authorities in several batches. By 1947, there were mass trials: in principle, any member of the *Waffen-SS* was condemned as a traitor to his country. In some cases, this led to death sentences or life imprisonment, but most got extremely long prison sentences.

Only a small number of Walloons volunteered for the fight against the Soviet Union. The attempt in October 1944 to use a propaganda campaign to enlist all collaborating Walloon organizations into a *Division* of 12,000 men, failed. Of the approximately 4,500 men, definitely only at most 50% were fit for combat.

Kommandeure:
10/44 – 02/45 *SS-Oberführer* Burk
02/45 – 05/45 *SS-Obersturmbannführer* Degrelle

Feldpost numbers:

Divisionsstab	38 918
SS-Freiwilligen-Grenadier-Regiment 69 (wallonische Nr. 1)	28 193
SS-Freiwilligen-Grenadier-Regiment 70 (wallonische Nr. 2)	16 821
SS-Freiwilligen-Artillerie-Regiment 28 (wallonische Nr. 1)	02 544
SS-Panzerjäger-Abteilung 28	43 857
SS-Pionier-Bataillon 28	25 151
SS-Nachrichtentruppe 28	36 637
SS-Feldersatz-Kompanie 28	18 909
SS-Verwaltungs-Kompanie [management company] *28*	04 712

29. Waffen-Grenadier-Division der SS "RONA" (*russische Nr. 1*)

Volkswehr [People's Militia] Brigade "RONA"[26]

As in all the districts[27] it occupied after the beginning of the *Ostfeldzug* [Eastern Campaign] on June 22, 1941, the German *Wehrmacht* set up a non-communist mayor in Lokot (south of Bryansk).

However, in the autumn of 1941, Ivan Voskoboinik, who held this position, decided, in contrast to most of the other local population mayors that he, together with his deputy Bronislav Kaminski, also wanted to be politically active. On November 25, 1941, they founded the National Socialist Russian Workers Party, but due to German *Ostpolitik* [Eastern policy] and its associated fundamental lack of interest in such activities, no initial manifesto was issued after the founding.

Hoping to take part in Russian policymaking, at least after a German military victory, Voskoboinik and Kaminski refrained from future political agitation by their party, but began instead to take action in the military area.

Here, too, this chapter in the history of Russian collaboration began in a way that was not unusual. Voskoboinik formed first a 20- and then 50-man strong *Ordnungsdienst* [security force], which not only was an auxiliary police force used in the district villages, but also fought the increasingly active Soviet partisans.

Without the knowledge of the Germans, the mayor expanded the *Ordnungsdienst* using volunteers from among former Red Army soldiers and civilians, into a several hundred-man troop. About eight weeks later, the group, unnoticed by the Germans, became active in the vast forest areas around Lokot and collected weapons and equipment – as the partisans did also – in the surrounding woods, from stocks left behind by the Red Army.

When Voskoboinik died on January 8, 1942, Kaminski took over the mayoral post and command of the local forces. A few days later, *AOK 2* [*Armeeoberkommando*: Army High Command] became aware of the nationalist combat group after a chance meeting of German *Eisenbahn-Baupioniere* [railway engineers] with members of the so-called Lokoter people's militia in the woods south of Bryansk.

The *Kommandant rückwärtiges Armeegebiet* (*Korück*) of the *2. Panzer-Armee, Generalleutnant* Bernhard, unlike many others, showed more foresight and was open to Kaminski and his independent operations. Ultimately, the 1,400-strong Lokot militia represented, along with the German *Sicherungs-*

[26] *Russkaya Osvoboditielnaya Narodnaya Armiya* (Russian People's Liberation Army).

[27] A *Rayon* is the lowest-level Soviet administrative district and corresponds approximately to a German *Landkreis* [county].

Bataillonen and the Royal Hungarian Light 102nd and 108th Divisions, an integral part of *Generalleutnant* Bernard's forces. The local militia companies, mostly wearing Red Army uniforms, were stationed in each village and were included in larger operations.

While things had remained quiet in the sector of *Heeresgruppe Mitte* since mid-April 1942, there were ever-increasing problems with Soviet partisan units in the area of the now-designated *Korück 532*. Therefore, in May 1942, the *4. Armee* north of Bryansk and the *2. Panzer-Armee* south of Bryansk, launched a full-scale attack against the partisans. The *PzAOK 2* [*Panzerarmeeoberkommando*: Panzer Army High Command] commissioned the *Kommandeur* of the *216. Infanterie-Division, Generalleutnant Freiherr* von und zu Gilsa, whose *Division* was deployed spread along a number of front sectors at that time, with this operation. Gilsa was to fight the estimated 20,000-strong partisan forces from Lokot (75km south of Bryansk) to Desna, in an area around 30km wide. The Lokot milita was among the forces put under his command for this. When the operation was completed in September 1942, Gilsa's *Gruppe* reported:

9,000 captured partisans and suspected partisans
4,000 enemy dead
200 *Geschütze*
500 *Maschinengewehre*
Large amounts of *Sprengmunition* [explosive ammunition] and a print shop.

Still during this operation, the *Oberbefehlshaber* of *2. Panzer-Armee, Generaloberst* Rudolf Schmidt, on July 19, 1942, gave Kaminski control of more *Rayon* and the title of *Oberbürgermeister* [senior mayor] of a *Selbstverwaltungsbezirks (SVB)* [Self-governing District]. This now included the *Rayon* of Mikhailovka, Navlya, Brassovo, Ssusemka, Ssevsk, Dimitrovsk, Dimitriyev, and Komarishi. In addition, the *PzAOK 2* from now on ran the Russian volunteer organization as *Volkswehr-Brigade "RONA."* Kaminski received no rank, but had the official position of a *Brigade-Kommandeur*.

In September 1942, the *Volkswehr-Brigade* already had around 6,000 men and:

8 tanks (Kv-I and T-34)
5 heavy armored reconnaissance vehicles (BT-5 and BT-7)
3 armored personnel carriers (BA-10 and BA-20).

When the *Gruppe* was taken from Gilsa and put under command of the *4. Armee*, the *Gruppe Rübsam* (Staff of *17. Panzer-Grenadier-Brigade*) took over the function of a tactical command and control unit in the Lokot *Selbstverwaltungsbezirk*.

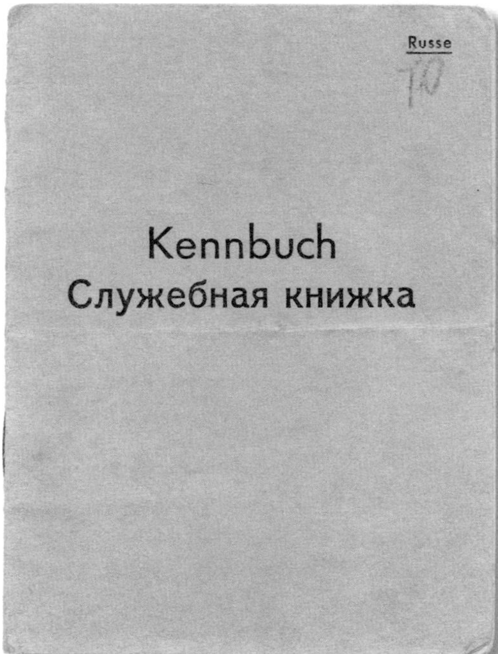

"RONA" sleeve badge (Cyrillic: POHA).

Dmitrij Nikulin was a militia member of I. /Volkswehr-Brigade "RONA" from April 20, 1943.

Kennbuch / Служебная книжка
zugleich Personalausweis / заменяет удостоверение личности
Nr. 111

für den / выдана кому: Volkswehrmann, Солдат Н. С.
(Dienstgrad / воинский чин)

Befördert / Произведен ab / с (Datum) (число, месяц, год) zum / в (neuer Dienstgrad) (новый чин)
Bescheinigung / Служебная отметка:

Dmitrij Nikulin
Дмитрий Никулин
(Vor- und Zuname / имя и фамилия)

Geb. am / Когда родился: 17.10.1926 in / где: d. Gorelaja Sloboda, Гор. Слобода
Ständ. Wohnort / Постоянное местожительство: Gorel. Sloboda, Гор. Слобода; Bezirk / Область: Orel, Орловская
Ledig, verheiratet / Холост, женат: ledig, холост; Kinder / Детей: keine, нет
Beruf / Профессия: Klempner, жестянщик; Erkennungsmarke / Опознавательный знак:

Personalbeschreibung / Приметы
Größe / Рост: 178
Gestalt / Внешний вид: schlank, прямой
Gesicht / Лицо: oval, овальное
Haar / Волосы: d. blond, т. русые
Bart / Борода, усы: keinen, нет
Augen / Глаза: braun, карие
Besond. Kennzeichen / Особые приметы: keine, нет

Д. Никулин
(Eigenhändige Unterschrift des Inhabers) (Собственноручная подпись)

Die Richtigkeit obiger Angaben bescheinigt: / Правильность вышеозначенного удостоверяет:
den / Число, месяц, год: 20.4.1943
Volkswehr-Batl. I
(Ausfertigender Truppenteil) (Воинская часть)
(Dienststempel) (Служебная печать)
(Unterschrift, Dienstgrad, Dienststellung) (Подпись, воинский чин, должность)

Anschrift der nächsten Angehörigen
Адрес ближайших родственников

Ehefrau / Жена:

Eltern / Родители: Peter Nikulin, Gorelaja Sloboda, Rn Rognedino
Петр Никулин, д. Горелая Слобода, Рогнединск...

Russe

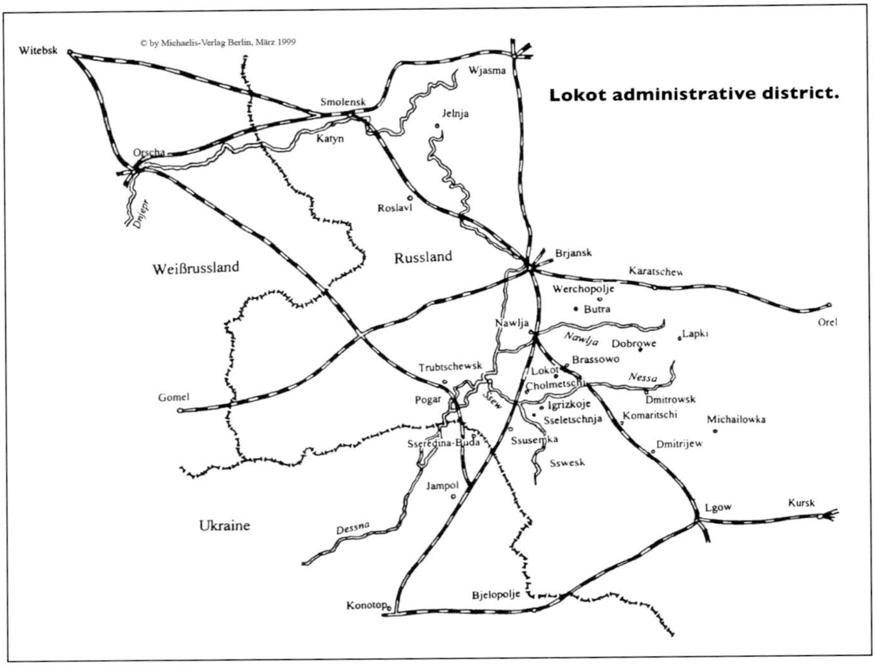

They were not initially involved in larger combined operations. Instead, the companies were mostly used independently. For example, a *Volkswehr-Kompanie* overwhelmed a partisan supply column at Orliya (15km west of Ssewsk) and captured, among other things eighty hundredweight of grain, thirty horses, and twelve cows. A former member remembers another operation against the Soviet partisans:

> *"The partisan for a long time mined the roads out of the villages, so that there were numerous accidents causing serious injuries or deaths among the villagers. Some people's militiamen set up a lookout and a few days later surprised two partisans who were laying new mines. A partisan was killed, the other was captured and tied up on a tree stump. We lay the mines he had brought with him around him and ignited them. That got around quickly and the partisans then were so afraid of us that they – if they had the mission, for example, of blowing up a bridge – went into the woods and there just blew up few trees and reported that their orders had been carried out."*

After Kaminski was given control of more Rayon in the summer, he kept reinforcing the militia and also recruited regularly in the villages of the

Selbstverwaltungsbezirk. Due to the forced enlistment, the combat power of individual troops differed widely. While there were some very motivated members, there were now also men in the companies who were neither interested in fighting nor in Nazi politics. Nevertheless, at this point there were no large-scale desertions. On December 31, 1942, the militia thus had thirteen battalions with a total of about 9,000 men.

In January and February 1943, they participated in *Unternehmen Eisbär I* to *III* [Operation Polar Bear], in the sector of *Gruppe Rübsam*, which had been ordered by the *2. Panzer-Armee*.

In the battles against the large Panschenko partisan unit near Dmitrijev-Mikhailovka, the *Volkswehr-Bataillone* were mainly used for protection to the north, along Bryansk-Roslavl rail line. At the same time, other *Volkswehr* elements – especially the *VIII. Battaillon* – was sent to the front for the first time. Deployed under *SS-Kampfgruppe Zehender* in the sector of the *XLVII. Armee-Korps,* and the *72. Infanterie-Division* in the sector of *XX. Armee-Korps*, the men were initially used for reconnaissance and later to dig trenches.

While the German forces were able to repel the attacks of two Soviet fronts (Army Groups) and the Red Army had subsequently halted further advances in the Orel area by the end of March 1943, the Komarishi, Dimitrovsk, Mikhailovka, and Ssusemka districts were taken away from the *Selbstverwaltungsbezirk* and put under the direct command of the *Wehrmacht*: they had become front line sectors. Since the enemy had captured the Ssewsk and Dmitrievin *Rayon* in previous battles, Kaminski now only controlled Navlya and Brassovo, with about 80,000 inhabitants, of whom 6,575 were refugees from other districts.

The initial levels of motivation gave way under pressure of the constant successes of the Red Army. This also resulted in unrest in the *Volkswehr*. The *Gruppe Geheime Feldpolizei 639* noted in its activity report in March 1943:

> *"On February 24, 1943, the 2. Kompanie of the Russian Volkswehr Karatschev abandoned their bases and went into the nearby forest to unite with the Banditen [partisans] there. On 26-27, almost all members of the company returned, except a few people who had stayed in the woods and had joined the Banditen. The seven ringleaders were sentenced to death by shooting by Korück 532, based on the interrogations and investigation carried out by the Außenkommando [external command] Karachev. The sentence was carried out on March 12, 1943."*

On March 22, 1943, *PzAOK 2* ordered a campaign against the partisans and Red Army bands which had broken through in the previous battles, and who remained in the *Armee* rear. The *Divisionskommando z.b.V.* [*zur besonderen Verwendung*: For special use] *442* (*Generalleutnant* Karl Bornemann) took over the overall command of the battle against the partisans in this area and recommended the removal of the Hungarian divisions, since they were in constant confrontation with the *Volkswehr*. The German leadership responded first by pulling out the Royal Hungarian 108th Light Division. The units were to use concentric attacks from the north, east, and south, to force the partisans together in the forests south of the Navyla-north of Sseredina Buda-Gremyach'ye and against the Desna and annihilate them. The time required for this action was, depending on weather and road conditions, set at four weeks. The 20,000 men deployed failed in their attempt to completely pacify the area and destroy the partisans.

The *Volkswehr*, which was still outfitted in Soviet uniforms and white armbands bearing an Iron Cross, now were issued German uniforms in larger numbers. Its strength had meanwhile fallen, due to the limited possibility for recruitment, to about 7,100 men.

It also became apparent now that the *Volksweh*r-Brigade was no longer a homogeneous force. This became evident at this point in signs of disintegration in the *VIII. Bataillon*, deployed at the front in the sector of the *72. Infanterie-Division* (*XX. Armee-Korps*) at Dimitrovsk. When all company and platoon leaders and sergeants were given furloughs for Easter 1943, the men also took off without leave; and some never returned. Since Dimitrovsk no longer belonged to the *Selbstverwaltungsbezirk*, Kaminski ordered the transfer of the battalion to Lokot, to re-assert his authority over the men. However, since they wanted to stay with their families in the Dimitrovs district, this set off another wave of desertions. It was only with difficulty that the soldiers were set in march to Lokot.

Starting May 16, 1943, elements of *Volkswehr-Brigade "RONA"* took part in the anti-partisan *Unternehmen Zigeunerbaron* [Gypsy Baron] in the forest area south of Bryansk, until June 4, 1943. In addition, Unternehmen Freischütz [Marksman] was run between May 20-30, 1943, north of Bryansk. Here, the *I., II., III.* and *XI. Volkswehr-Bataillone* were used in the fighting.

With the capture of only 193 rifles, twenty *Machinengewehre,* and thirty-three automatic rifles, and German losses of twenty-seven dead, the claim of about 1,800 enemy dead raises questions about the actual nature of the fighting. The figures for *Unternehmen Zigeunerbaron* also give rise to similar questions. It would appear that these involved, at least in part, full-scale mass executions of the so-called suspected "bandit" population.

As of June 14, 1943, *XII. Bataillon* of *Volkswehr-Brigade "RONA"* was involved in *Unternehmen Tannhäuser*. From June 25 to July 27, 1943, *Unternehmen Seydlitz* was carried out south of Dorogobuzh.

After the failed German summer offensive at Kursk (*Unternehmen Zitadelle* [Operation Citadel]) the Red Army managed to break through the *2. Panzer-Armee* front. On July 26, 1943, Hitler approved the evacuation of Orel. On August 20, 1943, the evacuation of the civilian population started from the former *Selbstverwaltungsbezirk* Lokot by way of Sseredina Buda-Lukashenkov-Prokopvka-Novgorod Sseversk-Pushkari-Gramyatsk to Pogar. While the *4.*

Members of the German liaison staff to Volkswehr-Brigade "RONA" in summer 1943.

Regiment der Volkswehr-Brigade "RONA" was destroyed in the fighting on August 26, 1943, in the sector of the *XX. Armee-Korps* at Ssvesk, the other *Volkswehr* units were sent by rail with the civilians from, Pogar to Vitebsk.

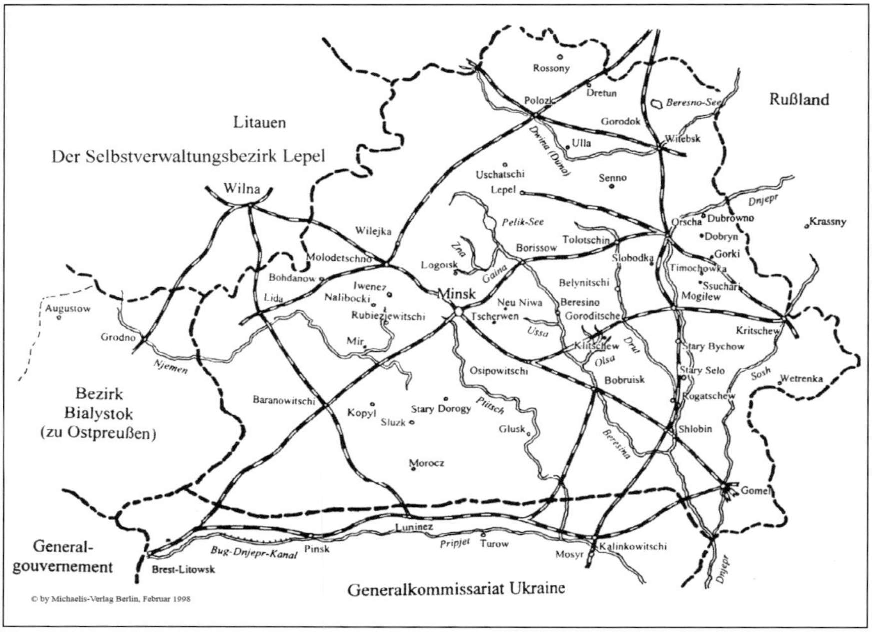

In early September 1943, most of the evacuated population and the *Volkswehr* were assembled in the area west of Vitebsk. This mass of some 30,000 people not only caused logistical problems. There were also growing signs of disintegration. Already in the first days, elements of the *VII. Volkswehr-Bataillon* made contact with the regional partisan leadership and deserted. *PzAOK 3* therefore regarded the *Volkswehr-Brigade* as a source of danger – even if Kaminski was considered an energetic *Kommandeur.*

Unternehmen Hubertus was launched on October 16, 1943, to free the area of Senno Chashniki and send the some 3,000 evacuees from Lokot remaining there to Chashniki, and attempt to largely pacify the Beshenkovichi-Senno-Usvaika River-Chashniki region. The *2. 3.* and *5. Schützen-Regiment* and the *Garde-Bataillon* were used for this operation. After some heavy fighting, all battle groups were assembled on October 27, 1943, in Lepel, which was again to be declared a new *Selbstverwaltungsbezirk*. The *Volkswehr* had thirty-four dead; the partisans, 562. Even taking into account that "successes" were usually claimed to be higher than they were, this raises questions about the scope of the fighting. *Hauptmann* Könneke of the German liaison staff reported about *Unternehmen Hubertus*:

> *"The Volkswehr conducted itself well in the attack. At times, the attacks were carried out courageously. The units were not all equal; decisive factor is always the personality of the unit leader.*
>
> *The Volkswehr main combat power is in their tanks and heavy weapons, since the [partisan] bands have nothing like that to use against them. The Volkswehr is not as good at defense. It lacks the necessary perseverance. Confidence in their own strength easily slackens if there is a shortage of ammunition."*

While the German *Wehrmacht* was fending off the most serious attacks at the front, Kaminski tried to consolidate his position in the new *Selbstverwaltungsbezirk* and to combat the Soviet partisans at the rear of the *3. Panzer-Armee*. He was only partly successful at both; life as it had been in the *Selbstverwaltungsbezirk* Lokot no longer existed. The morale of both the *Volkswehr* and the population had been shaken by the retreat: they felt like refugees and suspected that the war had been lost. A former member recalls:

> *"The conditions in Byelorussia were chaotic at times. Individual troops and leaders were in contact with the partisans. The morale of most of the officers had also begun to falter. I remember, for example, Major Turlakov, who was invited along with Oberstleutnant [Lieutenant Colonel] Belay to Berlin in winter 1943-44. When he saw the awful situation there and living conditions for the Russian prisoners and Ostarbeiter [Eastern workers], he came back a broken man. In a subsequent interview with Kaminski, he tore off his epaulettes and medals (including EK I) and explained that he was very likely on the wrong side! Kaminski and I reassured him, but could not prevent it when Turlakov, in the spring of 1944, jumped under the treads in front of a tank, and thus ended his life. One day, others hung signs on the houses: 'Against Bolshevism and foreign domination' – these signs had of course immediately to be taken down, by order of the German authorities."*

Unternehmen Frühlingsfest [Spring Festival] was launched on April 16, 1944. In the fighting, which lasted until May 12, 1944 in the Ushatchi region, the forces deployed on the German side suffered 175 killed and 625 wounded – the enemy losses were again many times those: 3,654 dead and 1,794 prisoners.

While about 40% of *Volkswehr-Brigade "RONA"* took part in *Unternehmen Frühlingsfest*, the elements not used in action accompanied the civilians on a mid-April 1944 rail transport to Dyatlovo (south of Lida). Kaminski's civilian followers were to be protected against the Red Army. By mid-May 1944, the troops previously used in *Unternehmen Frühlingsfest* also arrived here and *SS- und Polizeiführer Bialystok* was made economically responsible for them. A former interpreter remembers conversations between *SS-Obergruppenführer und General der Polizei* von Gottberg and *Brigade-Kommandeur* Kaminski:

Deployment of Volkswehr-Brigade "RONA" in February 1944.

"RONA" members with Freiwilligen from the Caucasus.

> *"One day, SS-Obergruppenführer und General der Polizei von Gottberg arrived from Minsk to meet Kaminski at Dyatlovo. The latter also planned to build up an autonomous Russian government here, as in Lokot. Von Gottberg would not hear of any self-governing territory. I was the interpreter for this discussion, although Kaminski spoke passable German. It also was about the following: In addition to the Soviet partisans, the Polish Home Army (Armia Krajowa) was already fighting in this area. As far as the Germans were concerned, they were all bandits, and they demanded Kaminski also fight against the Poles. Kaminski, however, refused categorically. Von Gottberg screamed at him and I translated without toning down what he said. Kaminski answered the same way – using Russian profanity. I translated, but did soften his expressions. Finally Kaminski managed it – at least at this point – that the 'RONA' did not have to fight the Poles."*

A former *"RONA"* staff officer recalls on this issue:

> *"It is true that Kaminski did not want to let RONA fight against the Armia Krajowa. His fight was directed against Stalin and Bolshevism, not against the national struggle of individual peoples. His slogan was: Against communism and foreign rule – which was, of course, contrary to the German beliefs. Kaminski said that there had been enmity between Russia and Poland for so long, and he did not contribute to further problems. He would not use the RONA against Poles nationalists!"*

When the Red Army pushed forward further westwards and reached Brest-Litovsk, the western border of the USSR on July 28, 1944, *Volkswehr-Brigade "RONA"* was moved further west, along with the civilians. Here, the question arose, where and how the some 21,000 civilians could be accommodated and fed. After many discussions, they finally planned to move the evacuated civilians to Pomerania and the *Volkswehr-Brigade* and their families (a total of about 10,000 people) to Hungary.

Waffen-Sturmbrigade der SS "RONA"

Always interested in expanding the *Waffen-SS, Reichsführer-SS* Himmler and the head of the *SS-Hauptamt* in Berlin, *SS-Obergruppenführer* Berger, began to get interested in the *Volkswehr-Brigade*. *SS-Obergruppenführer* von Gottberg also served, as a "medium" for the newly established *Freiwilligen-Leitstelle Ost* [Volunteer Headquarters East], under *SS-Obersturmbannführer* Dr. Fritz Arlt, as already noted. *Heeresgruppe Mitte* noted on this on May 29, 1944:

Celebrating Russian Easter at Kaminski's house on April 16, 1944.

Center, Oberst i.G. [: General staff service] Ludendorff together with the Brigade Kommandeur.

At center, Kaminski. Next to him, Generalmajor Heidkämper. At right, Oberst i.G. Ludendorff.

> *"According to instructions from OKW/WPr. [Wehrmachts-Propaganda: Armed Forces Propaganda] Vlasov could continue to be used as a propaganda figure in [sic] the enemy. Any singling out of the personality of Vlasov by those Russians cooperating with us is not desirable.*
>
> *The Kaminski movement, primarily in the sector of Heeresgruppe Mitte, has recently been strictly watched and supervised by the SS (SS-Obergruppenführer Gottsberg in Minsk). There is no intention, especially in leading positions, to bring about any fundamental clarification on this matter. We want above all to wait and see about the further development of the Kaminski movement."*

Some fourteen days later, the *Waffen-SS* had already issued the command to take control of the *Volkswehr-Brigade*. On June 17, 1944, as *Waffen-Sturmbrigade der SS "RONA,"* it was allocated the *Feldpost* number 45 155. The *Wehrmacht Verbindungskommando* [liaison command] was removed, and *SS-Sturmbannführer* Reußner replaced *SS-Hauptsturmführer* Loleit as liaison to the *Waffen-SS*.

The remaining around 5,000 men were to be used to form a *SS-Sturmbrigade neuer Art* with a *Grenadier-Bataillon (4 Kompanien)* and a *schwere Bataillon* (each with 1 *Infanteriegeschütz.-, Panzerabwehr-, Flak-* and *Pionierkompanie*).

However, the proposed reclassification was initially delayed by the launching of the Red Army summer offensive on June 22, 1944. A *Kampfgruppe* was organized using the elements of the *Waffen-Sturmbrigade* still at Dyatlovo, still referred to the *Volkswehr-Brigade der SS "RONA,"* which was briefly placed under command of *Kampfgruppe von Gottberg* and the *50. Infanterie-Division*.

Beginning July 4, 1944, the men fought off many partisan attacks between Lubcz and Nienievich from the Naliboki forest. This was followed up July 8th, 1944 with fighting against regular Soviet troops in the Vselyub and Nowogrodek line (southeast of Lida). Since the German *Kampfgruppen* were pushed back to Grodno in just a few days, the Russians were withdrawn from action and followed the units and families that meanwhile were now in the Czestochowa area.

29. Waffen-Grenadier-Division der SS "RONA" (*russische Nr. 1*)

The original plan to relocate *Waffen-Sturmbrigade "RONA"* and its dependent family members to an autonomous region in Hungary was abandoned. Ultimately, the German leadership intended to accommodate these approximately 10,000 people in Slovakia. In addition to the fact that Hungarians would be extremely sensitive to the relocation of Russian units and civilians into their territory, certainly not at the end of the day, the partisan threat in Slovakia was decisive. Due to the rush of events, the transported people initially were left scattered in different areas. By July 1944, troops and civilians were dispersed among Czestochowa, Krakow, and Ratibor. Kaminski now considered his most urgent task was to bring the families of his soldiers to safety. At the end of the month, he was ordered to meet Himmler in Rastenburg. The former *Ic* [*3. Generalstabsoffizier*: 3rd General Staff Officer] recalls:

> *"On July 30, 1944, Kaminski, with his chief of staff Oberstleutnant Schawykin and I, third staff officer, drove to Rastenburg. There, the next day, Kaminski got his appointment as Waffen-Brigadeführer and Kommandeur of the newly reorganized 29. Waffen-Grenadier-Division der SS 'RONA' (russische Nr. 1). In the personal discussion between Himmler and Kaminski, Himmler said – under the impact of the attempt to assassinate Hitler only ten days earlier – that he would be most happy to have a Leibwache [bodyguard] of RONA members. We got our new rank insignia from the SS uniform supply in Berlin. Schawykin was formerly a Red Army captain and had served as a platoon commander in the cavalry. In the RONA he moved up to be Chief of Staff and received the rank of lieutenant colonel. There may be disagreements about his military capabilities, but he had Kaminski's trust ..."*

SS-Obergruppenführer and *General der Polizei* von dem Bach also took part in these discussions and presented *Waffen-Brigadeführer* Kaminski with the *Bandenkampfabzeichen* [Anti-Partisan Guerrilla Warfare Badge] in *Bronze*. In his diary he noted for August 2, 1944:

> *"The day before yesterday I was back at the RF-SS [Reichsführer-SS], where I also met Guderian. In addition, the Russian Freischarenführer [guerilla leader] Kaminski was present, with whom I had to lead long negotiations."*

While talks between Himmler and Kaminski led to the matter that organizing a *Sturmbrigade n.A.* was foreseen and therefore *29. Waffen-Grenadier-Division der SS RONA (russische Nr. 1)*[28] was to be assembled at *Truppenübungsplatz* Neuhammer, an insurrection broke out in Warsaw.

It was initiated by the Polish government-in-exile in London, who feared for their position of power in a post-war Poland. Therefore, the capital was to be freed from German occupation by its own power and not by the Red Army, already stationed on the eastern bank of the Vistula. In all Warsaw districts, the Polish insurgents – insufficiently coordinated and prepared – took up a struggle, which cost over 200,000 lives in the following sixty-three days. The Poles were unable to achieve any significant successes anywhere. The all-important Vistula bridges thus remained in German hands, like all other strategic objectives.

[28] To achieve the authorized strength of approximately 12,300 men, the *Reichsführer-SS* was planning, in his capacity as head of the German *Polizei*, to integrate especially *Schutzmannschafts-Bataillone* into the *Division*.

To combat the uprising, *erste Generalstabsoffizier (Ia) Waffen-Sturmbannführer* Frolow organized around 1,700 men into the:

Waffen-Grenadier-Regiment der SS 72 (russische Nr. 1)
13.(Infanteriegeschütz-)Kompanie (2 Soviet 12.2cm guns)
14.(Panzerjäger-)Kompanie (8 Soviet 7.62cm Pak)
1.Panzer-Kompanie (4 T-34s and 1 Soviet assault gun)

On August 2, 1944, at 16:25 o'clock, *SS-Obersturmbannführer* Reußner reported that the Russian *Regiment* had reached Rakow (south-southwest of Warsaw) and had been deployed to free the Ochota city district.

For this, *Waffen-Grenadier-Regiment der SS 72 (russische Nr. 1)* was reinforced by the *2. /Panzerjäger-Abteilung 743* with twelve *Panzerabwehrkanonen* and the *1. /Panzer-Pionier-Sturmbataillon 500* and integrated into *Gruppe Reinefarth*.

On August 5, 1944, *Waffen-Grenadier Regiment der SS 72* (*russische Nr. 1*) began its attack on Ochata at eight o'clock. The *Regiment*, coming from the southwest along Radomer Street, reached Academy Square in the University district by way of Narutowicz Square. The *Kriegstagebuch* of the *9. Armee* has a polemical statement on this incident: *"Regiment Kaminski, from the south on the National Highway, had gotten drunk at the Makhorka factory."*

The behavior of the Russians, who did more plundering than fighting, demonstrated the complete lack of motivation that had meanwhile developed and their general lack of interest in fighting the *Armia Krajowa*. *Waffen-Brigadeführer* Kaminski left Rastenburg, arriving in Warsaw the same day with *Waffen-Obersturmbannführer* Schawykin, to have his *Regiment* taken out of the action by *SS-Obergruppenführer* and *General der Waffen-SS und Polizei* von dem Bach.[29] Already in Dyatlovo, Kaminski had not wanted his men to be deployed against the Polish *Armia Krajowa* and sacrificed in the streets of Warsaw. Bach agreed, under the condition that replacements would arrive for the *Regiment*. Kaminski initially remained in Warsaw and from then on led the *Regiment*, along with *Waffen-Sturmbannführer* Frolow.

During August 10-11, 1944, *Waffen-Grenadier-Regiment der SS 72* reached the area of Tytusa Street-Jerozolimskie Avenue-Central Station-Poznanska Street-Emilii Plater Street. As of August 17, 1944, the Russians – reinforced by 600 men from Czestochowa – were put under command of the newly formed *Kampfgruppe Rohr*.

Throughout the struggle, the Kampinos Forest – northwest of Warsaw – had a special strategic importance for the Polish Home Army and represented a potential danger for the German troops. After the German leadership had decided to withdraw the Russian *SS-Regiment* from Warsaw, the *9. Armee* planned to use the freed-up unit in the obstacle line to block the Kampinos Forest. The *Kriegstagebuch* of the *9. Armee* noted on August 27, 1944:

[29] *Waffen-Obersturmbannführer* Belaj was responsible for the troops who had not been deployed.

> *"Shielding Warsaw from the northwest against the influx of gangs from the Pusza Kampinoska, the AOK thinks to lead offensively with the Brigade Kaminski Regiment, previously used in the south city, which will end their use in Warsaw."*

The next day came the end of not only the *Regiment*'s deployment, but also the life of *Waffen-Brigadeführer* Kaminski, who had been boisterously praised by Himmler on August 3, 1944, in his Posen speech to the *Gauleiter* [district leaders]:

> *"Three troops have emerged, for me, out of this collapse in Minsk or behind Minsk. One was a Russian Brigade Kaminski, with 6,000-7,000 men, led by a Russian. I had to hear from my German command staff, how many cigar boxes with EK II and EK I the Russians picked up as souvenirs, which lay by the wayside because they had been thrown away!"*

Since Kaminski, with his confident demeanor, did not want to make himself out as a puppet of the German leadership, he was ordered, under a pretext, to meet *SS-Obergruppenführer* and *General der Polizei* von dem Bach, and on August 28, 1944, he was shot, along with his driver, his chief of staff Schawykin and divisional surgeon Dr. Sabora, who had accompanied him. This was reported as a partisan attack, but doubts quickly emerged about this version of events. In fact, the Russian side suspected that the *SS* had given the order for his liquidation.

Since it was not yet clear whether the *"RONA"* would be dissolved or should/could continue to operate under new leadership, the *SS-Führungshauptamt* initially installed the previous *SS- und Polizeiführer* of Lviv, *SS-Brigadeführer und Generalmajor der Polizei* Diehm, as acting *Division* leader. A month later, *SS-Obergruppenführer* Berger appointed *SS-Gruppenführer* Jürs commander of the *29. Waffen-Grenadier-Division der SS "RONA" (russische Nr. 1)*. Jürs was to re-organize it in the German *Schutzzone* [protected zone] in Slovakia, and lead it from there into action in the central Slovakia region.

When it was realized, however, that this formation was useless without Kaminski's leadership, the *Reichsführer-SS* decided to dissolve it. Himmler had changed his plans in the recent weeks. He, who always wanted to set up new major units, ordered, after a conversation with General Vlasov on September 16, 1944, the formation of the *600.* and *650. Infanterie-Division (russische)*. He appointed Vlasov at the same time as commander of the Russian Liberation Army, *ROA*. To organize these new *Divisionen*, Himmler ordered the delivery of all the smaller Russian units to *Truppenübungsplatz* Münsingen – including the remaining about 2,000 *"RONA"* members, who still had twelve T-34 tanks and two armored Kv-Is.

This ended the history of the Russian Liberation Army. Initially formed and deployed as a militia, its leaders then attempted to organize a cohesive unit.

Kaminski's sovereign political thinking ended tragically for him, and led to the disbandment of the unit.

Kommandeure:

06/44 – 08/44	*Waffen-Brigadeführer* Kaminski
08/44	*SS-Brigadeführer* Diehm
08/44	*SS-Gruppenführer* Jürs

Feldpost numbers:

Brigade-/Divisionsstab	45 155

29. Waffen-Grenadier-Division der SS (*italienische Nr. 1*)

Italienische (SS-)Freiwilligen-Legion

As a result of the shift in power in Italy in summer 1943, there was a complete restructuring of the Italian units based in the German sphere of influence. On September 22, 1943, the head of the *SS-Hauptamt* announced that all Italians who wanted to serve in the *Waffen-SS* should be assembled at *Truppenübungsplatz* Münsingen. Since it initially was only a group of *Freiwilligen*, the unit was to be named the ***Italienische Freiwilligen-Legion*** **[Italian Volunteer Legion]**.[30] The *Freiwilligen* – often fascists, but partly also opportunists (e.g., to be released from internment) – were called *"Legionäre [Legionnaires] der italienischen Freiwilligen-Formationen."*

In fact, there was no initial plan to form a *Waffen-SS Division*, but rather set up, in collaboration with the *Ordnungspolizei*, so-called anti-partisan militias under command of the *Waffen-SS*. To this end, the head of the *SS-Hauptamt* drew up a *"Program for the formation of Italian militia units by the Waffen-SS"* on October 2, 1943.

By the end of October 1943, there were some 15,000 demobilized Italians willing to elinst in the *Waffen-SS* at *Truppenübungsplatz* Münsingen. Of these, some 9,000 were found to be unfit and usually were sent to work in the arms industry. The remaining 6,000 men formed thirteen *Miliz-Bataillone* [militia battalions], which in November 1943, were sent back to northern Italy to the area west of Turin. Placed under command of the *Höheren SS- und Polizeiführer Italien*, by early December 1943 they were – now designated the ***Italienische SS-Freiwilligen-Legion*** – used for fighting partisans. The *KTB/OKW* [*Kriegstagebuch Oberkommando West*] noted here on December 15, 1943:

> *"The OB [Oberbefehlshaber] Südwest was informed that the Reichsführer-SS, on the orders of the Führer, is forming an Italian SS-Legion in Italy, whose organization is to be supported."*

The Legionnaires, or militiamen – these terms, as with membership in the *Waffen-SS* or *Ordnungspolizei*, varied even among German departments – wore Italian uniforms with badges similar to those of the *Waffen-SS*: red instead of black collar patches and a white eagle on a red background, holding a fasces rather than a swastika.

---

[30] The designations *"italienische Freiwilligen-Legion"* and *"italienische SS-Freiwilligen-Legion"* do not represent, as with the volunteer *"Niederlande"* or *"Flandern" Legions*, the name of a formation, but rather were, as for the so-called *"Lettischen SS-Legion"* formulations, a group of *Freiwilligen*, whose deployment and future organization had not yet been clearly defined.

Himmler's reluctance[31] to officially recognize the Italians as members of the *Waffen-SS* was demonstrated not only by the altered badge, but also by his decree that externally, the units should not be designated as *SS* troops. Thus, *Oberbefehlshaber Südwest* was still reporting on June 1, 1944, *"that the designation SS in conjunction with Italian formations is banned, in accordance with the wishes of the Reichsführer-SS in the sector of Oberbefehlshaber Südwest."*

It is also extremely unusual that the *Freiwilligen* were given *Heer* ranks until the end of 1944.[32]

Italienische Freiwilligen-Sturmbrigade (Milizia d'Armata)

In February 1944, the *Reichsführer-SS* ordered the combination of various militia units into an *SS-Sturmbrigade n.A.* Since Himmler, however, still wanted to dispense with the designation *"SS"* for the Italian units, the official name was ***Italienische Freiwilligen-Sturmbrigade***.

The typical structure of an *SS-Sturmbrigade n.A.* with a *Grenadier-Bataillon (mot.)* and a *schwere Bataillon (mot.)*. was not realized, due to the difficulties in delivering heavy weapons, as well as the *Reichsführer-SS*'s profound skepticism of the Italians' combat power and motivation.

Still under formation in early March 1944, the *I. /Italienische Freiwilligen-Sturmbrigade*, with a strength of:

Führer	***sonstige Dienstgrade***	**Total**
32	608	640
5.0%	95.0%	100%

Was approved for combat duty against the Allied Nettuno beachhead. Equipped with:

421	M 91 rifles (Ital.)
131	sub-machine guns (Ital.)
139	Beretta pistols (Ital.)
50	light Beretta machine guns (Ital.)
10	grenade launchers 8.14cm
6	*Panzerabwehrkanonen* 7.5cm

The reinforced *Bataillon* reached Latisana and was put under command of *SS-Kampfgruppe Diebitsch*. On April 18, 1944, the unit was placed under command

[31] Presumably it was Himmler's distrust of the Italians as fighters, which led to the decision that neither uniforms nor unit designations would indicate any affiliation with the *Waffen-SS*! This would only change for both only after a trial period.

[32] See the appendix on comparison of ranks.

of the *715. Infanterie-Division* and reinforced by the end of the month by Italian *Bataillon Debica*, which had been formed at *SS-Truppenübungsplatz* Heidelager.

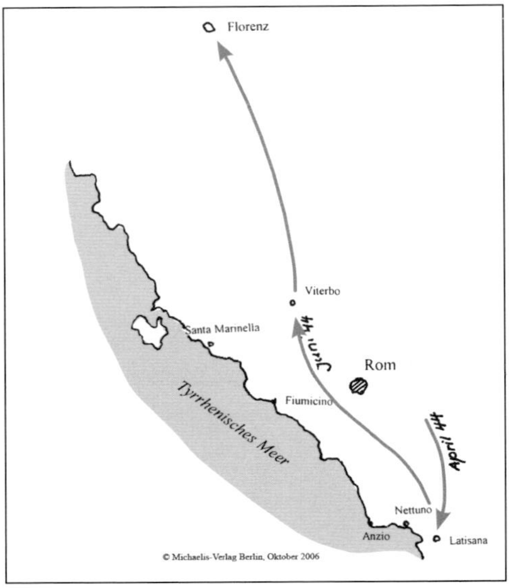

When the Allies broke through the German positions after a massive artillery bombardment on May 23, 1944, the *HKL* had to be pulled back. The *Kommandeur* of the *715. Infanterie-Division, Generalmajor* Hildebrandt, compiled a report on May 31, 1944, on the Italians under his command. He also reported on an American war crime:

"After detailed discussions with Oberst Mangold, who carried out the necessary findings, I report:

1. *In the surprise attack with preparatory smokescreens on May 20, 1944, some Italians, about fifteen men, approached the Americans with hands up. These Italians were shot down by the Americans.*

2. *In the large-scale attack on May 23, 1944, after heavy preparatory artillery barrage with tanks, the 2. and 3. SS-Italia collapsed and fled to the rear. Elements were detained at the Artillerie Abteilungsgefechtsstand and Regimentsgefechtsstand [Artillery and Regimental command posts].*

3. *It is likely that German soldiers shot at the retreating Italians. We can not assemble impeccable evidence, since Leutnant Burghardt, who commanded this position, was killed and the staff's entire records, telephone records, etc., were destroyed.*

Inspection of Waffen-Grenadier-Brigade der SS (italienische Nr. 1) by SS-Obergruppenführer Wolff and Marshal Graziani.

Höchste SS- und Polizeiführer SS-Obergruppenführer Wolff awards an Italian Waffen-Untersturmführer the EK I.

4. *SS-Italia Oberfeldwebel Cavic, Leutnant Gulli (EK 2), both fought well, both killed, also Hauptmann Fischotti with some men. Oberstleutnant Degli Oddi was at all times with Hauptmann Tornow (Bataillon-Kommandeur). His conduct was good."*

While the German troops tried to halt the Allied troops in front of Rome, the two Italian *(SS-)Bataillone* were withdrawn from action and marched through Viterbo to Florence. By train, the soldiers reached Pinerolo (about 30km southwest of Turin) on June 25, 1944. Here, the previous *I. /Italienische Freiwilligen-Sturmbrigade* formed the *II. /Infanterie-Regiment 1,* and *Bataillon Debica* formed the *Füsilier-Bataillon* of the *Waffen-Grenadier-Brigade der SS (italienische Nr. 1)* which was being organized.

Waffen-Grenadier-Brigade der SS (*italienische Nr. 1*)

Because it was impossible to realize the structure of an *SS-SturmBrigade n. A.* due to the lack of heavy weapons, Himmler ordered in early May 1944, the formation of a ***Waffen-Grenadier-Brigade der SS (italienische Nr. 1)***. This was to be organized as follows:

Stab
Infanterie-Regiment 1 (I. – II. Bataillon)
Infanterie-Regiment 2 (I. – II. Bataillon)
Artillerie-Abteilung
Füsilier-Bataillon
Pionier-Kompanie
Nachrichten-Kompanie
Panzerjäger-Abteilung
Ersatz-Bataillon

It is interesting that *Wehrmacht* ranks and unit designations – up to that of *Brigade* – were used without the addition of *"SS-."*

Although Himmler still basically wanted to avoid use of the designation *"SS"* externally for the Italian *Freiwilligen* in the *Waffen-SS*, he did state in early May 1944 that the *Milizia d'Armata* units set up by the *Höchsten SS- und Polizeiführer Italien* are *"Waffenverbände der SS with all rights and obligations."*

Intended for fighting partisans, the organization of *Waffen-Grenadier-Brigade der SS (italienische Nr. 1)* did not include any unit training at a *Truppenübungsplatz*. Instead, the units were used to combat insurgents in the Piedmont, in the region in between Turin-Levanna-Pellice-the French border (about 2,500 square kilometers).

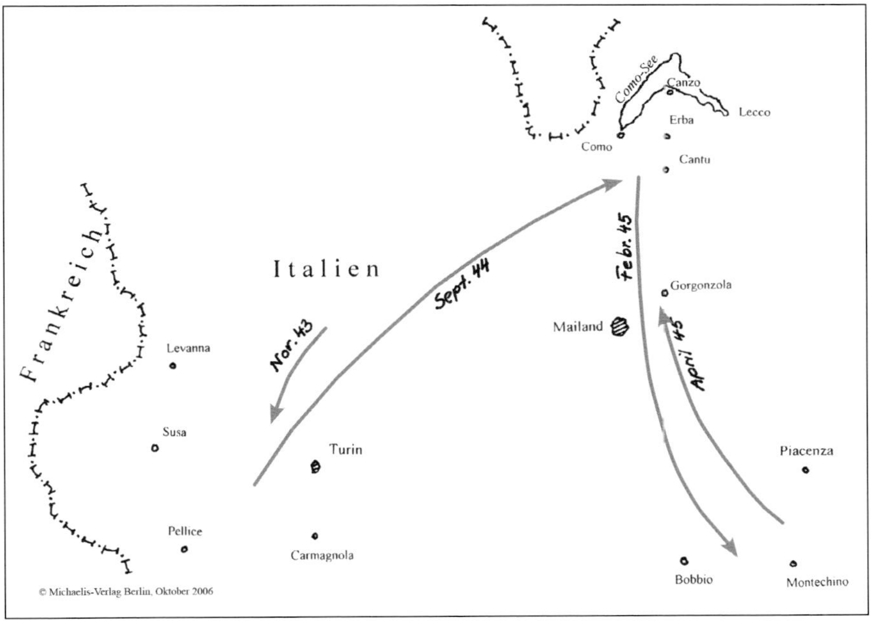

The last major operation in the Piedmont was carried out in September 1944, when a *Kampfgruppe* was deployed against the Mauri band of partisans in the area of Carmagnola (about 25km south of Turin).

The troops were then transferred to Lombardy and put under command of *Generalkommando Lombardia* (formerly *LXXXVII. Armee-Korps*). In further anti-partisan operations, the units were moved into the following areas:

Brigadestab Cantù	(about 12km south of Como)
Infanterie-Regiment 1	Cantù
Infanterie-Regiment 2	Meda (about 20km south of Como)
Artillery Regiment	Asso in Como
Füsilier-Bataillon	Missaglia in Lecco (25km NE of Como)
Panzerjäger-Abteilung	Canzo (about 15km NE of Como)
Pionier-Kompanie	Cantù
Sanitäts-Kompanie	Erba (about 10km east of Como)
Nachschub-Kompanie	Erba
Nachrichten-Kompanie	Montorfano in Como

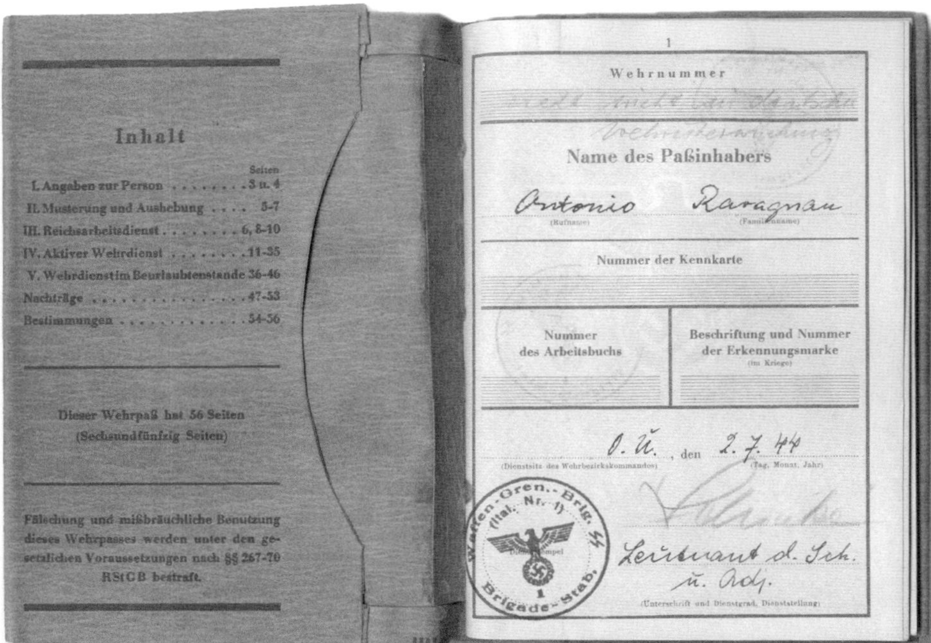

Inhalt

Seiten
I. Angaben zur Person . . . . 3 u. 4
II. Musterung und Aushebung 5-7
III. Reichsarbeitsdienst 6, 8-10
IV. Aktiver Wehrdienst 11-35
V. Wehrdienst im Beurlaubtenstande 36-46
Nachträge 47-53
Bestimmungen 54-56

Dieser Wehrpaß hat 56 Seiten
(Sechsundfünfzig Seiten)

Fälschung und mißbräuchliche Benutzung dieses Wehrpasses werden unter den gesetzlichen Voraussetzungen nach §§ 267-70 RStGB bestraft.

1

Wehrnummer

Name des Paßinhabers

Antonio Ravagnan
(Rufname) (Familienname)

Nummer der Kennkarte

Nummer des Arbeitsbuchs

Beschriftung und Nummer der Erkennungsmarke (im Kriege)

O.U., den 2.7.44
(Dienstsitz des Wehrbezirkskommandos) (Tag, Monat, Jahr)

Waffen-Gren.-Brig. (ital. Nr. 1) SS Brigade-Stab

Leutnant d. Sch. u. Adj.
(Unterschrift und Dienstgrad, Dienststellung)

Wehrpaß [military service record book] of Italian SS-Freiwilliger Antonio Ravagnan.

2

Von den Bestimmungen auf Seite 54, 55 und 56 habe ich Kenntnis genommen

Antonio Ravagnan
(Eigenhändige Unterschrift des Inhabers — Rufname, Familienname)

Größe in Zentimetern 167 Augenfarbe braun
Körperbauform schlank Haarfarbe braun
Besondere Kennzeichen (z. B. Brillenträger)

Blutgruppe

3

I. Angaben zur Person

1	Familienname	Ravagnan
2	Vornamen (Rufnamen unterstreichen)	Antonio
3	Geburtstag, -monat, -jahr	12. 9. 1912
4	Geburtsort, Verwaltungsbezirk (z. B. Kreis, Reg. Bezirk)	Venezia / Venezia
5	Staatsangehörigkeit (auch frühere)	ital.
6	Religiöses Bekenntnis	kath. — Zahl der leb. Kinder
7	Familienstand	led.
8	Beruf (nach Berufsverzeichnis)	erlernter: Fischer; zuletzt ausgeübter: dto.
9	Eltern	Vater: Luca Ravagnan, Fischer; Mutter: Sofia R., Moliuari

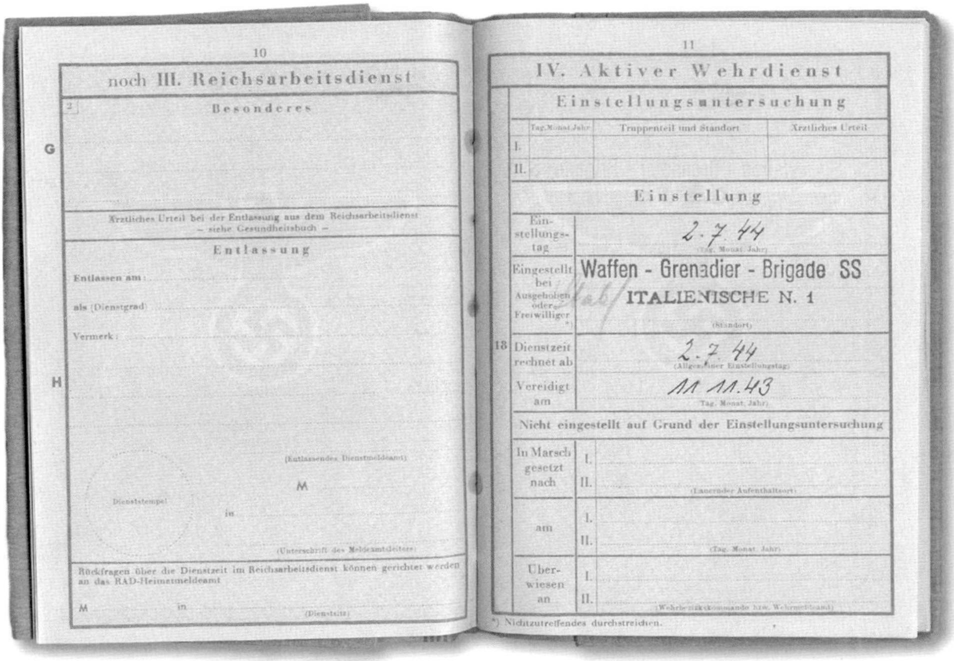

Ravagnan was inducted in Waffen-Grenadier-Brigade der SS (italienische Nr. 1) on February 7, 1944.

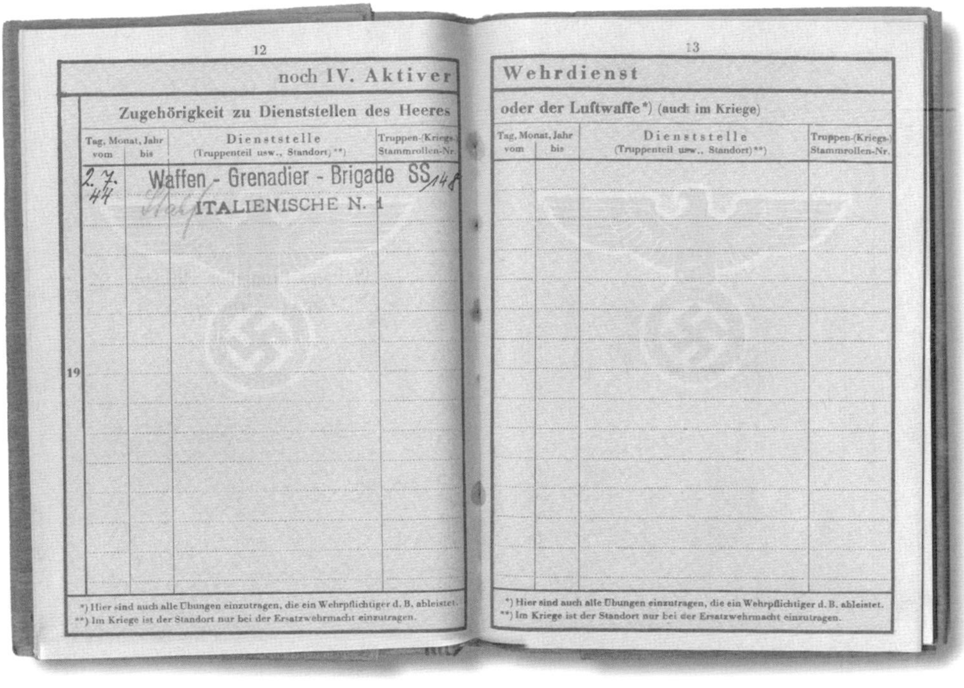

On November 27, 1944, *Waffen-Grenadier-Brigade der SS (italienische Nr. 1)* reported a strength of:

Führer	*Unterführer*	*Männer*	**Total**
282	756	3,094	4,132
6.8%	18.3%	74.9%	100%

At the end of January 1945, *SS-Standartenführer* Heldmann – *Kommandeur* of the *Brigade* since November 1944 – was ordered to set up a *Kampfgruppe* for deployment south of Piacenza. The barely *Regiment*-strength *Kampfgruppe* was assembled under the command of *SS-Obersturmbannführer* Binz and loaded on trains in Como on February 6, 1945. They reached the region of Bobbio-Montechino (respectively about 30km to the southwest-southeast of Piacenza) by rail. Here they relieved elements of the *162. (Turk.) Infanterie-Division* and secured the supply routes to the front. This led to repeated skirmishes with partisans. Due to the Allied advance, *SS-Kampfgruppe Binz* pulled back starting April 25, 1945, on both sides of the Via Emilia towards Milan and was split up five days later, northeast of Milan at Gorgonzola. Some elements were taken prisoner by American forces.

29. Waffen-Grenadier-Division der SS (*italienische Nr. 1*)

On February 10, 1945, Himmler ordered, for the purpose of deception, that the *Waffen-SS Brigade* be renamed as *Divisionen*. This also included *Waffen-Grenadier-***Brigade** *der SS (italienische Nr. 1)*, which now would be designated ***29. Waffen-Grenadier-Division der SS (italienische Nr. 1)***. Placed under command of *SS- und Polizeiführer Oberitalien-West* [Upper Italy-West] it was then ordered to be reorganized into a two-part *Grenadier-Division* with the official *SS* troop designations:

Waffen-Grenadier-Regiment der SS 81 (italienische Nr. 1)
Waffen-Grenadier-Regiment der SS 82 (italienische Nr. 1)
Waffen-Artillerie-Regiment der SS 29 (italienische Nr. 1)
SS-Füsilier-Bataillon 29
SS-Panzerjäger-Abteilung 29
SS-Pionier-Kompanie 29
SS-Nachrichten-Kompanie 29
SS-Sanitäts-Kompanie 29
SS-Feldersatz-Bataillon 29

Except for *SS-Kampfgruppe Binz*, the fragments of the remaining *Division* sections were again used to secure the Piedmont region. Initially, always suffering from lack of arms and equipment, the unit had, according to a report of April 9, 1945, with a strength of some 4,500 men:

6,200	*Gewehre*
1,200	*Maschinenpistolen*
1,200	*Pistolen*
330	*leichte Maschinengewehre*
60	*schwere Maschinengewehre*
45	*Granatwerfer* 8.14cm
14	*Flugabwehrkanonen* 2cm
24	*Panzerabwehrkanonen* 4.5cm
6	*Panzerabwehrkanonen* 7.5cm
17	*Gebirgsgeschütze* 7.5cm

Thus, the *Division* had almost twice as many weapons as it had soldiers, a curious situation in April 1945. The first units disbanded even before the German surrender in Italy at the end of April 1945. The rest were taken as Allied prisoners of war.

The training of the Italian *SS-Freiwilligen-Verband* reflected Himmler's distrust of the Italian soldiers. For external appearances, their membership in the *Waffen-SS* was to be essentially withheld, pending probation. As part of the new reorganization of foreign-national formations, it was first ordered that a *Brigade* be formed, and only later, a *Division*. Except for the deployment of two *Bataillone* at the Nettuno beachhead, the units were only used in the anti-partisan campaigns in northern Italy. Set up at a time of general war-weariness, the units were made up of some fascists and many opportunists who mostly wanted to get out of internment in 1943. Any benefit for Germany must be considered as moderate at best.

Kommandeure:

05/44 – 10/44	*SS-Brigadeführer* Hansen
11/44 – 05/45	*SS-Standartenführer* Heldmann

***Feldpost* numbers:**

Divisionsstab	82 640
Waffen-Grenadier-Regiment der SS 81 (italienische Nr. 1)	87 670
I. Bataillon	83 851
II. Bataillon	81 304
III. Bataillon	81 456
Waffen-Grenadier-Regiment der SS 82 (italienische Nr. 2)	86 922
I. Bataillon	81 984
II. Bataillon	83 761
III. Bataillon	82 354
Waffen-Artillerie-Regiment der SS 29 (italienische Nr. 1)	80 203
I. Abteilung	81 568
II. Abteilung	80 465
SS-Füsilier-Bataillon 29	57 239
SS-Pionier-Kompanie 29	59 436
SS-Nachrichten-Kompanie 29	58 260
SS-Panzerjäger-Abteilung 29	87 772
SS-Feld-Ersatz-Bataillon 29	85 373

30. Waffen-Grenadier-Division der SS (*russische Nr. 2*)

Schutzmannschafts-Brigade "Siegling"

When the Red Army succeeded in rapidly occupying almost the entire area of the *Generalkommissariat Weißruthenien* [White Ruthenia or Byelorussia] as part of its summer offensive launched on June 22, 1944, the *Höhere SS- und Polizeiführer Russland-Mitte und Weißruthenien* lost its entire sector of responsibility. It is interesting that already on July 28, 1944, Himmler ordered the closing down of this command – which had its headquarters in Plock [German: Schröttersburg], East Prussia, since July 11, 1944. This was one indication of his awareness that there would be no more positive turn of events in the war for Germany – although he had found other words for the *Gauleiter* in Posen a few days later.

While the German *SS-Polizei-Regimenter* of the former *Höheree SS- und Polizeiführers Russland-Mitte und Weißruthenien* were deployed at the front line, the foreign-national *Schutzmannschaften*[33] [Police forces] were ordered to assemble in the area northeast of Warsaw at Serok-Nasielsk-Modlin.

Amidst all the chaos that had broken out after the collapse of the German front in Byelorussia, to impose some order within the numerous foreign national units, these troops were organized at the end of July 1944, into a *Schutzmannschafts-Brigade*.

Within a few days, the former *Kommandeur* of *Schutzmannschafts-Bataillons 57* and last *SS- und Polizeiführer Weißruthenien und Pripjet, SS-Sturmbannführer and Major der Schutzpolizei* Siegling, pulled together a *Brigade* structured as follows:

Brigadestab

1. Regiment

Schutzmannschafts-Bataillone 57, 60 and 61

Elements of weißruthenischen Heimwehr-Btl. 34

2. Regiment

Schutzmannschafts-Bataillone 62, 63 and 64

3. Regiment

Schutzmannschafts-Bataillons 65, 66 and 67

[33] The foreign national *Polizei-Hilfstruppen* [auxiliary police] were designated *Schutzmannschaften* by command of the *Reichsführer-SS* and chief of the German *Polizei* as of November 6, 1941. In addition to individual service in the countryside and cities, there were complete units, referred to as *Schutzmannschafts-Bataillone*, which were mostly used to fight partisans.

4. Regiment
weißruthenische Heimwehr-Bataillone 23 and 34
Personnel of the former Polizei-Gebietskommandantur [Police Area Command]
Artillerie-Abteilung
Schutzmannschafts-Artillerie-Abteilung 56
Reiter-Abteilung
Kosaken-Reiter-Abteilung 68 [Cossak Cavalry]

The *Brigade* was never used, but it was transferred about two weeks later to the *Waffen-SS*.

30. Waffen-Grenadier-Division der SS (*russische Nr. 2*)

After Hitler appointed the *Reichsführer-SS Kommandeur* of the *Ersatzheer* [Army Reserve] starting July 20, 1944, Himmler went about performing this new task with elan, as he considered it should be done. Seeking troops not currently deployed, he found *Schutzmannschafts-Brigade "Siegling"* and suggested to Hitler organizing it into a *Waffen-SS Division*. After Hitler agreed, the *Reichsführer-SS* ordered that the unit be transferred from the *Ordnungspolizei* to the *Waffen-SS* on July 31, 1944. The *SS-Führungshauptamt* announced on August 18, 1944:

> *"On command of the Reichsführer-SS, the Schuma-Brigade 'Siegling,' comprised of units and formations of Freiwillge Ukrainian, Russian and White Ruthenian origin, with effect as of 8/1/44 will have its personnel and materiel transferred to the Waffen-SS. Schuma-Brigade 'Siegling' was renamed the 30. Waffen-Grenadier-Division der SS (russische Nr. 2) and newly reorganized.*
>
> *SS-Obersturmbannführer Siegling has been appointed as Kommandeur of the 30. Waffen-Grenadier-Division der SS (russische Nr. 2)."*

Although the organization command itself spoke of Ukrainian, Russian and Byelorussian *Freiwilligen*, the additional title was *"russische Nr. 2."* This documented that the *SS-Führungshauptamt*, in the designation of its foreign-national units – for propagandistic purposes – paid little attention to their actual ethnic composition.[34] With respect to the *30. Waffen-Grenadier-Division der SS (russische Nr. 2)*, it was to be termed this, based on a communication from the *III. /4. Regiment*. Of the 583 men, there were:

[34] This can be seen, for example, with the *11. SS-Freiwilligen-Panzer-Grenadier-Division "Nordland."* Only about 15% of those serving in *SS-Panzer-Grenadier-Regimenter 23 "Norge"* and *24 "Danmark"* were Norwegians or Danes. The rest were ethnic Germans from Romania.

447	White Russians
53	Russians
15	Ukrainians
65	Poles
3	Tartars

The *Division* was to have the following authorized organization:

Waffen-Grenadier-Regiment der SS 75 (russische Nr. 4)
Waffen-Grenadier-Regiment der SS 76 (russische Nr. 5)
Waffen-Grenadier-Regiment der SS 77 (russische Nr. 6)
Waffen-Artillerie-Regiment der SS 30 (russische Nr. 2)
SS-Füsilier-Bataillon 30
SS-Pionier-Bataillon 30
SS-Panzerjäger-Abteilung 30
SS-Nachrichten-Abteilung 30
SS-Vesorgungs-Regiment 30
SS-Veterinär-Kompanie 30
SS-Sanitäts-Kompanie 30
SS-Feldersatz-Bataillon 30

Since it was impossible to organize an operational front-line *Division* due to the lack of heavy weapons and equipment, as well as the specialists trained to use them, and the lack of individual and unit training, it was decided to use this formation, as others had previously been deployed, for anti-partisan operations. On August 4, 1944, the *Kriegstagebuch des Oberbefehlshabers West* already noted the planned delivery of the two Russian *Waffen-Grenadier-Divisionen der SS*:

> *"Order tor the transfer of the 29. and 30. Waffen-Grenadier-Division der SS (russische Nr. 1 und 2) to the sector of OB West, to fight terrorists (Divisionen are currently deployed for the suppression of the uprising in Warsaw;[35] strength 6,000-7,000, and 9,000 men). Further orders per Ic."*

With their integration into the *Waffen-SS*, the former *Schutzmannschaften* and *Ordnungspolizisten* rank designations were amended to those of the *Waffen-SS*.

The *Division* members changed their former black *Schutzmannschaft* uniforms[36] for green *Polizei* uniforms and were transferred by rail by way of Ilawa [German: Deutsch-Eylau] -Torun [Thorn] -Inowrocław [Hohensalza] -Halle-Worms-Hanau-Frankfurt-Strasbourg to the Belfort-Besançon-Dole region.

[35] Here, the German authorities were wrong. Since there were doubts at the front about the reliability of the former *Schutzmannschaften*, no troops of *30. Waffen-Grenadier-Division der SS (russ. Nr. 2)* were used for the suppression of the Warsaw Uprising.
[36] Black-colored Polish, Lithuanian, or Latvian uniforms.

The first units were already being used to fight partisans by August 24, 1944. Two days later, *Oberbefehlshaber West* again explicitly instructed *Heeresgruppe G* that Himmler, with justified concern, had only released the *Division* for anti-partisan *operations:*

> *"30. SS-Panzer-Grenadier-Division, on the orders of the Reichsführer-SS and Chef Heeresrüstung and Befehlshaber des Ersatzheeres [Chief of Army Equipment and Commander of Replacement Army], is under command of the Militärbefehlshaber Frankreich [Military Command France] only for combating 'gangs' [partisans].*
>
> *Other deployments ordered in an emergency with Ob. West, KTB [Kriegstagebuch] Ia Nr. 7311/44 geh. Kdos. [geheime Kommandosache: secret orders] of 8/24, but with the warning that reliability in fighting against the 'Allies' is undetermined."*

Since half of the *Division* was still on the trains, the first *Bataillone* rebelled. On August 27, 1944, the *II. Bataillone* of the *1.* and *2. Regimenter* assassinated the German *Rahmenpersonal* and fled to join the Résistance. The next day, most of the *4. Regiment* deployed to fight French partisans in the area of Pont de Roide-St. Hippolyte-Maiche deserted to Switzerland. *Generalfeldmarschall* Model reported to the *SS-Führungshauptamt* on August 28, 1944:

> *"30. SS-Panzer-Grenadier-Division is fleeing to the gangs by the Bataillon, beating German officers to death, completely unreliable. Division is disarmed. Immediate deportation to the Reich for labor essential."*

What had been feared had occurred: the foreign-national *Division* members had no motivation anymore to fight for Germany, and especially not to fight against the Western Allies. Even as the transfer of the *Division,* including unloading all thirty-one transport trains from East Prussia to France, was completed on August 30, 1944, it had already been ordered out of the Point de Roide area, to go to Alsace by way of Audincourt-Belfort to be re-organized in *Wehrkreis* [Military District] *V*.

SS-Obersturmbannführer Siegling had all *"unusable and unreliable elements"* withdrawn from the *Division* and formed from these two *Schanz* [Entrenchment]-*Regimenter* with a total strength of thirty-seven officers and 2,331 other ranks. They were initially placed, unarmed, under the command of *Transportkommandantur* [Transport Command] Karlsruhe and then used to expand the Westwall defenses.

The long-overdue reorganization of the *Division* was carried out using the remaining 6,200 men. The now two-part formation was comprised of:

Divisionsstab	Garrison: Markolsheim
Waffen-Grenadier-Regiment der SS 75	Garrison: Mussig
I. Bataillon (remnants of former *1. Regiment*)	
II. Bataillon (remnants of former *2. Regiment*)	
III. Bataillon (*Bataillon Murawjew*[37])	
Waffen-Grenadier-Regiment der SS 76	Garrison: Saasenheim
I. Bataillon (remnants of former *3. Regiment*)	
II. Bataillon (remnants of former *4. Regiment*)	
III. Bataillon (Ost-Bataillon 654[38])	
SS-Aufklärungs-Abteilung 30 (for Cossack *Reiter-Abteilung 68*)	Garrison: Mackenheim
SS-Panzer-Grenadier-Abteilung 30	Garrison: Elsenheim
1 Panzer-Grenadier- and *1 Panzerspäh-Kompanie*	
SS-Artillerie-Abteilung 30	Garrison: Hessenheim
2 Batterien 12.2 cm *Feldhaubitzen (r.)*	
SS-Pionier-Kompanie 30	Garrison: Heidolsheim
SS-Nachrichten-Kompanie 30	Garrison: Markolsheim
SS-Feldersatz-Bataillon	Pionier-Übungsplatz Breisach
SS-Versorgungs-Regiment 30	Garrison: Markolsheim

The *Division* had barely any heavy weapons. Instead of an *Artillerie-Regiment* with four *Abteilungen*, there was only one *Artillerie-Abteilung*. There was no *Panzerjäger-Abteilung* at all. These circumstances had very negative results in later deployments.

The unit was again reorganized, already on October 19, 1944, as a *Infanterie-Division neuer Art 1944*. Thus, the two *Grenadier-Regimenter* were reduced to two *Bataillone*, and a third *Regiment* formed.

As French formations reached Montbéliard, near Belfort, on November 17, 1944, *SS-Obersturmbannführer* Siegling offered *Heeresgruppe G* the use of his *30. Waffen-Grenadier-Division der SS (russische Nr. 2)*. This was received very skeptically, due to previous experience with the Russians, and approved after consultation with the *Kommandeur* of the *19. Armee*, only for deployment in a second *Auffanglinie* [second or rear line of defense]:

> *"30. SS-Freiwilligen-Division will be released to the Armee for use in the Larg position to prevent a breakthrough of enemy points of attack to the northeast. The Division is to be deployed through the Armee."*

[37] The so-called *Bataillon Murawjew* was formed on September 12, 1944, with three officers and eighty-eight men of the *1. Regiment*, six officers and 754 men of the *2. Regiment,* and two officers and thirty-seven men of the *Aufklärungs-Abteilung*.

[38] The *Ost-Bataillon 654* was formed on October 23, 1943, in the area west of Staraya Rusa from the Russian *Sicherungs-Abteilung 510* which reached it in the summer and transferred to Chaumont (France). With orders as of February 17, 1945, the *Bataillon* was dissolved and the Russian members sent to the *600. Infanterie-Division (russische)*. This was the only *Heer* unit to which the *SS* unit was transferred.

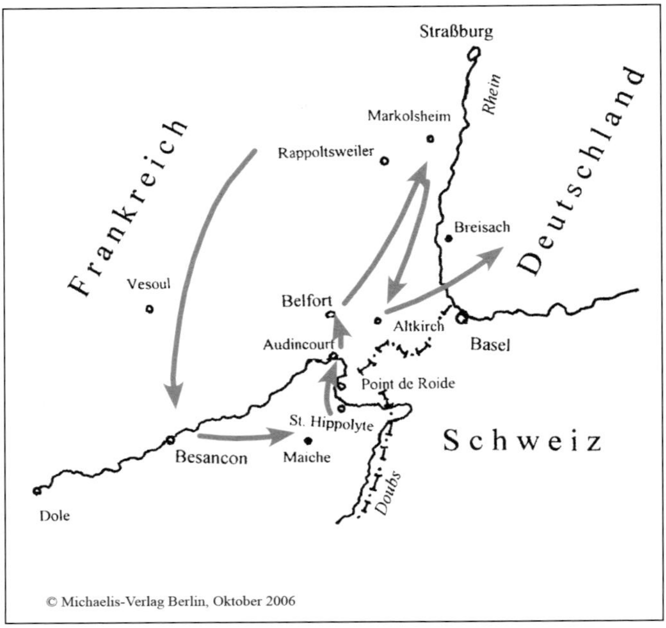

As the enemy pushed through to Mulhouse on November 20, 1944 and established bridgeheads over the Rhone-Rhine Canal in Brittany and Montreux Chateau, the *30. Waffen-Grenadier-Division der SS* was sent to *LXIII. Armee-Korps* for an all-out defense of the Larg position and took over the positions of the 198. Infanterie-*Division*. The *Waffen-Grenadier-Regiment der SS 76 (russische Nr. 5)* moved into the Dammerkirch-Altkirch-Hirtzbach line. *Waffen-Grenadier-Regiment der SS 75 (russische Nr. 4)* was deployed along the Rhine-Rhone Canal between Montreux Chateau and Wolfersdorf. However, *Generalfeldmarschal* Model gave the express command that they could not be used to attack.

Nevertheless, *Waffen-Grenadier-Regiment der SS 76* was transferred out of the Altkirch-Hirtzbach area by way of Hirsingen-Largitzen, for a limited foray at Friesen-Überstraß. There was heavy local fighting in Hirsingen and Largitzen. *SS-Aufklärungs-Abteilung 30* pushed forward along the Ill River to Waldighofen.

While the *198. Infanterie-Division,* by its attacks moving through Chavanatte reached the forest area south of the Grosne-Suarce road on November 21, 1944, the *30. Waffen-Grenadier-Division der SS (russische Nr. 2)* was thrown back to the Hindlingen-Hirtzbach line by French 1st Armored Division counterattacks.

In the extremely heavy offensive and defensive combat, the soldiers of the *LXIII. Armee-Korps* succeeded in destroying forty-one French 1st Armored *Division* tanks. Of these, *30. Waffen-Grenadier-Division der SS (russische Nr. 2)* destroyed six. The *Kriegstagebuch der Oberbefehlshabers West* reported here:

Divisions Kommandeur SS-Obersturmbannführer Siegling awarded four Russian Waffen-Grenadiere of separate Bataillone the Tapferkeitsauszeichnung [Bravery Citation] for Eastern peoples.

> *"30. SS-Waffen-Grenadier-Division (russische Nr. 2) – led by SS-Obersturmbannführer Siegling – has distinguished itself in the fighting at the Burgundian Gate with its bravery and steadfastness. It repeatedly repulsed heavy enemy attacks and thereby destroyed six enemy tanks. A mention in the Wehrmachtbericht supplement is requested."*

However, no mention was made. The results were all the more surprising, since the *Division* was mostly armed with carbines, some machine guns, and *Panzerfäusten*. It had only five *SS-Artillerie-Abteilung 30* 12.2cm guns for heavy weapons.

By November 23, 1944, the French troops had recovered from the unexpected German attack, and launched a counterattack. They were able to break into the *198. Infanterie-Division* wedge formation to the Swiss border between Courtelevant and Seppois. Moreover, the French were able to force back the *30. Waffen-Grenadier-Division der SS (russische Nr. 2)* from several positions. Their fighting strength was reduced by the fierce artillery and tank fire. The next day, the Russian *Waffen-Grenadiere* pulled back further north to Spechbach-Bernweiler. The *Kriegstagebuch* of the *19. Armee* documented on November 26, 1944:

> *"Chef Höheres Kommando Eifel indicates by way of contrast the seriousness of their own situation, especially with 30. Waffen-Grenadier-Division der SS (russische Nr. 2). The Russians run at the appearance of tanks, without firing a shot, from their positions and some fight against us. If no reinforcements are sent, the Generalkommando believes it can no longer take responsibility for the front."*

The Russian's panicked behavior showed that the German Führer and Unterführer had again lost control over the units. The foreign national soldiers' motivation had again fallen to the depths. The lack of vital *Panzerabwehrkanonen* also led to a sense of helplessness.

Finally, the troops of *LXIII. Armee-Korps* fell back to the Doller sector. The Russian soldiers were at the same time engaged in fierce defensive battles around the villages Buetweiler, Balschweiler, and Bernweiler and tried to ward off tank attacks from Balschweiler and Bernweiler in the direction of Burnhaupt-le-Bas [German: Niederburnhaupt]. When the *Division* was pulled out of the southern front on November 28, 1944, to be used with the *LXXXX. Armee-Korps* at Ribeauvillé [German: Rappoltsweiler], *SS-Obersturmbannführer* Siegling prevented any further deployment of his unit: *"Troops no longer fit for action, instead, deploying them would be dangerous!"*

However, Siegling formed a *Kampfgruppe* of those men still fit for duty – mostly German *Rahmenpersonal* – who were sent to the *LXXXX. Armee-Korps*. The rest of the *30. Waffen-Grenadier-Division der SS (russische Nr. 2)* gave up their weapons and equipment and marched across the Rhine at Neuenburg;

they reached *Truppenübungsplatz* Münsingen on December 2, 1944. They were followed there on December 7, 1944, by those units still in action. In Münsingen, the Russian *Division* members were ordered to join the *600. Infanterie-Division (russische)* and the remaining German and especially Byelorussian men transferred to *Truppenübungsplatz* Grafenwöhr for reorganization.

30. Waffen-Grenadier-*Division* der SS (*weißruthenische Nr. 1*)

When some 1,000 Russian *Division* members were ordered, right at *Truppenübungsplatz* Münsingen, to join the *600. Infanterie-Division (russische)*, the *30. Waffen-Grenadier-Division der SS (russische Nr. 2)* was disbanded on December 31, 1944, at *Truppenübungsplatz* Grafenwöhr.

SS-Versorgungs-Regiment 30, which had over 100 wagons, was ordered to join *25. Waffen-Grenadier-Division der SS Hunyadi (ungarische Nr. 1)* at *SS-Truppenübungsplatz* Neuhammer. The *SS-Aufklärungs-Abteilung 30 (Kosaken-Reiter-Abteilung 68)* was commanded to join *26. Waffen-Grenadier-Division der SS Hungaria (ungarische Nr. 2)* and reached *Truppenübungsplatz* Schieratz on January 7, 1945.

Waffen-Grenadier-Brigade der SS ***(weißruthenische Nr. 1)*** was organized from the remaining German *Rahmenpersonal* and Byelorussian soldiers (especially the former *Schutzmannschafts-Bataillone 60, 64, 65, 66,* and *67*). With a strength of about 2,000 members, it comprised:

Waffen-Grenadier-Regiment der SS 75 (weißruthenische Nr. 1)
1 Aufklärungs-Schwadron
1 Panzerjäger-Kompanie
1 Feldersatz-Kompanie

To deceive enemy reconnaissance, on March 9, 1945, Himmler ordered it to be renamed ***30. Waffen-Grenadier-Division der SS (weißruthenische Nr. 1)***. It was never deployed. Rather, the formation was dissolved in early April 1945. The *Kriegstagebuch des OKW* noted in general terms: *"In early April, formation of non-German Divisionen was ended."*

This ended the history of this second Russian *Division der Waffen-SS*. Only intended to combat partisans, the foreign-national members, some 1,600km from home, showed little movation to fight for the collapsing German *Reich*.

SS-Obersturmbannführer Siegling formed a *Bataillon* out of the *Rahmenpersonal*, which was put under command of the *38. SS-Grenadier-Division Nibelungen*. Starting April 21-26, 1945, *Polizei-Bataillon* Siegling was stationed at Kehlheim on the Danube (Bad Gögging) as the right-hand neighbor of the *II. /SS-Grenadier-Regiment 95*. Moving by way of Landshut and Wasserburg, in May 1945 it reached the Chiemsee area and was taken prisoner by American forces.

Kommandeure:
08/44 – 05/45 *SS-Obersturmbannführer* Siegling

Feldpost numbers:

Divisionsstab	14 471
Waffen-Grenadier-Regiment der SS 75 (russische Nr. 4)	08 385
I. Bataillon	66 415
II. Bataillon	66 408
III. Bataillon	67 827
Waffen-Grenadier-Regiment der SS 76 (russische Nr. 5)	01 069
I. Bataillon	64 868
II. Bataillon	67 283
III. Bataillon	65 794
Waffen-Grenadier-Regiment der SS 77 (russische Nr. 6)	03 844
I. Bataillon	65 253
II. Bataillon	67 002
III. Bataillon	66 134
SS-Artillerie-Abteilung 30	05 607
SS-Aufklärungs-Abteilung 30	31 251
SS-Feldersatz-Bataillon 30	41 526

31. SS-Freiwilligen-Grenadier-Division

The *SS-FHA* halted the organization of the *23. Waffen-Gebirgs-Division der SS "Kama" (kroatische Nr. 2)* on September 24, 1944, because the Bosniaks were basically unreliable. When nearly 10,000 *Volksdeutsche* [ethnic Germans living in other countries] from Hungary were to be used to bring the *"Kama" Division* up to full strength, Berlin decided on October 4, 1944, to use them form their own – purely *Volksdeutsche – SS-Freiwilligen-Grenadier-Division*, which was then designated ***31.***

There were some 845,000 people of German descent then living in Hungary, most of whom had been organized into a *Volksgruppe* under Dr. Franz Basch. Germany and Hungary had already reached an agreement on February 1, 1942, that all *Volksdeutsche* born in the years 1912-1925 (17 to 30 years old) were to report to the *Waffen-SS*, unless they were already serving in the Hungarian Army. This recruitment drive resulted in great success – within five weeks, the around 17,000 new recruits provided the *Waffen-SS* with the manpower for a full *Division*.

This result would be repeated a year later. However, since drafting just the men born in one year (1926) provided about 6,000 potentially able-bodied men, the second agreement – which followed on June 1, 1943 – raised the age limit to thirty-five years old. This theoretically made available a total of six more cohorts, some 36,000 men, for the *Freiwilligen* registration and physicals. As some of them were already in the Hungarian Army, the new Hungarian Prime Minister Kallay approved their being discharged if they would volunteer for the *Waffen-SS*. The first transport trains left Hungary beginning September 7, 1943. This recruitment campaign, which lasted until February 8, 1944, enlisted approximately 20,000 men – often no longer entirely voluntarily – in the *Waffen-SS*.

Just a few weeks later, on April 14, 1944, a third agreement with the succeeding Prime Minister Sztójay introduced general conscription for Hungarian *Volksdeutsche* into the *Waffen-SS*. This made all men from 17 to 60 years old obligated to serve! The former *Höhere SS- und Polizeiführer in Ungarn, SS-Gruppenführer und Generalleutnant der Polizei* Winkelmann recalled after the war:

> *"In the spring of 1944 – I do not know exactly whether it was in April or not – I heard that negotiations were being held in the German Legation to conclude an intergovernmental agreement on the Volksdeutsche serving in the Waffen-SS. The negotiations were led by the Waffen-SS-Befehlshaber in Hungary, SS-Gruppenführer Keppler and the leader of the SS-Ergänzungskommando [Replacement Recruitment Command] in Hungary, Heermann. I ascertained that: Himmler had instructed the SS-Hauptamt (Berger) to take care that an agreement between Hungary and Germany would be reached to ensure that the Volksdeutsche in Hungary are drafted into the Waffen-SS. I would point*

out that already earlier – before March 19, 1944 – there had been campaigns to enlist Volksdeutsche in the Waffen-SS. These were, however, voluntary enlistments. The SS-FHA gave the above order to the SS-Ersatzkommando in Hungary and turned to Keppler with the request he support it. Therefore Keppler called on Honvédminister Csatay and got an agreement in principle from the Hungarian government. After repeated modification of the text, serving in the Waffen-SS became mandatory for all those who were Volksdeutsche, by descent and way of life. There was no consideration of whether those concerned should actually continue to acknowledge themselves as part of Volksdeutschtum. The following procedure was set up between the Hungarian War Ministry and the SS-Ergänzungskommando in Hungary: The local organs of the German Volksbund [People's Federation] pulled together local registries of all the Volksdeutsche in question. These registers went to the SS-Ergänzungskommando, which submitted them to the Ergänzungsabteilung [Replacement Recruitment Department] of the Kriegsministerium [Ministry of War].

They then presented the register to the local notaries for their opinion. They struck out the people they no longer considered Volksdeutsche. At the same time, they also proposed some names. The register went back to the Kriegsministerium, which brought it to the attention of the SS-Ersatzkommando. Since Heermann was complaining almost daily that the notaries were striking off men from the lists who were clearly German and the Kriegsministerium in this case would not accept them, I told Heermann he should be satisfied for the time being with those for whom he had gotten authorization. We could deal with the other matter later.

That's what happened. Meanwhile, Himmler instructed me to use all my power to speed up the implementation of the agreement. He had the feeling that the Hungarian authorities would reject everything, and I had to deal with it all. I tried to set the record straight: Hungarians fulfill their obligations, and it is natural that there are differences of opinion. According to the agreement, this needs to be clarified by mutual consent. Moreover, the process is tied to a complicated proceding, which cannot be shortened. I said it would probably take four to six weeks before the physicals could be done. Only then would the men be inducted by the Hungarian Ministry of War. The conscripts up to the age of forty-five were assigned to the Waffen-SS by the SS-Ersatzkommando, which was under command of the SS-FHA[39] and those older than that to the Ordnungspolizei."

At this time, those who were 36-45 were to be registered for the *Waffen-SS,* and those 46-50 for the *Ordnungspolizei*. From the first group, of some 35,000 drafted,

[39] In contrast to the so-called *"Germanic"* countries, where recruitment was done within the scope of the *SS-Hauptamt – Amt VI*, the former *"Germanische Freiwilligen-Leitstelle" [Germanic Volunteers Headquarters]*.

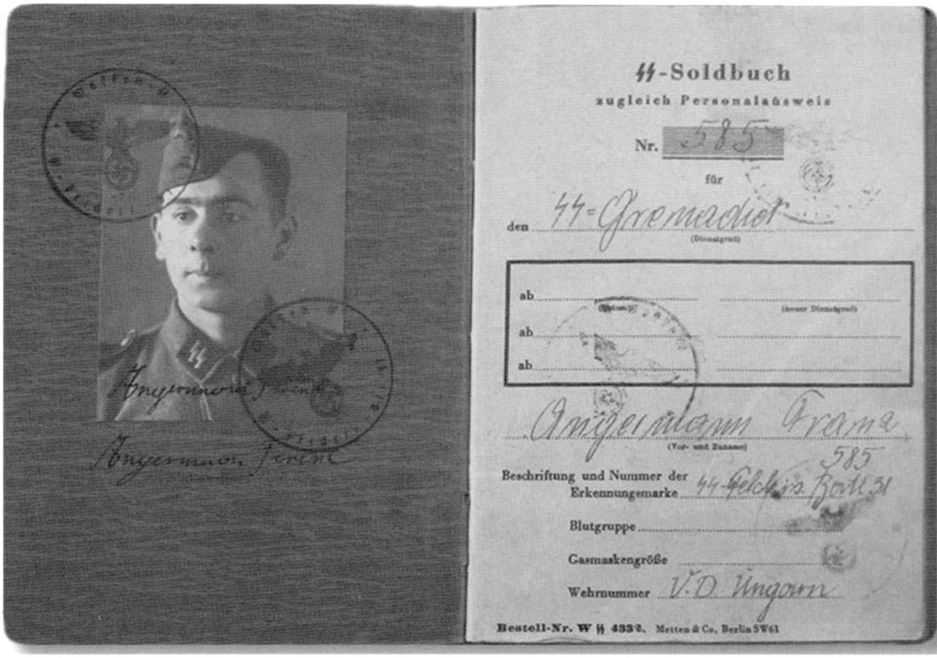

In 1944, Jan Verneulen joined the 27. SS-Freiwilligen-Grenadier-Division Langemarck and ultimately served in the SS-Freiw.-Gren.-Regiment 66.

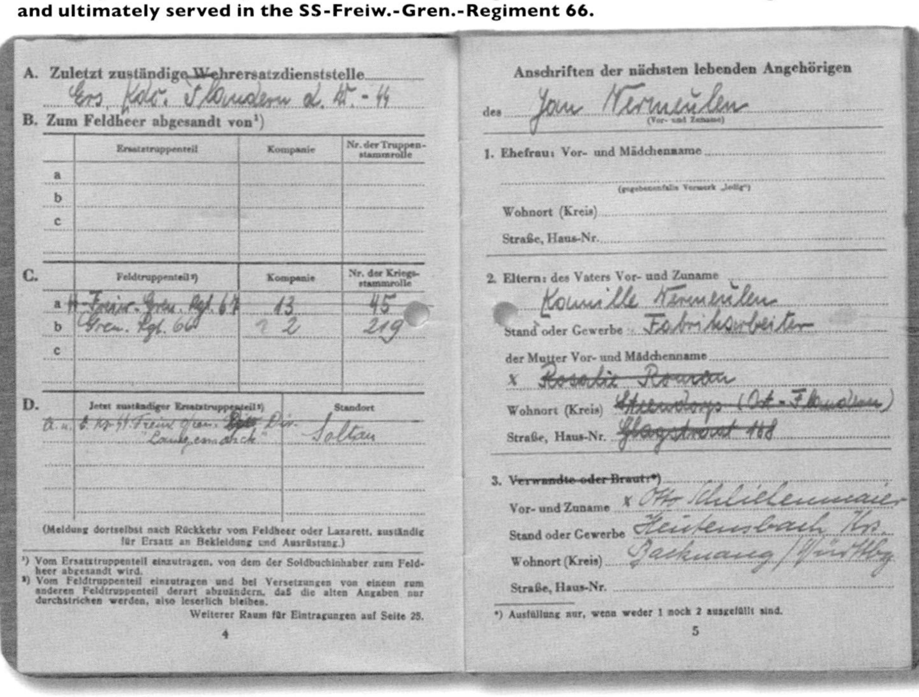

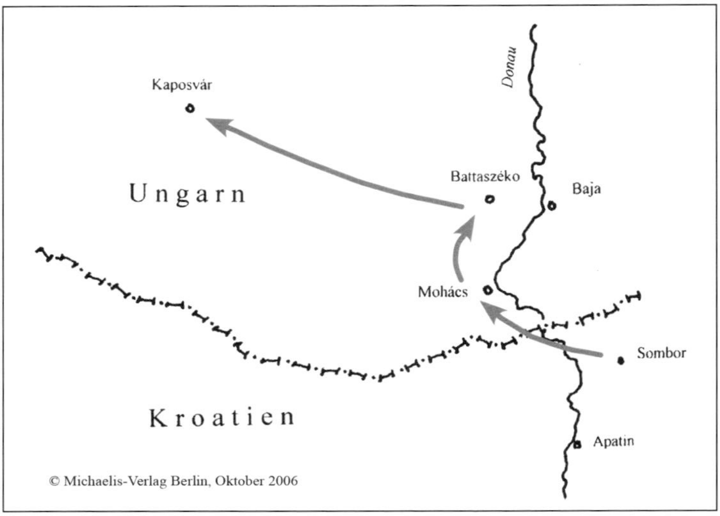

about 50,000 were inducted in the *Waffen-SS*, while about 15,000 of the 30,000 men of the older age groups went to the *Ordnungspolizei*.

Of the approximately 35,000 men who were drafted into the *Waffen-SS*, as already mentioned about 10,000 would go to reinforce the *23. Waffen-Gebirgs-Division der SS "Kama" (kroatische Nr. 2)* up to its authorized strength, and were already at the *Rekrutendepot* [recruiting depot] Sombor. Now, the *31. SS-Freiwilligen-Grenadier-Division,* gradually being reinforced by more *Volksdeutsche* recruits, could be organized, with:

Divisionsstab
SS-Freiwilligen-Grenadier-Regiment 78 (I. – III. Bataillon)
SS-Freiwilligen-Grenadier-Regiment 79 (I. – III. Bataillon)
SS-Freiwilligen-Grenadier-Regiment 80 (I. – II. Bataillon)
SS-Freiwilligen-Artillerie-Regiment 31 (I. – II. Abteilung)
SS-Divisions-Füsilier-Bataillon 31
SS-Panzerjäger-Abteilung 31
SS-Pionier-Bataillon 31
SS-Nachrichtentruppe 31
SS-Feldersatz-Bataillon 31
SS-Versorgungstruppen 31

Even before it was possible to start organizing the units, the men were ordered to the area of Mohaces, about 20km to the northwest. During the transfer starting October 7, 1944, on the initiative of *Divisionskommandeur SS-Oberführer*

Lombard, about 80,000 *Volksdeutsche* civilians were evacuated with them from Bačka.

On November 1, 1944, the *Volksdeutsche* men, more or less well trained for about six months, occupied security lines near Mohacs-Battaszéko. When the Red Army took the offensive in this sector on November 7, 1944, and two days later established their first bridgeheads over the Danube, elements of the *31. SS-Freiwilligen-Grenadier-Division* were put under command of *LXVIII. Armee-Korps (2. Panzer-Armee)* on November 12, 1944, for combat deployment.

Heavy fighting followed, in which the men suffered severe losses due to their lack of heavy weapons and inadequate training and leadership. The *LXVIII. Armee-Korps* understandably described the *31. SS-Freiwilligen-Grenadier-Division* as *"inadequate under fire."*

The major offensive launched by the Red Army on November 27, 1944, shattered, those elements of *31. SS-Freiwilligen-Grenadier-Division* deployed in the area between Battaszéko and Kaposvár. On December 21, 1944, the unit was transferred to the Celje-Gonobitz-Slovenska Bistrica-Maribor [German: Cilli-Gonobitz-Slovenska Bistrica-Marburg] region (*Wehrkreis XVIII*), to "continue" its organization.

Under command of *Höhere SS- und Polizeiführer Alpenland, SS-Obergruppenführer und General der Polizei* Rösener to carry out anti-partisan operations in this region – especially in the Bacher Mountains – somehow, a combat-ready frontline unit was supposed to be formed. Since this was impossible anyway, its reclassification to an *ID 45* on January 16, 1945, also changed nothing.

Due to the transfer on February 16, 1945, the *Division* had received no training as a formation. Beyond that, the German armaments industry was no longer able to supply heavy weapons. By this time, it was deployed solely as *Infanterie.*

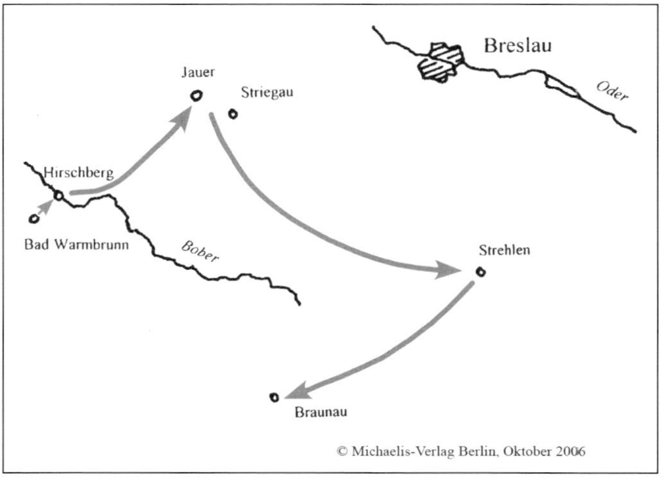

SS-Panzerjäger-Abteilung 31 at the end of the war in 1945.

Nevertheless, the *Division* was again ordered to the front and transferred to *Heeresgruppe Mitte* at 500km distant Görlitz. By the end of February 1945, the first units were being unloaded at Cieplice [Bad Warmbrunn], southwest of Jelenia Góra [Hirschberg]. A *Kampfgruppe* was formed from the two *SS-Freiwilligen-Grenadier-Regimenter 78* and *79* and placed under command of *XXXXVIII. Panzer-Korps (17. Armee)* and replaced elements of the *269. Infanterie-Division* at Jawor [Jauer].

At the same time, *SS-Freiwilligen-Grenadier-Regiment 80* was to be organized using the Hungarian *SS-Freiwilligen* in *SS-Füsilier-Bataillon 31* and using members of *SS-Polizei-Regiment Brixen*. The latter followed the *Kampfgruppe* on March 6, 1945, towards Strzegom [Striegau] (south of Jawor) and relieved a *Regiment* of the adjacent *208. Infanterie-Division*. The Red Army offensive launched here on March 15, 1945, quickly destroyed *SS-Freiwilligen-Grenadier-Regiment 80*, which had had no front-line experience.

On April 6, 1945, the *Divisionskampfgruppe* took over positions about 70km further east at Strzelin [Strehlen], which were under the *100. Jäger-Division* [Hunter or Ranger Division]. They thus came under command of the *XVII. Armee-Korps*. Meanwhile, their first heavy weapons arrived; some *Artillerie-Geschütze*, 14 *Jagdpanzer* 38 *Hetzer* and some 7.5cm *Panzerabwehrkanonen (mot.)*.

Although there were no major battles on the front up until May 6, 1945, the retreat led to dramatic scenes. *SS-Oberführer* Lombard gave the order to break away from the enemy and, avoiding Prague, to reach Plzeň [Pilsen], more than 300km away. Here, the units would surrender to the American armed forces. In countless columns including civilians and *Wehrmacht* members alike, the members of *31. SS-Freiwilligen-Grenadier-Division* first tried to reach Hradec Kralove [Königgrätz] going by way of Broumov-Nachod-Josefov [Braunau-Nachod-Josefstadt]. Others marched westwards through Trutnov [Trautenau] to Paka. On the march, they were in constant battle with Czech partisans. Former *SS-Unterscharführer* Gensicke (*Divisionsstab*) recalls:

> *"The Czechs were rampaging at the defenseless German population and us soldiers. We were then collected at a sports field. Here individual SS members were grappled around their legs, dragged face down over the dirt track, and then shot! On the way to Teplice, anyone who left the column to get a drink or to escape, was shot. It was horrible."*

Like most of the units organized in the *Waffen-SS* in 1944, this was first and foremost an effort to pull together any human resources available. They were to be trained, in the broader context, based on what was possible, but this did not happen due to the hasty orders for front-line deployment. Unorganized both in terms of numbers and quality, the *Division* was – with no heavy weapons – de facto simply used as infantry in *Kampfgruppen*.

Kommandeure:
09/44 – 05/45 *SS-Oberführer* Lombard

Feldpost numbers:

Divisionsstab	19 970
SS-Freiwilligen-Grenadier-Regiment 78	45 334
I. Bataillon	36 293
II. Bataillon	20 797
III. Bataillon	44 219
SS -Freiwilligen-Grenadier-Regiment 79	48 865
I. Bataillon	21 714
II. Bataillon	37 565
III. Bataillon	31 597
SS-Freiwilligen-Grenadier-Regiment 80	24 378
I. Bataillon	24 378
II. Bataillon	33 535
SS-Freiwilligen-Artillerie-Regiment 31	38 377
I. Abteilung	34 775
II. Abteilung	23 497
III. Abteilung	47 259
IV. Abteilung	32 713
SS-Panzerjäger-Abteilung 31	48 064
SS-Füsilier-Bataillon 31	22 397
SS-Pionier-Bataillon 31	43 199
SS-Freiwilligen-Versorgungs-Regiment 31	40 349
SS-Nachrichten-Abteilung 31	39 839
SS-Feldersatz-Bataillon 31	41 036

32. SS-Freiwilligen-Grenadier-Division "30. Januar"

To reinforce the Oder front, the *SS-FHA* issued the order to organize the ***SS-Panzergrenadier-Division "30. Januar"*** on January 26, 1945. The cadre was to train the two already-existing *SS-Panzergrenadier-Regimenter Schill* and *Kurmark*. Primarily due to the lack of fuel, these two Regimenter were reclassified as horse-drawn units. For its organization at *Truppenübungsplatz* Kurmark, the formation was designated by early February 1945 as ***32. SS-Freiwilligen-Grenadier-Division "30. Januar."*** It is surprising that this unit was thus confirmed as a *Freiwilligen-Division* – up till then, this was unusual for an SS-*Division*, which were almost entirely made up of *Reichsdeutsche* [Reich Germans] personnel.

Although *Truppenübungsplatz* Kurmark was appointed as the formation area, it only served as a reporting center and temporary accommodation for the incoming units. There was no training as a unit. This was typical for practically all-new formations from summer 1944 on. Therefore, the units were deployed made up of troops, most of whom had received only a few weeks of basic training.

When both *Grenadier-Regimenter* – initially still designated as *Schill* and *Kurmark* – were ordered in early February 1945 to the sector of *319. Sicherungs-Division* on the Oder front, to destroy the Soviet bridgeheads at Wiesenau-Vogelsang, *SS-Standartenführer* Mühlenkamp was commissioned with organizing the new formation. The organization followed that of an *Infanterie-Division 45*:

Divisionsstab
SS-Freiwilligen-Grenadier-Regiment 86[40] with *I.* and *II. Bataillon*
SS-Freiwilligen-Grenadier-Regiment 87[41] with *I.* and *II. Bataillon*
SS-Panzerjäger-Abteilung 32[42]
  1. Kompanie (10 Pak 7.5 cm mot. Z. [*motorisiert Zug*: motorized Platoon])
  2. Kompanie (11 Sturmgeschütze III)
  3. Kompanie (11 Sturmgeschütze III)[43]
SS-Freiwilligen-Artillerie-Regiment 32
SS-Pionier-Bataillon 32 SS-Nachrichtentruppe 32 SS-Versorgungsregiment 32

[40] This involved renaming *SS-Panzergrenadier-Regiment Schill* which was formed in summer 1944 at *SS-Panzergrenadier-Schule Kienschlag* at *SS-Truppenübungsplatz* Böhmen to suppress the Slovak National Uprising and transferred in January 1945 to the *Ostfront*.
[41] The *Regiment* was formed from *SS-Panzergrenadier-Regiment "Kurmark"* as an *Alarmeinheit* from January 25, 1945, out of members of *SS-Panzergrenadier-Ausbildungs- und Ersatz-Bataillone 1*, *3* and *16* at *Truppenübungsplatz "Kurmark."*
[42] The detachment cadre was from *SS-Panzerjäger-Abteilung 16*, which arrived at the front in February 1945.
[43] Instead of a *Flak-Batterie, SS-Panzerjäger-Abteilung 32* had a second *Sturmgeschütz-Kompanie*.

Positions along the Oder, March 1945.

The *Division* was deployed under various units. These included, besides the *Volkssturm, SS-Flak-Abteilung 550,* and *SS-Grenadier-Regiment "Becker."*[44]

Ernst Gädtke recalls his first deployment as a member of *SS-Panzer-Jäger Division 32* with elements of *SS-Freiwilligen-Grenadier-Regiment 86:*

> *"Around noon on February 7, 1945, we arrived in Pohlitz and were prepared for an impending attack on Vogelsang bridgehead. We did not take part in the attack, however, because our gun had engine damage. It was fixed in Pohlitz. We stayed there overnight. I remember from this day, that groups of strangely uniformed and armed men of the Volkssturm, who fell back, totally exhausted and battle weary. On February 8-9, 1945, we took part in several attacks using four guns, intended to recapture the Vogelsang. On the afternoon of February 9, 1945, enemy fire immobilized the last of our guns and made them useless for fighting. We could barely maneuver in the soft, moist soil beside the road and the paved paths; we got stuck and were as good as defenseless on the side facing the enemy. Although we were able to tow the guns away in the dark, they were useless for any more fighting."*

At the end of February 1945, *SS-Oberführer* Ax took over command of the front-deployed troops of *32. SS-Freiwilligen-Grenadier-Division "30. Januar"* from the *Stab* of *391. Sicherungs-Division*. There were three enemy Oder bridgeheads, at Brieskow, Wiesenau, and Vogelsang, in the *Division* sector.

The hasty deployment in February 1945, to attempt to seal off the bridgeheads, and later their almost daily attacks, not strategically conceived, to demolish the bridgeheads, resulted in extremely high losses among the men, who had barely any war experience. As a result, *32. SS-Freiwilligen-Grenadier-Division "30. Januar"* suffered in the first three weeks of action in February 1945 alone:

314 killed
1,385 wounded
87 missing[45]
Total: 1,786 men

---

[44] SS-*Kampfgruppe Becker* was organized in February 1945 for the Oder front with 900 members of *SS-Führerschule des Wirtschafts- und Verwaltungsdienstes* in Arolsen. It was reinforced with remaining personnel from *SS-Polizei-Regiment 34* to form *SS-Grenadier-Regiment Becker*. Initially under the staff of *Division Raegener*, it was to be put under command of the third *Grenadier-Regiment (88)* of *32. SS-Freiwilligen-Grenadier-Division*. However, in the military classification as of April 1945, there is no mention of this *Regiment*.

[45] As can be read in the reports of the missing, the *Kompanien* often had no personal details for their members! A sign that the men were allotted ad hoc to the frontline troops and were killed or missing, before the orderly room even got their personnel records!

In March 1945, the numbers rose even higher to:

407 killed
1,447 wounded
<u>336 missing</u>
Total: 2,190 men

In just two months, the *SS* formation therefore had a total of nearly 4,000 casualties. This corresponded to the strength of two *Grenadier-Regimenter*. The constant supply of replacements from *Ausbildungs-* and *Ersatzeinheiten* made it possible not only to offset the losses, but even bring the *Division* up to its authorized strength.

The former *SS-Untersturmführer* Polle remembers the high losses:

> *"My Zug was in SS-Panzergrenadier-Regiment Schill from the beginning. After seeing action in Slovakia, there was only a paltry handful of us at Vogelsang. My proud Pionierzug [Engineer Platoon] had been completely wiped out, used as infantry in my absence. I myself was then Bataillonsadjutant and later Führer of the 13. /SS-Freiwilligen-Grenadier-Regiment 86 in Mixdorf. As a Stoßtrupp [Assault Detachment] section Führer in the assault on the E-Werk [Elektricität Werk: electricity power station] at Vogelsang, which functioned as a forward observation position for the Soviet artillery, I had warned about our lack of preparedness. I was then relieved from duty – the Stoßtrupp operation was a total disaster. Due to this idiotic command, many of my comrades, including those who had been through the whole war, still lost their lives at the last minute!"*

On March 17, 1945, the *32. SS-Freiwilligen-Grenadier-Division "30. Januar"* reported a combat strength of 2,846 men. Since *SS-Flak-Abteilung 550* and *SS-Grenadier-Regiment Becker* were not included in this figure, it represents the sum of nine *Kampfbataillone* (including the three *Artillerie-Abteilungen*). Thus, each *Bataillon* had an average strength of about 300 men.

A month later, the *Division* announced a strength of 14,500 men, with 2,000 of them members of *SS-Panzergrenadier-Ausbildungs- und Ersatz-Bataillon 9*, under its command. The authorized strength of about 12,500 men was achieved by using replacements transferred from the *Luftwaffe* and *Kriegsmarine* to the *Waffen-SS*. Since most of them had little infantry experience, the reinforcement was mostly in numbers alone.

When the Red Army launched its operation to take Berlin on April 16, 1945, the attacks on the *32. SS-Freiwilligen-Grenadier-Division "30. Januar"* positions were initially fought off. But in the next few days, the troops had to retreat to the line along Lichtenberg-Markendorf-Kaisermühl-north Rießen-Pohlitz. Many mixed *Kampfgruppen* were pulled together in the withdrawal.

The Oder front, April 1945.

The E-Werk at Vogelsang.

SS-Sturmmann Baumgart

SS-Junker Harnisch

On April 20, 1945, the *Divisionskommando* received a transfer order to the hard-pressed *XI. SS-Armee-Korps*. When the enemy succeeded the next day in encircling *9. Armee* in the Guben-Müllrose-Fürstenwalde-Königswusterhausen-Lübben area, *V. SS-Armee-Korps* ordered the *Division* to split up. *SS-Regiments-Gruppe 87* with:

Stab/SS-Grenadier-Regiment 87
I. /SS-Grenadier-Regiment 86
I. /SS-Grenadier-Regiment 87

These units remained in the 20km-long Oder positions, while *SS-Regimentsgruppe 86* marched towards Erkner with:

Stab/SS-Grenadier-Regimenter 86
II. /SS-Grenadier-Regiment 86
II. /SS-Grenadier-Regiment 87

On April 22, 1945, *SS-Regiments-Gruppe 87* was also ordered to surrender the positions between Ziltendorf and Vogelsang, which had received few attacks during the Soviet offensive, to units of the *Volkssturm* and to follow *SS-Regiments-Gruppe 86* to the area southeast of the *Müggelsee* [Lake Müggel]. Without encountering much fighting, the *Kampfgruppe* reached Beeskow, to again move into defensive lines. On April 25, 1945, they reached the Prieros area. What remained of *SS-Regiments-Gruppe 86* also had marched here by way of Niederlehme-Königswusterhausen-Gräbendorf.

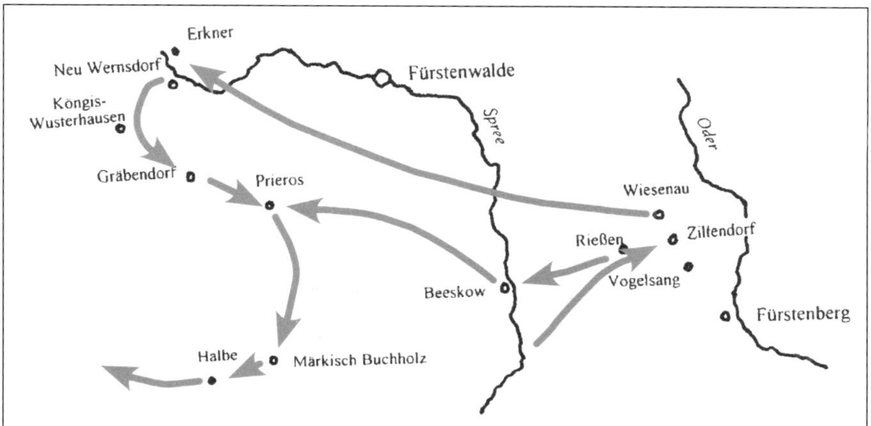

Without getting involved in larger battles, the soldiers marched together with civilians through woodland and forest paths towards Hermsdorf. After heavy fighting on April 27, 1945, the remnants of the *Division*, leaving behind about 700 wounded and attending medical personnel, gave up the area. All cohesion among the troops was now completely lost. From Maerkisch-Buchholz, the ragtag units moved into *Forsthaus* [forester's house] Hammer. This served as command post for the *Oberbefehlshaber* of *9. Armee, General der Infanterie* Busse. On the evening of April 28, 1945, he ordered the troops to break through to the west. While the last armored troops of *XI. SS-Armee-Korps* was to break out of the Soviet pocket, what remained of *32. SS-Freiwilligen-Grenadier-Division "30. Januar"* was to cover the breakout to the east.

The remnants of *9. Armee* broke out of the Halbe pocket in the night of April 29, 1945, amidst infernal scenes. On April 30, 1945, about 400 members of the *Division* gathered at Kummersdorf. Together with *Heer* formations and countless civilians, the *SS* members attempted to reach the *12. Armee* near Dobbrikow. Since any further fighting was senseless, they attempted to cross the Elbe. Then-*SS-Junker* [Officer Candidate] Günter Adam remembers making his way from Kummersdorf to the Elbe:

> *"The next morning we arrived, as one of them said, the area around Kummersdorf. Men who had just been killed lay everywhere; they could have just fallen last evening, or during the night. An eerie place. But then we met a larger Waffen-SS troop. SS-Brigadeführer Wagner was at the front, in a command car. This man was trustworthy and we stayed with this crew. We moved quickly and overpowered any resistance. Large clusters of ordinary soldiers, often without any weapon, hung on to us – but they apparently did not want any fighting. As soon as it broke out, they were gone. In front of Beelitz, there was a severe battle to break through, and some, including myself, lost contact with the main group. We also made it, and a little later were in the arms of our comrades of the 12. Armee. We were dead tired and it was already dark when we reached a wide road. There was little vehicle traffic on it. A completely overloaded truck stopped not far ahead of us and we ran towards it. Since the cargo space was totally full, I found a place on the fender. It first went towards Belzig and then on to Burg. When we arrived there the next day, we suddenly heard: 'The Führer is dead!' We could not or would not believe it, but this news was confirmed to us from all sides. We were stunned, many of us were crying, we had believed in the Führer even then and hoped for Wunderwaffen [miracle weapons]. Now, was it all over? Our attempt to cross the Elbe here failed and we went north to Tangermünde. Here we passed over to Ami [slang for Americans]."*

Thus, the *Division* deployment ended only thirteen weeks after the command was given to form it. The fact that the first units were sent into action already in February 1945, instead of getting eight months of training as a unit at a *Truppenübungsplatz*, clearly shows just what could be expected from the formation. The high losses, of about 4,000 men in the first eight weeks, speak for themselves.

Kommandeure:

01/45	*SS-Standartenführe*r Mühlenkamp
02/45	*SS-Standartenführer* Richter
02/45	*SS-Oberführer* Ax
02/45 – 05/45	*SS-Standartenführer* Kempin

Feldpost numbers:

Divisionsstab	05 662
SS-Freiwilligen-Grenadier-Regiment 86	26 667
I. Bataillon	33 920
II. Bataillon	35 520
SS-Freiwilligen-Grenadier-Regiment 87	07 776
I. Bataillon	08 964
II. Bataillon	10 036
SS-Freiwilligen-Grenadier-Regiment 88	38 416
SS-Feldersatz-Bataillon 32	05 066
SS-Panzerjäger-Abteilung 32	37 196
SS-Freiwilligen-Artillerie-Regiment 32	11 586
I. Abteilung	16 881
II. Abteilung	18 539
III. Abteilung	19 714
SS-Pionier-Bataillon 32	20 686
SS-Nachrichtentruppe 35	21 641

33. Waffen-Grenadier-Division der SS "Charlemagne" (*französische Nr. 1*)

Französisches SS-Freiwilligen-Grenadier-Regiment

Even as Himmler called for *SS Freiwilligen* in the "Germanic" countries, and allowed *Freiwilligen* who were not qualified for the *SS* nor had any explicit interest in the *SS* to join the *Freiwilligen-Legionen*, French *Freiwilligen* initially were paid no attention for racial-ideological reasons. The *Reich* government told the German ambassador in Paris, Otto Abetz, after its proposals to approve a Legion, as part of the *"Crusade against Bolshevism"* – such as was done in Spain or Croatia – of 30,000 *Freiwilligen* that: *"It [...] [is] not desired politically to take such a large number of French* Freiwilligen *[...] into the German* Wehrmacht.*"*

On July 11, 1941, Hitler finally approved, primarily for propagandistic reasons, the formation of French infantry regiment 638 under the *Heer*.[46]

Some fifteen months later, in February 1943, Himmler also changed his attitude towards the French. Following proposals by the head of the *Germanischen Leitstelle* [control center] in the *SS-Hauptamt, SS-Sturmbannführer* Riedweg, he envisaged the formation of a French *SS-Freiwilligen-Division*, but it should comprise *"Only men of especially good race [and] Germanic appearance."*

It is interesting that Hitler retained his negative attitude towards any large-scale French formation and in turn only approved one the size of a *Grenadier-Regiment*. After long delays, in part due to the talks with the French government, the *SS-FHA* first announced on September 18, 1943:

> *"The Führer has ordered the formation of a French SS-Freiwilligen-Grenadier-Regiment. The planned formation of the French SS-Freiwilligen-Division will initially not be done."*

Already by July 22, 1943, the French Vichy government passed a law that allowed French citizens to enlist in the *Waffen-SS*:

> *"The French are allowed to enlist voluntarily and to combat Bolshevism outside the national territory in the German government-formed troops (Waffen-SS), within a French unit."*

Three weeks later, on August 14, 1943, French daily newspapers reported:

[46] With effect from August 10, 1944, the *Regiment* was transferred to the *Waffen-SS*.

> *"A French Regiment of the Waffen-SS has now been organized as part of the struggle by European youth against the international foe, Bolshevism. The age limit for Freiwilligen is 17-40 years old; the minimum height is set at 1.65m. Waffen-SS Freiwilligen are exempt from labor duty. French officers and non-commissioned officers will keep their ranks and any volunteer from the rank and file is eligible for a career as Unterführer or Führer, subject to performance and probation. Provision for and care of family members is subject to the applicable laws. Unmarried Freiwilligen, although they are not supporting a family, will receive a gratuity paid into an account that they can have available in France. The first enthusiastic voluntary enlistments have shown a crucial group of French youth has realized that German fighting youth regard them as friends and comrades."*

As a result, some 5,000 *Freiwilligen* signed up, who were initally assembled at *SS-Ausbildungslager* [training camp] Sennheim (Alsace). Besides the numerous members of French right-wing movements, adventurers and many a criminal enlisted. About 50% of them were eventually rejected in the physicals. Heinrich Wolf, a former member of the *12. SS-Panzer-Division "Hitlerjugend,"* encountered a former German *Regiment Führer* in the Heilbronn POW camp in 1945:

> *"I met interesting people in the medical camp. These included an SS-Obersturmführer and Oberleutnant der Waffen-SS, (according to the entry in his Soldbuch, which he showed me). Because of his bad case of furunculosis, this man probably could not be deported to the Kornwestheim camp. Poor food and malnutrition has different effects: sometimes cellulitis, sometimes furunculosis. This officer told me that he had been involved in organizing the French SS-Freiwilligen. I replied that inducting so many foreigners would have degraded our troops more or less to a Foreign Legion. The Obersturmführer violently contradicted my objection. We requested each Freiwilliger's criminal record and also judged them based on appearance, so that those who seemed to be adventurers or otherwise gave an unfavorable impression, would be rejected from the outset, so that only about one in two of those who voluntarily enlisted as an Ostfrontkämpfer [Eastern front fighter], was accepted. But they were supposed to have been 'idealists' and 'great guys'."*

On orders as of October 15, 1943, the *SS-Hauptamt* was to try to recruit ninety French officers and 300 French NCOs. This was relatively unsuccessful, but on January 10, 1944, a few *Freiwilligen* were sent to the *"1. Special training course for French officers at the SS-Junkerschule Tölz"* until March 11, 1944. At the same time, the French *SS-Freiwilligen-Grenadier-Regiment* with two *Grenadier-*

Training and swearing-in of French SS-Freiwilligen in Wildflecken.

Bataillone was transferred from Sennheim to *SS-Truppenübungsplatz* Böhmen. Here, as of March 30, 1944, it was reclassified as an *SS-Sturmbrigade neuer Art.*

Französische SS-Freiwilligen-Sturmbrigade

In addition to the *SS-Sturmbrigade n.A.*, with a *Grenadier-Bataillon (mot.)* and a *schwere Bataillon (mot.)*, a so-called *Ausbildungs-Bataillon* was organized for the excess men. Former French Lieutenant Colonel Gamory-Dubourdeau, born in 1885, was named as *Brigade Kommandeur*, who took part as a *Freiwilligen-Hauptsturmführer* in the first special training course in Tölz. When he finished the course, he was named as *Freiwilligen-Sturmbannführer*.

In April 1944, the *Französische SS-Freiwilligen-Sturmbrigade* was ordered to the *SS-Panzergrenadierschule* Kienschlagor for further training. As of June 30, 1944, this formation, without the French *Ausbildungsbataillon* that remained at *Truppenübungsplatz* Böhmen (about 700 men), had:

Führer	***Unterführer***	***Männer***	**Total**
30	44	1,614	1,688
1.78%	2.61%	95.61%	100%

The ratio between *Unterführer* and *Mannschaften* is particularly striking. It can be seen that the proposed induction of nearly 400 French officers and NCOs had not been realized.

When the *SS-FHA* ordered the *Brigadekommando* to form an approximately 1,000-man strong *Kampfgruppe* on July 28, 1944 and transfer it to the hard-pressed *Heeresgruppe Nordukraine*, most of the French *SS Freiwilligen* already had a year of service behind them. In peacetime, this period which would be sufficient for the unit training of an entire *Division*.

At the beginning of August 1944, the French *Marsch-Bataillon* [March Battalion], led by *Freiwilligen-Hauptsturmführer* Cance, had reached Turka on the Stryj River, and was put under command of *SS-Kampfgruppe Schäfer* (an element of the *18. SS-Freiwilligen-Panzergrenadier-Division*), stationed to the northwest. This moved directly into the Sanok area (about 50km southwest of Przemysl) to re-establish contact with the neighboring *17. Armee*. This could only be achieved after pulling back the front and shortening their own lines. As a result, the French marched mid-August 1944, as part of *SS-Kampfgruppe Schäfer*, to the *LIX.Aremm-Korps* and moved into defensive positions on the Wisloka River south of Mielic. When the Red Army launched an offensive, in the wake of a two-hour barrage on August 20, 1944, the units withdrew. Just two days later, *SS-Kampfgruppe Schäfer*, reduced to two (*Volks-)deutsche* and one weak French *Bataillon*, was stationed in the area south of Dabrowa (about 20km north of

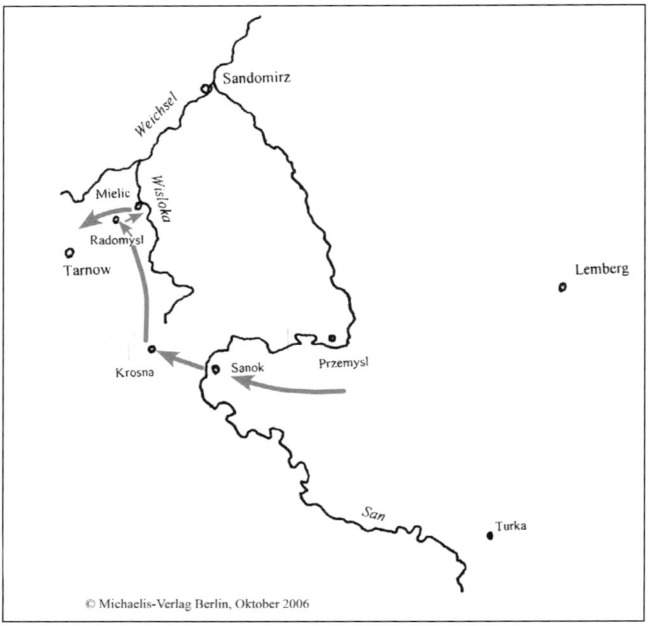

Tarnow). After see-saw battles, the *Kampfgruppe* was pulled out of the *HKL* at the end of August 1944 and the French *SS-Freiwilligen* were ordered, after barely four weeks of fighting, back to *SS-Truppenübungsplatz* Kienschlag.

Waffen-Grenadier-Division der SS "Charlemagne" (*französische Nr. 1*)

While the first French *SS-Freiwilligen* were fighting on the *Ostfront*, the order came, with effect from August 10, 1944, to combine the French *Freiwilligen-Legion* (*Legion Volontaires Francaise*), under command of the *Heer*, and the French *SS-Freiwilligen-Sturmbrigade* into a *Waffen-Grenadier-Brigade der SS*. The former *Kommandeur* of French *Grenadier-Regiment 638*, Colonel Puaud, was awarded the rank of *Waffen-Oberführer* and appointed *Kommandeur* of *Waffen-Grenadier-Brigade der SS "Charlemagne" (französische Nr. 1)*.

Its new designation as a ***Waffen-Verband der SS*** indicates a new ranking by the *SS-FHA*. The majority of the French, after taking in the many men *"unsuitable for the SS,"* did not represent the more *"Germanic"*-related type of *Freiwilligen*. Therefore, the designation as an *SS-Freiwilligen-Sturmbrigade* was changed to a *Waffen-Grenadier-Brigade der SS*. This was also reflected in their equipment and armaments. As *Grenadiere*, they were the lowest in the hierarchy of the fighting

Andre Baylé

Members of I. /Französische SS-Freiwilligen-Sturmbrigade, summer 1944.

troops. This did not change the propaganda tune, however *"Infantry, the crown of all weaponry."*

The new *Grenadier-Brigade* was to be organized as follows:

Stab
Waffen-Grenadier-Regiment der SS 57 (französische Nr. 1) (I. – II. Btl.)
Waffen-Grenadier-Regiment der SS 58 (französische Nr. 2) (I. – II. Btl.)
SS-Panzerjäger-Abteilung 57
SS-Artillerie-Abteilung 57
SS-Nachrichten-Kompanie 57
SS-Pionier-Kompanie 57
SS-Feldersatz-Kompanie 57

The first *Regiment* was formed using the remaining elements of the *Französischen SS-Freiwilligen-SturmBrigade* returning from deployment and the *Ausbildungsbataillon*. The second *Regiment* (command language: French) was formed using French *Grenadier-Regiment 638*, turned over from the *Heer*. The only two combat support *Kompanien* of the *SS-Freiwilligen-Sturmbrigade* went to the *Panzerjäger-Abteilung*, while the *2. (Sturmgeschütz-)Kompanie* consisted only of unarmed cadre of personnel.

At the end of September 1944, the units moved to *Truppenübungsplatz* Wildflecken in the Rhön region. The newly formed French *SS-Grenadier-Ausbildungsund Ersatz-Bataillon* remained in Greiffenberg and moved to Wildflecken only on February 15, 1945.

From October 1944, numerous other French formations had been arriving at Wildflecken, some of which had been evacuated from France. These included approximately:

1,200 *Marine* members
2,200 members of the *NSKK [Nationalsozialistisches Kraftfahrkorps*: National Socialist Motor Corps] and *OT [Organisation Todt]* and
2,500 militia members.

To coordinate all the related issues and problems, the French *SS* units *Inspektion* [Inspectorate] was formed on October 10, 1944. *SS-Brigadeführer* Krukenberg was appointed *Inspekteur* due to his excellent knowledge of French. One important task for the *Inspekteur* was to resolve, along with *Waffen-Oberführer* Puaud, the differences among the individual French party factions in the *Brigade*. Some of the men refused to be transferred to the *Waffen-SS*, and at times there were political tensions within the various units.

Finally, the men were checked individually, and those members classified as unacceptable were pulled out of the military units. The primary reasons for this were:

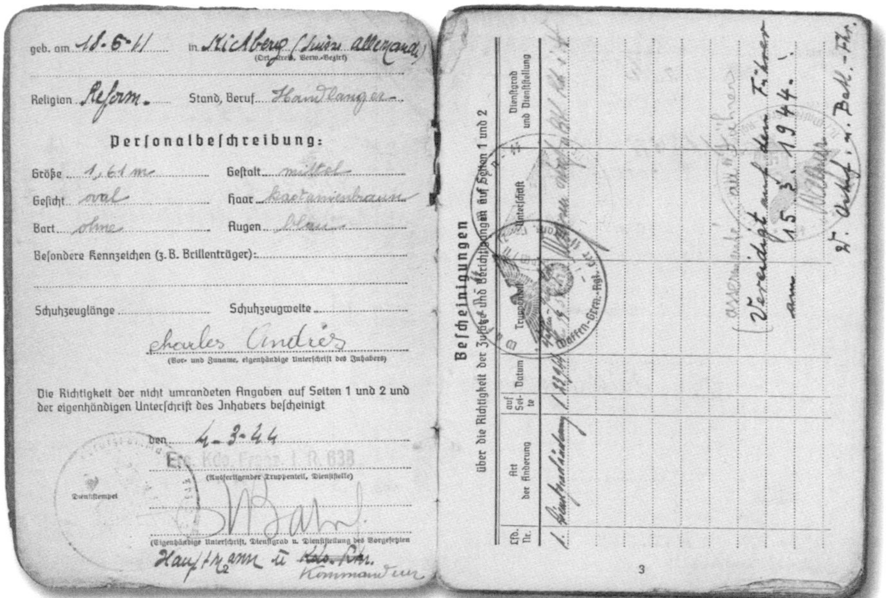

Karl Andres joined the LVF on March 4, 1944, and was transferred to the Französische SS-Freiwilligen-Sturmbrigade in summer 1944.

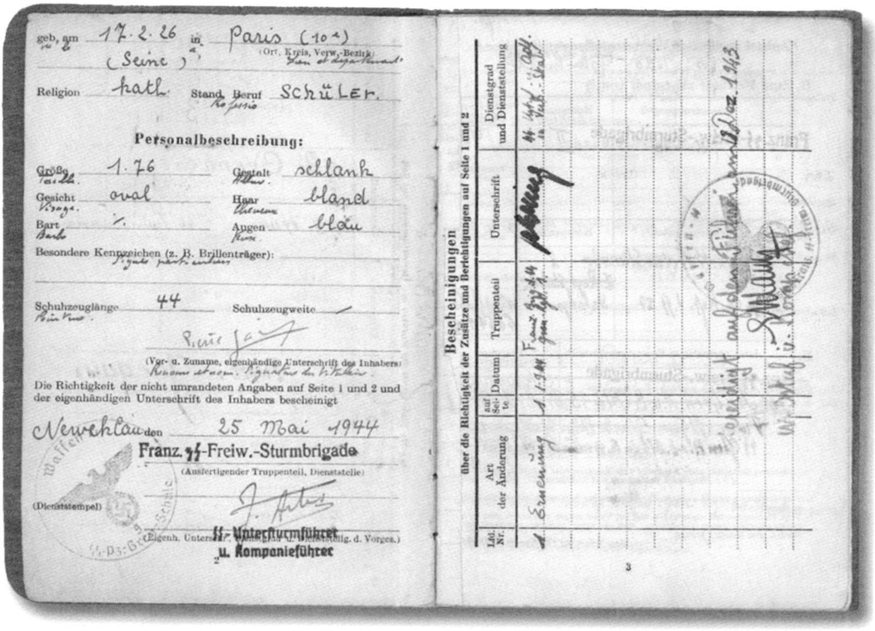

Soldbuch of an eighteen-year-old French SS Freiwilliger, who joined the Französische SS-Freiwilligen-Sturmbrigade in May 1944.

defeatist statements
Interception/listening in on prohibited transmitters
refusal to join the SS
bad attitude
inconsistency
unauthorized removal from the troops
lack of discipline

Overall, about 500 French were removed from the *Brigade* and either sent to the *SS* and *Polizei* prison camp at Danzig-Matzkau or to the compulsory labor service.

Military training of the remaining 5,400 new *Marine, NSKK, OT,* and Militia members was limited to just infantry training. Training for teamwork among *Grenadiere*, combat support units, and heavy weapons could not be realized due to lack of equipment. Because of the German military situation, there was also a poor supply of uniforms and food.

Already by the winter 1944/45, all training was halted – the motivation of many men fell to zero.

33. Waffen-Grenadier-Division der SS "Charlemange" (*französische Nr. 1*)

On February 10, 1945, Himmler ordered the 8,000-strong *Grenadier-Brigade* be renamed *33. Waffen-Grenadier-Division der SS "Charlemagne" (französische Nr. 1)*. It was organized as an *Infanterie-Division 45*, but for the units, nothing changed in comparison with the *Brigade*. The *Brigade* units were not even renumbered from 57 to 33. Since the formation was supplied neither with personnel nor materiel, only the name changed.

A week later, the *SS-FHA* issued movement orders to the newly formed Heeresgruppe Weichsel, on January 21, 1945. Starting February 22, 1945, some 4,000 men of the *33. Waffen-Grenadier-Division der SS* arrived at *Truppenübungsplatz* Hammerstein and there were put under command of the *XVIII. Gebirgs-Korps (2. Armee)*.

The next night, as Soviet tanks pushed through to Człěchòwò [German: Schlochau] (about 20km east of Czarne, to reach the Baltic Sea via Biały Bór [Baldenburg]), the *Kommandierende General* of *XVIII. Gebirgs-Korps* already ordered the first French troops to secure the area southeast of Czarne. To do this, *Waffen-Grenadier-Regiment der SS 57* was placed under command of *32. Infanterie-Division*, which deployed it on the right flank of the *15. Waffen-Grenadier-Division der SS (lettische Nr. 1)*. A former French *Freiwilliger* remembers the battles for Elsenau:

> *"The struggle was truly bitter and the Russians gained ground only with difficulty. They began to comb through the cemetery. A French prisoner of war was killed here; he had spontaneously voluntarily joined us and the Waffen-SS. The Russians kill all the wounded who fell into their hands. Now members of an undetermined nationality appeared on the Russian side. Some insulted us in excellent French: Surrender, you herd of pigs!"*

The *Division* was not deployed cohesively. After the first *Regiment*, then *Waffen-Grenadier-Regiment der SS 58* followed to the front, and finally the rear services were used to form *SS-Kampfgruppe Katzian*, which was used to protect the flanks during the retreat. Deployed to fight only as infantry against an enemy equipped with heavy weapons and tanks, the units had to fall back to Szczecinek on February 27, 1945.[47]

The next day the troops marched back towards Belgard, which they reached without major fighting on March 1, 1945. *Waffen-Oberführer* Puaud was overwhelmed by the situation, so *SS-Brigadeführer* Krukenberg, *Inspekteur* of the French *SS* formations, took command of the assembled elements of *33. Waffen-Grenadier-Division der SS*.

When the Red Army reached the Baltic at Koszalin, by way of Baldenburg, thus splitting *Heeresgruppe Weichsel* in two, the greatest part of the French *SS* formation came under command of *Korpsgruppe von Tettenau (3. Panzer-Armee)*. They gave the order to immediately occupy defensive positions eastwards along the Parsęta River at Karlino [Körlin]. About 500 men remained in the *2. Armee* sector and on March 4, 1945, as *SS-Kampfgruppe Obitz*, were put under command of *4. SS-Polizei-Panzer-Grenadier-Division (VII. Panzer-Korps)* in the Prudnik area (northwest of Gdynia).[48]

Events came thick and fast. On the same day, Soviet tank formations were again able to break through the front in the *3. Panzer-Armee* sector to Kołobrzeg [Kolberg]. They thus surrounded not just the German formations but also the French *SS* units. Deployed in *Kampfgruppe*, the men again sought to make contact with the German *HKL*. In this effort, the units fell apart.

While *SS-Kampfgruppe Fenet* managed to reach the German front at Dievenow by way of Gryfice [German: Greifenberg] on March 11, 1945, the bulk of the *Division* was shattered in the fighting west of Belgard. Around 100 French got into the *Festung* [fortress] Kolberg and fought there until they were evacuated March 18, 1945 together with *Alarmeinheiten* and *Volkssturm*. Anyone remaining was sent to the French *SS-Grenadier-Ausbildungs- und Ersatz-Bataillon* at Wildflecken. On March 16, 1945, *SS-Kampfgruppe Fenet* reached Jargelin, near

[47] An *Artillerie-Batterie* and a few *Pak* 7.5cm provided support. Of these, four *Pak* and two *lFH [leichte Feldhaubitze]* 10.5cm were lost at Szczecinek.

[48] After *Waffen-Hauptsturmführer* Obitz was wounded, *Waffen-Hauptsturmführer* Martin led whoever remained. From Hela, the French moved through Copenhagen and on April 10, 1945, reached Neustrelitz, where the *Division* was to be reorganized.

Anklam, by way of Swinemünde and from there marched on five days later to Neustrelitz, where *33. Waffen-Grenadier-Division der SS "Charlemagne"* was to be re-organized. *SS-Brigadeführer und Generalmajor der Waffen-SS* Krukenberg summed up the previous fighting very euphemistically on March 27, 1945:

> *"We have drastic days of bitter fighting and forced marches behind us. We have not fought as a little troop in the German Armee, but as an independent French division. With the name of Charlemagne, the reputation for bravery and endurance of the French has been confirmed once again. The duration of the fighting has united us. [...]*
>
> *We have everywhere helped to hold back or halt the surging tide of Bolshevism. This fight could not have been carried out without serious losses, and many of our comrades have not yet been able to reach our current lines. Let's hope that General Puaud and other heroic fighters with him are soon back amongst us. The battle has welded us together. The fact that our Division has fused together in glorious battles will redound to our advantage, as we now form one block, a cohesive team.*
>
> *Far away from our homeland, we were able to attach new glory to our banner. We know that all French people, who, like us, stand up for the freedom of the fatherland and for the New European Order, look at us with pride. [...] The fame of the LVF in the east, the success of the French SS-Sturmbrigade in the Carpathians, the struggles of the French Militia in our country, must create a block, sealed by French blood shed in Pomerania, which must lead to the birth of a tradition that is worthy of the revolutionary idea for which we fight.*
>
> *Our faith in National Socialist victory is unshakeable. It will become even more determined when the situation becomes more difficult.*
>
> *By the side of our German comrades who are fighting for the same ideal, we follow the Führer, the liberator of Europe."*

This order of the day, which recalls the spiritual outpourings of a National Socialist leadership officer, had little demagogic effect on the French collaborators in *Waffen-SS* uniforms. Of the approximately 4,000 *Division* members deployed in Pomerania, some 3,000 were killed, wounded, scattered, or taken prisoner. Replacements from the French *SS-Grenadier-Ausbildungs- und Ersatz-Bataillon* in Wildflecken were to make it possible to organize at least a ***Waffen-Grenadier-Regiment der SS "Charlemagne" (französisches)*** at Neustrelitz. Aware of the lack of motivation, *SS-Brigadeführer* Krukenberg left it up to the French members whether they wanted to continue to serve in a *Bau-* [construction] or a *Kampf* [combat] *bataillon*. About 400 men reported for the *Arbeits* [work] *Bataillon* – about 700 men for the *Kampfbataillon*. Despite this, skepticism about the French ran like a common thread through the German ranks: The *Kampfbataillon* was

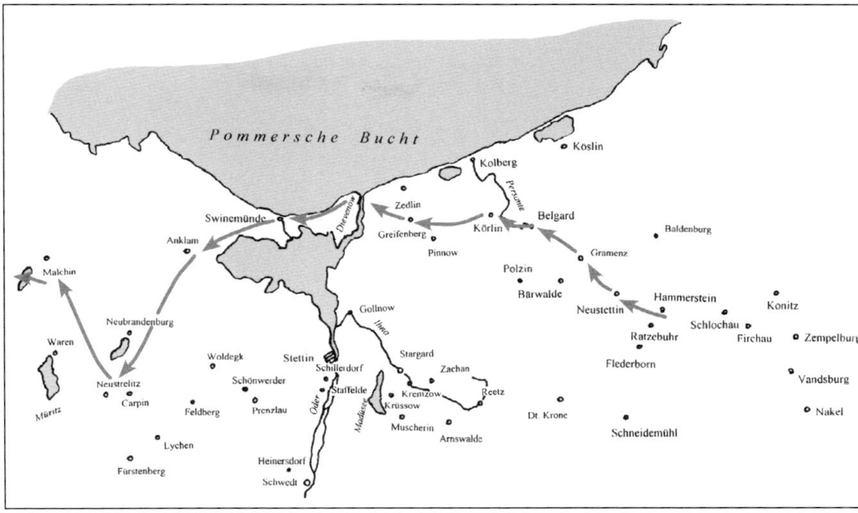

never again deployed on the front lines, but rather helped the *Baubataillon*, under command of *Korück 3. Panzer-Armee*, construct tank traps at Neustrelitz.

On April 11, 1945, the formation, now only used to dig trenches, organized itself like the former French *SS-Freiwilligen-Sturmbrigade* into:

I. /Waffen-Grenadier-Regiment der SS 57
II. /Waffen-Grenadier-Regiment der SS 58
schweres Bataillon with
- *1 (Pak-)Kompanie*
- *1 (Jagdpanzer-)Kompanie*
- *1 (Flak-)Kompanie*
- *1 leichte Artillerie-Batterie*

While the remaining members in the sector of the *3. Panzer-Armee* removed to Güstrow by way of Malchin, *SS-Brigadeführer* Krukenberg was given the order on April 24, 1945, to take over command of *11. SS-Freiwilligen-Panzergrenadier-Division "Nordland"* in Berlin. About ninety French *SS* men volunteered to accompany him. Loaded on trucks, the men reached the district of Neukölln the next day set up, under command of the *11. SS-Freiwilligen-Panzergrenadier-Division)*, a command post at the local town hall. While the units marching through Mecklenburg toward the line of demarcation units reached Bad Kleinen and disbanded there, the men in Berlin experienced the final battles there, first at Hermannplatz and later on the grounds of the *Reichsluftfahrtministerium* [Air Ministry]. In close combat, they managed to damage or destroy many Soviet tanks. When the attempt to break through over the Weidendammer bridge failed, the last of the French went into Soviet captivity.

The French *SS-Grenadier-Ausbildungs- und Ersatz-Bataillon* left *Truppenübungsplatz* Wildflecken on March 31, 1945, before American units arrived, trying to reach Neustrelitz. Due to the situation, when they were already on the march, the about 1,200-man strong *Bataillon* was ordered fourteen days later to move not to Mecklenburg, but rather to Regensburg.

On April 29, 1945, *SS-Kampfgruppe Hersche*, organized from the French *SS-Grenadier-Ausbildungsund Ersatz-Bataillon*, was put under command of the *38. SS-Grenadier-Division "Nibelungen."* On May 2, 1945, the *Kompanien* occupied positions at Wasserburg am Inn, and finally fell back across the Chiemsee towards Bad Reichenhall. When U.S. troops occupied the city on May 4, 1945, *SS-Kampfgruppe Hersche* was among those they took prisoner. When handed over to French troops, twelve French *SS* members fled and, re-arrested by members of the French 2nd Armored Division, were shot on May 8, 1945.

The history of the French formations in the *Waffen-SS* was characterized by general mistrust from the German side. The various collaborationist French organizations also found no consensus among themselves; as a result, the order to enforce the combination of *Freiwilligen* from the militia, the *Wehrmacht* and *Waffen-SS* did not result in any increase of motivation, which was by now generally lacking. Never reaching authorized strength in terms of personnel or materiel, the *Division* was destroyed within about three weeks of its initial deployment. Used afterwards only to dig trenches, ninety French in late April 1945 volunteered for the final battles in and around the *Reich* capital.

Kommandeure:

08/44 – 02/45	*Waffen-Oberführer der SS* Puaud
03/45 – 05/45	*SS-Brigadeführer* Krukenberg

Feldpost numbers:

Stab	47 335
Waffen-Grenadier-Regiment der SS 57 (französische Nr. 1)	66 641
I. Bataillon	41 592
II. Bataillon	35 411
Waffen-Grenadier-Regiment der SS 58 (französische Nr. 2)	02 951
I. Bataillon	03 865
II. Bataillon	05 492
SS-Panzerjäger-Abteilung 57	66 885
SS-Artillerie-Abteilung 57	00 290
SS-Nachrichten-Kompanie 57	14 309

SS-Pionier-Kompanie 57	64 680
SS-Feldersatz-Bataillon 33	65 920
SS-Versorgungstruppen 57	13 630
SS-Veterinär-Kompanie 57	11 498
SS-Sanitäts-Kompanie 57	66 453
SS-Feldpostamt 57	11 498
Französisches SS-Grenadier-Ausbildungs- und Ersatz-Bataillon	46 765
Inspektion der französischen SS-Verbände	65 448

34. Waffen-Grenadier-Division der SS "Landstorm Nederland" (*niederländische Nr. 2*)

Landwacht Niederlande

In early-1943, the Netherlands resistance movement was becoming evermore active. In addition to destroying and damaging German military installations, they also threatened and murdered collaborators, among others. *General* Seyffardt was one prominent victim as he had supported the formation of the Dutch *SS-Freiwilligen-Brigade*.

The *Reichsminister* for the occupied Dutch territories Artur Seyss-Inquart demanded that the occupation forces be reinforced. His proposal to bring the *SS-Wach-Bataillon 3 Nordwest*, made up of Dutchmen, up to *Regiment*al strength, was rejected by Himmler, because of the formation of the *4. SS-Freiwilligen-Panzergrenadier-Brigade "Nederland."*[49] For this, he approved, in his capacity as head of the German *Polizei*, formation of a Dutch *Hilfspolizeitruppe* [Auxiliary Police troop].

Under command of *Höhere SS- und Polizeiführer Nordwest SS-Obergruppenführer* Rauter, as of March 1943, Dutchman aged 17 to 45 years old could volunteer to enlist in the so-called ***Landwacht Niederlande***. In contrast to the *Waffen-SS*, both age and fitness requirements were loosened. Thus, to join the so-called *Polizeihilfsdienst*, not even the level of: *"k.v. [kriegsverwendungsfähig: fit for active duty] Heer"* was necessary.

The idea that these troops, who served under command of the *Befehlshaber* of the *Ordnungspolizei* in the Netherlands, *Generalmajor der Polizei* Dr. Lankenau, would be used primarily to protect property, lessened their aversion to them as collaborators. Therefore, not only right-wingers volunteered, but also those who were politically neutral or even opposition-minded Dutchman. For the latter, the economic benefits were decisive for deciding to enlist.

By April 6, 1943, the first 1,643 *Freiwilligen* had been registered for the *Regiment*-strong Landwacht. They formed:

1 Regimentsstab	Location: Haag
I. Bataillon	Location: s'Hertogenbosch
II. Bataillon III. Bataillon	Location: Veenendaal
13. (Infanteriegeschütz) Kompanie	Location: Weert
14. (Panzerjäger-) Kompanie	Location: Vught
15. (Flak-) Batterie[50]	Location: Vught

[49] He feared that potential Dutch *Freiwilligen* would rather enlist in the unit that up to then remained at home, rather than for the *Ostfront*.

[50] The *Flak-Batterie* was only added in 1944.

The units were deployed as planned, to guard important war installations, German agencies or to protect personnel.

SS-Grenadier-*Regiment* 1 "Landstorm Nederland"

On October 16, 1943, the *Landwacht Niederlande* was renamed, on the proposal of *Höheren SS- und Polizeiführer Nordwest SS-Obergruppenführer* Rauters, the ***"Landstorm Nederland."*** This was to emphasize the military character of the *Regiment*-strength unit, in contrast to that of a purely *Hilfspolizei* one.

As part of this change, the three *Bataillone* were transferred from *Ordnungspolizei* control to the *Waffen-SS* as ***SS-Grenadier-Regiment 1 "Landstorm Nederland."*** However, it remained subordinate to the *Höhere SS- und Polizeiführer Nordwest*. On December 31, 1943, the *Regiment* reported:

	Führer	***Unterführer***	***Männer***	**Total**
Actual	26	48	1,764	1,838
	1.41%	2.61%	95.98%	100%
Authorized	42	311	1,628	1,981
	2.11%	15.65%	82.24%	100%

Since there was a serious shortage of *Führer* and *Unterführer*, about 200 convolescents from 4. *SS-Freiwilligen-Panzergrenadier-Brigade Nederland* were transferred to *"Landstorm Nederland."* Because of the disastrous living standards the Dutch civilian population sometimes suffered, an additional some 1,000 *Freiwilligen* signed up in winter 1943-44, so that on June 30, 1944, *SS-Grenadier-Regiment 1 Landstorm Nederland* had the following strength:

	Führer	***Unterführer***	***Männer***	**Total**
Actual	32	226	2,910	3,168
	1%	7.14%	91.86%	100%

The approximately 1,200 more *Freiwilligen* than were needed for the authorized strength, were assembled and trained in the *SS-Feld-Ersatz-Bataillon*. However, the *Regiment* still lacked over 50% of its *Führer* and *Unterführer*, which limited its combat readiness.

When the Allies reached northern Belgium at the end of August 1944, the *Befehlshaber Niederlande, General der Flieger* [General of Aircraft] Christiansen ordered the *LXXXVIII. Armee-Korps,* which was under his command, as well as *Höheren SS-und Polizeiführers Nordwest* troops to hold back the advance of the British Armed Forces into the Netherlands along the Hasselt-Antwerp line, until the arrival of the *1. Fallschirm-Armee* [Paratroop Army].

Landstorm Nederland members being sworn in on April 20, 1943.

SS-Standartenführer Kohlroser, Kommandeur of SS-Grenadier-Regiment I "Landstorm Nederland."

To assist in this operation, *I./SS-Grenadier-Regiment 1 "Landstorm Nederland,"* with a combat strength of 438 men, was deployed on September 4, 1944, on the east flank of *LXXXVIII. Armee-Korps*, and occupied positions in the *85. Infanterie-Division* sector, between Hasselt and Beeringen, behind the Albert Canal. Providing little resistance to the British formations, the *Bataillon* finally pulled back to the Netherlands by way of Hechtel, and shifted to Apeldoorn in October 1944.

The *II./SS-Grenadier-Regiment 1 "Landstorm Nederland"* was placed under command of the *719. Infanterie-Division* on the west flank of the *Korps* near Antwerp on September 7, 1944. After heavy fighting, the *Bataillon* pulled back through Herenthals towards the Netherlands. In the Baarle-Nassau area, the units were deployed in the *HKL* until the end of October 1944; then they were transferred through Breda to the Apeldoorn area, for the formation of *SS-Freiwilligen-Grenadier-Brigade "Landstorm Nederland."*

The *III. /SS-Grenadier-Regiment 1 "Landstorm Nederland"* was put on alert for the defense against the Allied airborne Operation Market Garden and placed under command of *Sperrverband* [obstacle construction unit] *Harzer*. Skirmishes with British troops started on September 17, 1944, at Oosterbeek. When the fighting ended, the unit remained under command of *Sperrverband Harzer* until it was transferred to the *9. SS-Panzer-Division "Hohenstaufen"* in early October 1944. It was then transferred to the Apeldoorn assembly area.

SS-Freiwilligen-Grenadier-Brigade "Landstorm Nederland" (*niederländische Nr. 2*)

To have stronger formations at their disposal to defend the Netherlands, the *SS-FHA* ordered on November 2, 1944, the expansion of *SS-Grenadier-Regiment 1 "Landstorm Nederland."* A number of *Höhere SS- und Polizeiführer Nordwest* troops were therefore ordered to Apeldoorn for the formation of *SS-Freiwilligen-Grenadier-Brigade "Landstorm Nederland."* The *Brigade* was to be organized as follows:

Brigadestab
SS-Freiwilligen-Grenadier-Regiment 83 (niederländische Nr. 3)
  I. Bataillon (former *II. /SS-Grenadier-Regiment 1 L.N.)*
  II. Bataillon (former *II. /SS-Grenadier-Regiment 1 "L.N.")*
SS-Freiwilligen-Grenadier-Regiment 84 (niederländische Nr. 4)
  I. Bataillon (former I. /SS-Grenadier-Regiment 1 "L.N.")
  II. Bataillon (former SS-Wach-Bataillon 3)

SS-Freiwilligen-Artillerie-Regiment 60 (niederländische Nr. 2)
I. Abteilung
II. Abteilung
SS-Panzerjäger-Abteilung 60
1. *Kp.* (former *1. SS-Pz.Jäg.Kp. Nordwest)*
2. *Kp.* (former *2. SS-Pz.Jäg.Kp. Nordwest)*
3. *Kp.* (former *SS-Flak-Bttr. L. N.) SS-Nachrichten-Kompanie 60*
SS-Pionier-Kompanie 60 SS-Sanitäts-Kompanie 60 SS-Feldersatz-Bataillon 60

The *Brigade*'s authorized strength, with its de facto inclusion of nine *Bataillone*, was about 5,400 men. To achiever this, around 2,800 *Freiwilligen,* often members of the former *Germaansche SS in het Nederlande* equivalent to the *Allgemeine-SS* [General SS] in Germany, were mobilized in the next few weeks.

Since the *Regiment* had so far only had an *SS-* designation, the *Brigade* was now run as an *SS-Freiwilligen* formation. This addition to its name was not due to any change in the fitness standards for the *Landwacht*, even "*kv-Heer*" was not required but rather corresponded to the general designation for so-called "Germanic" *Waffen-SS* formations in Western Europe.

The men were put under command of *XXX. Armee-Korps (15. Armee)* in November 1944 as *SS-Freiwilligen-Grenadier-Brigade "Landstorm Nederland."*

34. SS-Freiwilligen-Grenadier-Division "Landstorm Nederland" (*niederländische Nr. 2*)

The formation was already, in the course of renaming the *Waffen-SS Brigaden*, raised to *34. SS-Freiwilligen-Grenadier-Division "Landstorm Nederland"* by February 10, 1945. Its authorized organization as an *Infanterie-Division 45* called for:

Divisionsstab
SS-Freiw.-Grenadier-Regiment 83 (niederländische Nr. 4) with *I. - III. Bataillon*
SS-Freiw.-Grenadier-Regiment 84 (niederländische Nr. 5) with *I. - III. Bataillon*
SS-Freiw.-Grenadier-Regiment 85 (niederländische Nr. 6) with *I. - III. Bataillon*
SS-Freiw.-Artillerie-Regiment 34 (niederländische Nr. 2) with *I. - IV. Abteilung*
SS-Panzerjäger-Abteilung 34[51]
SS-Pionier-Bataillon 34
SS-Nachrichtentruppe 34

[51] As of April 2, 1945, *SS-Panzerjäger-Abteilung 34* had eleven 7.5cm *Pak* on *Selbstfahrlafette* [self-propelled anti-tank guns].

In fact, it was impossible to carry out the reorganization in terms of both personnel and materiel. The *Brigade* retained this structure from November 1944. On February 13, 1945, the *Division* took over the positions of the *331. Infanterie-Division* in the Rhenen-Tiel-Zaltbommel line. The *Divisionsstab* was quartered in Amerongen. Except for reciprocal *Spähtrupp* [reconaissance patrol] operations, there was no combat. On February 23, 1945, the *Wehrmachtbericht* surprisingly reported about one such operation:

> *"Dutch Waffen-SS Freiwilligen, in a surprising foray in central Holland, raided an enemy strong point and brought back a large number of prisoners from the 49th British Infantry Division."*

The former *SS-Unterscharführer* Rolf Lohmeyer recalls the *Spähtrupp* operations:

> *"Shortly after my 21st birthday, I was transferred from the 4. SS-Polizei-Panzer-Grenadier-Division to the 34. SS-Freiwilligen-Grenadier-Division 'Landstorm Nederland.' My Kompanie was stationed at a farm in a fruit-growing area near Ochten, on the Waal River (about 40km west of Nijmegen). Position warfare prevailed, and the no man's land was the so-called summer dike of the Waal.*
>
> *Here, I reported to SS-Obersturmführer Hebel, my new Kompaniechef [company commander], a Dutch officer of our troop. My first impression was that he was a practical man, but not very accessible. I was Kompanietruppführer [company HQ platoon leader], so I was often near the Kompanieführer.*
>
> *Things weren't going well for the Dutch after the 'hungry winter' of 1944-45, mainly because the railway workers had been on strike since last September, so that hardly any food was arriving because there was no transport. Only the black market flourished. Fishing boats brought potatoes over the Ijsselmeer from Dutch Friesland and earned a lot of money with their black market trade. During that winter, people even paid insane amounts of money for potato peelings. Our Kompanie quarters were in a farmyard that had been shot to pieces. Mostly we stayed in the cellar, where we used some couches for a makeshift camp. The cellar, supported with beams, also offered some protection against fragments of exploding grenades.*
>
> *One night, Hebel sent me on a Spähtruppunternehmen [reconaissance patrol] on the south side of the Waal. It was held off until about 2:00 o'clock, because until then the moon shone so brightly that the river shone like a mirror and any movement could be seen. The boat glided through the night, driven by silent strokes of the oars. We were all a bit uneasy. After a quarter of an hour, we could see the opposite shore. I stood in the bow with the MPi [machinenpistole] and was the first to jump out. We reached the winter dike*

and crept cautiously up it. There were a few houses right on the dike. We hurried past the houses and hid in a hay shed. We were supposed to spend the next day here and then return to our side the next night. I lifted up a roof tile, pushed it back and took up my field glasses. It was the best conceivable observation post. I saw the approach road, where the British supply lines were rolling along. Five hundred meters away there was a house that some Tommies used during the day. One had a field telephone apparatus on his back. Then they got out of my sight and disappeared around the farmhouse. Would they go into the building on the other side?

I was planning to search the house in the evening and possibly take some prisoners. We waited until 21:00 then crept out of the shed. While my comrade Onderstaal stayed in the farmyard with a ready-to-fire Panzerfaust, van der Meulen and I walked into the house. We stopped and listened. We could clearly hear the BBC London call sign. It was probably an Englishman in the house. I pushed open the door to the living room and, with my MPi at the ready, sprang into the room. Van der Meulen, just behind me, ran into the opposite corner with his MPi. There were three people in the room. The farmer's wife, whom I had already seen in the yard, screamed in horror when she saw us. Van der Meulen asked in Dutch, if there were Englishmen in the house. They're 500m away, one of them said. All three civilians were very agitated. Van der Meulen reassured them: They had nothing to fear; we would do nothing to them. If they would tell us which English units were stationed here, we would disappear. One of the farmers knew that the English soldiers wore a white bear on their sleeve badges and were called the 'Polar Bears.' After we had eaten something, I said that we would be picked up by our people in the dinghy in two hours. We should be on the river by then. We would take one of the men with us as a hostage, so that no one would alert the English. The woman could not understand why her family was being threatened, while next door lived a black marketeer, de zwarte Pit. We should take him with us. I did not allow any discussion and ordered one of the men to come along. He grabbed a bread knife, turned around quickly and stabbed me. The first stab hit my arm. I dropped the MPi. The farmer kept stabbing, six or seven times in my arm, in my face. When I got over the first shock, I grabbed the bare knife with my right hand. I kicked the farmer in the stomach with my foot. He fell to the ground. His brother had used this second to attack van der Meulen. He shot his attacker in the legs. Onderstaal heard the shots from outside, came into the house, saw I was seriously wounded and immediately helped me. We ran to the swampy bank of the Waal, waded through a drainage ditch and shot off a flare. While Tommy was shooting up the area with machine guns, I collapsed. I fell down and could not get up. Everything around me was wet and cold. Convinced that it was over for me, I ordered Onderstaal and van der Meulen, to leave me lying there and try everything to get across the river.

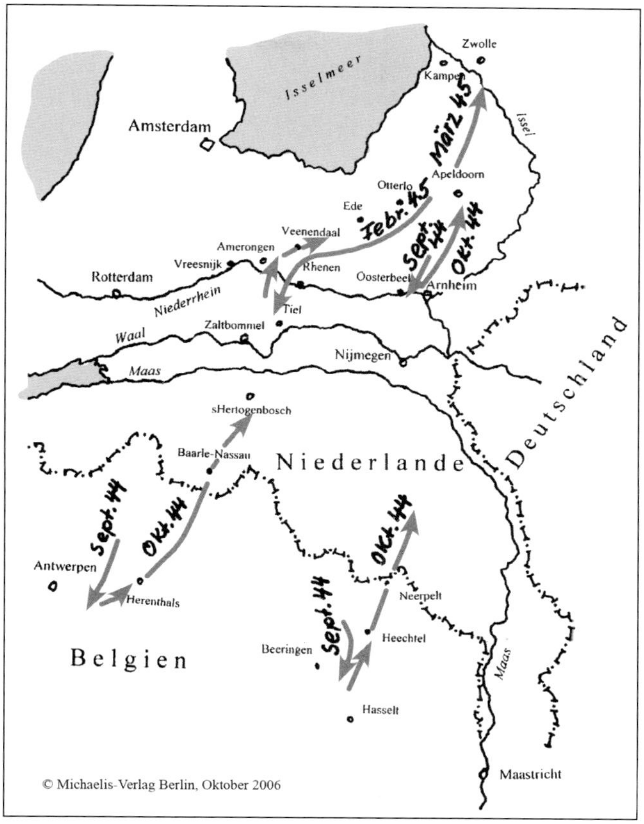

Then I handed them my map case and passed out. I regained consciousness when our men lifted me out of the dinghy and I heard them saying that we were back home."

On March 23, 1945, the Allies launched Operation Plunder, to envelop the Ruhrgebiet [Ruhr region of Germany] from the north. The enemy succeeded in making a thrust at Emmerich in between the *25. Armee* and *1. Fallschirm-Armee*. Since it was impossible to maintain a cohesive front, the *25. Armee* was forced to form a new front along the line from Kampen-Arnhem along the Issel River. Individual units of the *34. SS-Freiwilligen-Grenadier-Division* were deployed here, to the southwest of Zwolle.

As British troops advanced across the Waal, *SS-Freiwilligen-Grenadier-Regiment 83*, which had been deployed there, retreated over the Lower Rhine. Thus, the two *Grenadier-Regimenter* were stationed along a line between Rhenen and Vreeswijk.

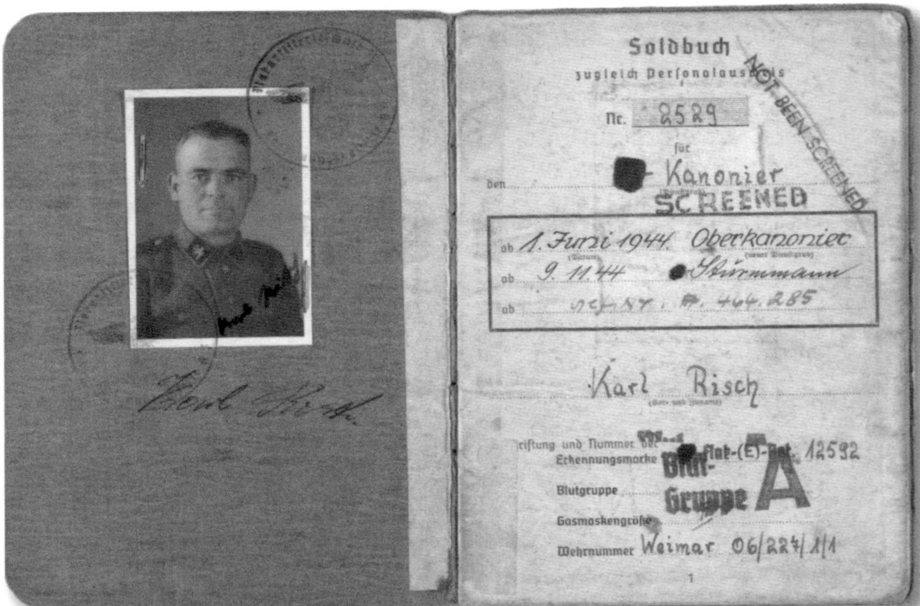

Soldbuch
zugleich Personalausweis
Nr. 2529
für
den Kanonier
SCREENED
NOT BEEN SCREENED
ab 1. Juni 1944 Oberkanonier
ab 9.11.44 Sturmmann
Karl Risch
Erkennungsmarke ... Flak-(E)-... 12592
Blutgruppe Blut-Gruppe A
Gasmaskengröße
Wehrnummer Weimar 06/224/1/1
1

Karl Risch, an Oberkanonier [chief gunner] in SS-Flak-Ausb. und Ers.-Rgt. in Munich, was transferred in June 1944 to SS-Flak-Batterie/"Landstorm Nederland."

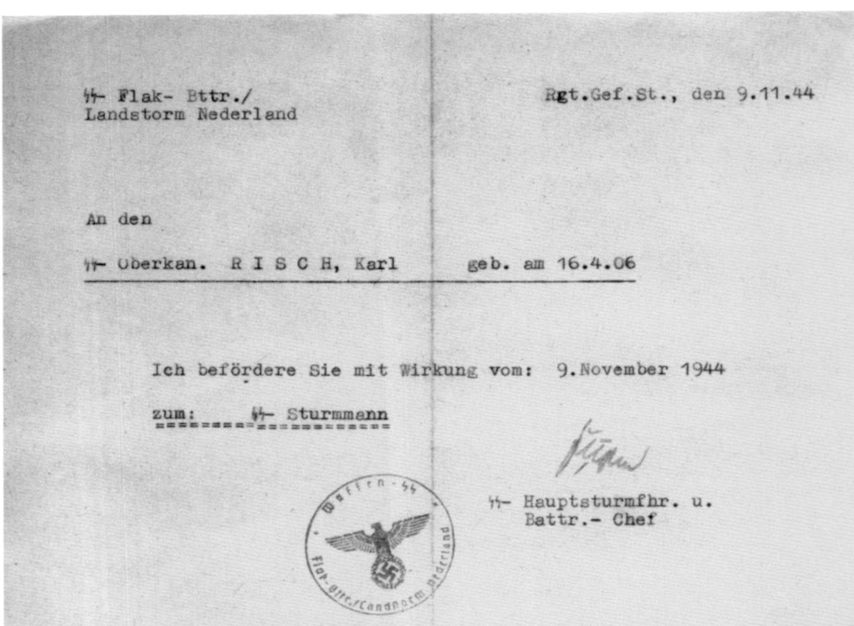

ϟϟ-Flak- Bttr./
Landstorm Nederland

Rgt.Gef.St., den 9.11.44

An den

ϟϟ-Oberkan. R I S C H, Karl geb. am 16.4.06

Ich befördere Sie mit Wirkung vom: 9.November 1944

zum: ϟϟ-Sturmmann

ϟϟ-Hauptsturmfhr. u.
Battr.- Chef

When the enemy succeeded in crossing the river at Vreeswijk, the *34. SS-Freiwilligen-Grenadier-Division* fell back to the area of Veenendaal-Otterlo-Ede on May 4, 1945. The next day, *Festung Niderland* [Fortress Netherlands] capitulated.[52] In a strength of:

Führer	*sonstige Dienstgrade*	Total
212	5,744	5,956
3.56%	96.44%	100%

The *Division* marched into British captivity on May 10, 1945. While the British behaved correctly, their own countrymen forced the collaborators to run the gauntlet. This was not helped by the fact that many had joined the unit for opportunistic reasons. Deployed in trench warfare, its structure was sufficient for an infantry formation, although it had no artillery support due to lack of guns. The commander of the British 49th Infantry Division, Brigadier General Crosse, wrote a report about disarming *34. SS-Freiwilligen-Grenadier-Division "Landstorm Nederland" (niederländische Nr. 2)* at the time:

> *"In my first conversation with the German Divisionskommandeur, Oberführer Kohlroser, on May 7, I made clear that I likely found the task just as distasteful as he did. Therefore, as I said, the faster we complete the job, the better it would be.*
>
> *His troops were to make all their weapons and equipment, personal belongings and baggage ready for inspection. My units would then appear and check everything according to the lists previously prepared by the Germans. Then, all their baggage would be put in a concentration camp built by their own people under my supervision. Kohlroser argued that this would be very humiliating; he would prefer to lead his troops as a complete formation to the camp, where they would allow my units to disarm them, and afterwards they would march into the camp. I told him that if he decided to act this way, I would concentrate an overwhelming armed force, disarm his men by force and immediately open fire at the slightest disturbance, with disastrous consequences for his men. On May 10, when the disarmament was to begin, I took the German Division commander with me during my inspection of his units. As unlikely as it might have seemed, they had all cooperated 100%. All of their weapons and equipment were ready for inspection in an orderly fashion. Honor guards stood at attention when I appeared, and always when I found something to object to, the man responsible stood at attention – a very embarrassing situation.*

[52] On April 9, 1945, the *25. Armee* sector was declared *"Festung Niederlande."*

An officer I caught smoking off to the side, was later specially sent me to apologize. The march of the mighty Wehrmacht into the camp, however, was a pathetic spectacle. The officers and men, without their weapons, marched in order and in lockstep, but still their transport was a sorry affair. We used every possible means of transport: two-wheeled handcarts, one-horse carriages, farm wagons and even a dismantled car drawn by horses. But we had to solve some strange problems. The Germans had stolen a number of cows, which they were taking with them. No one knew who owned them, so for the time being we let the Germans keep the cows in the camp. One village even wanted to keep its German mayor because he had always been decent to the inhabitants, and they did not want him to go now. During all this time, the Dutch resistance movement was going on about how they wanted to continue annihilating Germans. They wanted control of the Germans, they wanted gasoline and German weapons. All in all, it made one to think that we should thank Heaven that we were born Englishmen, and not Germans."

Kommandeure:
02/45 – 05/45 *SS-Oberführer* Kohlroser

Feldpost numbers:

Divisionsstab	19 003
SS-Freiwilligen-Grenadier-Regiment 83 (niederländische Nr. 4)	38 800
I. Bataillon	25 943
II. Bataillon	21 666
SS-Freiwilligen-Grenadier-Regiment 84 (niederländische Nr. 5)	15 089
I. Bataillon	27 195
II. Bataillon	42 810
SS-Freiwilligen-Artillerie-Regiment 34 (niederländische Nr. 2)	
I. Abteilung	39 149
II. Abteilung	44 150
SS-Panzerjäger-Abteilung 34	15 855
SS-Nachrichten-Kompanie 34	00 529
SS-Pionier-Kompanie 34	04 780
SS-Sanitäts-Kompanie 34	00 978
SS-Feldersatz-Bataillon 34	01 852
SS-Versorgungstruppe 34	01 141
SS-Veterinär-Kompanie 34	05 275

35. SS-Polizei-Grenadier-Division

Polizei-Brigade "Wirth"

When the Red Army launched a major offensive from the Baranov bridgehead on January 12, 1945, the German forces could do nothing to oppose the onslaught. *Alarmeinheiten* were thrown together in utmost haste, from *Ausbildungs- und Ersatz-* as well as *Polizeitruppen* and the *Volkssturm*, to attempt to hold the enemy advance before it got to the Oder. A *Polizei-Brigade* was also pulled together, primarily from remnants of *Polizei* units formerly used in the *General-gouvernement*, as well as elements from the *Polizei-Waffen-Schule II* Dresden-Hellerau.

Under the command of the former *Kommandeur of Polizei-Waffen-Schule II, Oberst der Schutzpolizei* Wirth, the units below were assembled and sent to the *XXXX. Panzer-Korps (9. Armee)*. At the end of January 1945, the *Polizei-Brigade* was deployed in the *HKL* across from the Odereck bridgehead north of Zielona Góra.

Brigadestab
Polizei-Regiment z.b.V. [zur besonderen Verwendung: for Special Deployment] *1 (I. – III. Bataillon)*
Polizei-Regiment z.b.V.2 (I. – III. Bataillon)
Polizei-Artillerie-Abteilung
Polizei-Panzerjäger-Abteilung
Polizei-Nachrichten-Kompanie
Polizei-Pionier-Kompanie
Polizei-Sanitäts-Kompanie
Polizei-Feldersatz-Bataillon

35. SS-Polizei-Grenadier-Division

About two weeks after the improvised organization of *Polizei-Brigade "Wirth,"* the *SS-FHA* ordered on February 10, 1945, that it be reinforced into the *35. SS-Polizei-Grenadier-Division*. It was impossible to carry out any training as a unit at a *Truppenübungsplatz*, to practice cooperation between the combat support units and the fighting troops. Instead, at the end of February 1945, the *Polizisten* remained stationed west of the Neisse, in positions built along the Oder tributary as far as Guben. To comply with the organization of an *Infanterie-Division 45*, those *Division* elements it still lacked were supplied in the time that followed. Various other units, including *Volkssturm* were also ordered to the defensive sector. Wirth handed over command to *SS-Standartenführer* Pipkorn and returned to *Polizei-Waffen-Schule II* Dresden-Hellerau. *SS-Standartenführer* Pipkorn had been *Chef des Generalstabes II. SS-Panzer-Korps* until October 1944 and therefore lacked the necessary tactical knowledge to lead a *Division*.

On March 16, 1945, both *Polizei-Grenadier-Regimenter z.b.V.1* and *2* were given the *Ordnungspolizei* consecutive numbers *29* and *30*. This meant that there was a *Waffen-SS Divisionsstab* leading *Ordnungspolizei* units.

By the end of March 1945, the *35. SS-Polizei-Grenadier-Division* was sent to the *SS-Polizei-Regiment 14*. Now equipped with three *Grenadier-Regimenter*, it was transferred to the *Waffen-SS* on April 6, 1945. In this transfer, the units were renamed:

SS-Polizei-Regiment 29 as *SS-Polizei-Grenadier-Rgt. 89*
SS-Polizei-Regiment 30 as *SS-Polizei-Grenadier-Rgt. 90*
SS-Polizei-Regiment 14 as *SS-Polizei-Grenadier-Rgt. 91*

The *Division* units were from now on uniformly numbered as 35.

On April 14, 1945, the *Reichsführer-SS* liaison officer reported to Hitler the formation strength as:

	Führer	***Unterführer***	***Männer***	**Total**
Actual	203	1,423	6,958	8,584
	2.36%	16.58%	81.06%	100%
Authorized	352	1,947	9,581	11,880
	2.96%	16.39%	80.65%	100%

An additional about 1,500 men, including *Flak-Abteilung 1203*, were also assigned to the formation. Besides lacking some 30% of its authorized strength, *Division* combat readiness was limited by its members' lack of training and their age. The greater number were older men, physically overwhelmed by front-line deployment.

In mid-April 1945, the *Division* – under command of the *V. Armee-Korps* – reported the following weaponry:

63	*schwere Maschinengewehre* (8 alleged)
412	*leichte Maschinengewehre* (25 alleged)
47	*mittlere Granatwerfer* 8.14cm
2	*leichte Infanteriegeschütze* 7.5cm
12	*leichte Feldhaubitzen* 18
6	*Feldkanonen* 7.5cm
4	*leichte Geschütze* 7.62 cm (r.)
6	*Pak* 5cm
16	*Pak* 7.5cm

12 *Pak* 8.8cm
12 *Flak* 2cm (9 alleged)
12 *Flak* 8.8cm (*Flak-Abteilung 1203*)

Due to the Red Army advance launched on April 16, 1945, *V. Armee-Korps* was pulled out of the *4. Panzer-Armee* sector and put under command of the *9. Armee*. By April 21, 1945, the unit was encircled in the area of Guben-Müllrose-Fürstenwalde-Königswusterhausen-Lubben. To protect the constantly expanding southern flank of the *9. Armee,* on April 21, 1945, *V. Armee-Korps* ordered that *35. SS-Polizei-Grenadier-Division* be split into two *Kampfgruppen*. While *Oberstleutnant der Schutzpolizei* Fleckner, with:

SS-Feldersatz-Bataillon 35
SS-Wach-Bataillon 4
II. /Waffen-Grenadier-Regiment der SS 73[53]

These units remained in the positions on the Neisse River, *SS-Standartenführer* Pipkorn marched with the:

SS-Polizei-Grenadier-Regimente 89-91
Most of the *Division* units

In an attempt to retake the territory occupied by the Red Army, *SS-Polizei-Grenadier-Regiment 91* was able to penetrate the area, but was virtually shattered in the street fighting which followed.

Kampfgruppe Fleckner was wiped out while it was still on the Neisse River, in the fighting at the Groß Breesen bridgehead (about 10km north of Guben) and retreated starting April 23, 1945, towards Lieberose. On April 25, 1945, the men reached Groß Köris and Neubrück and security detachments pushed forward to

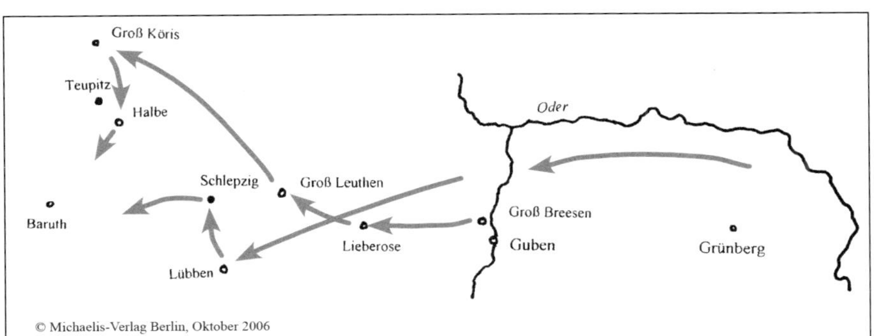

[53] Temporarily under command of *36. Waffen-Grenadier-Division der SS.*

Löpten, Teupitz and Halbe. To the south, in the evening, *SS-Polizei-Grenadier-Regiment 89* tried to break through to *SS-Kampfgruppe Pipkorn* at Schlepzig, westwards along the Berlin-Dresden *Autobahn* [highway]. Moving by way of Krausnick-Staakow, the men reached the area east of Baruth. Here the units met up with the remnants of *SS-Kampfgruppe Fleckner*, marching southwest from the Halbe area. The two groups were destroyed in an attempt to force a breakthrough at Baruth. Any remaining cohesion collapsed – *SS-Standartenführer* Pipkorn was killed in the action.

The *35. SS-Polizei-Grenadier-Division* was also in fact nothing more than an ad hoc motley collection of any troops somehow available – including many *Ordnungspolizei* members. Bearing little resemblance to any *Infanterie-Division* in terms of fighting capacity, the units were given totally pretenious designations that did not correspond to their real situation, even in terms of numbers.

Kommandeure:

03/45	*Oberst der Schutzpolizei* Wirth
03/45	*SS-Standartenführer* Pipkorn

Feldpost numbers:

Divisionsstab	34 435
SS-Polizei-Grenadier-Regiment 89	39 346
I. Bataillon	64 215
II. Bataillon	66 285
III. Bataillon	64 742
SS-Polizei-Grenadier-Regiment 90	65 942
I. Bataillon	35 916
II. Bataillon	37 510
SS-Polizei-Grenadier-Regiment 91	04 486
I. Bataillon	10 851
II. Bataillon	57 461
SS-Divisions-Füsilier-Bataillon 35	39 788
SS-Panzerjäger-Abteilung 35	35 487
SS-Polizei-Artillerie-Regiment 35	43 834
I. Abteilung	45 125
II. Abteilung	46 491
III. Abteilung	47 018
SS-Pionier-Bataillon 35	64 017
SS-Nachrichtentruppe 35	36 603

36. Waffen-Grenadier-Division der SS

SS-Sonderkommando "Dirlewanger"

On March 29, 1940, Himmler informed the *Reichsjustizminister* [Minister of Justice] of a radical new decree by Hitler:

> *"The Führer has decreed that all poachers, especially of Bavarian and Ostmark [annexed Austria] origin, who have broken the law, not by using snares, but by hunting with rifles, may, if they serve in Waffen-SS Scharfschützen-Kompanien [Sniper Companies] for the duration of the war, be exempted from serving their sentences and be pardoned for good behavior."*

As a result, on July 1, 1940, the first such offenders were used to form the so-called *Wilddiebkommando* [poacher command] *Oranienburg*.[54] It is notable that these "probationary shooters" were not required to meet *SS* fitness standards. Any man up to forty-five years old could be drafted, if they were at least 1.65m tall.

The intention to use these men as sharpshooters was eventually dropped and the unit, under the leadership of convicted criminal Dr. Dirlewanger was transferred as the *SS-Sonderkommando Dirlewanger* to *SS- und Polizeiführer Lublin*. This used the *Kommando* to guard the Jewish labor camp at Stary Dzikow. In spring 1941, it was transferred to guard a Jewish labor camp in Lvov.

These operations again exposed the negative character traits of most of the members including *SS-Hauptsturmführer* Dirlewanger. This led to the *SS- und Polizeigerichts VI* in Krakow conducting several investigations of the *SS-Sonderkommando* members.

As a result, the men were withdrawn from the *Generalgouvernement* on January 29, 1942, and transferred to *Höhere SS- und Polizeiführer Russland-Mitte*. Initially billeted in a former nursing home in Mogilev, the men were finally quartered in the castle at Lohoisk, north of Minsk.

Small in numbers, the unit was reinforced with sixty former Ukrainian Red Army soldiers in May 1942. Regularly deployed in the *Höheren SS- und Polizeiführer* territory to confiscate agricultural goods and labor and for large-scale anti-partisan fighting, the *SS-Sonderkommando* participaed in Byelorussia and elsewhere in the following operations:

07/20 – 08/07/42	*Unternehmen Adler* [Operation Eagle]
08/14 – 08/20/42	*Unternehmen Greif* [Griffon]
09/02 – 09/05/42	*Unternehmen Nordsee* [North Sea]

[54] The term Oranienburg comes from the fact that the *Kommando* was set up at the Sachsenhausen concentration camp.

Members of SS-Sonderbataillon "Dirlewanger" in Byelorussia.

10/04 – 10/08/42	*Unternehmen Regatta*
10/11 – 10/23/42	*Unternehmen Karlsbad*
11/06 – 11/08/42	*Unternehmen Frieda*
01/06 – 01/14/43	*Unternehmen Franz*
01/18 – 01/27/43	*Unternehmen Erntefest I* [Harvest Festival]
01/30 – 01/15/43	*Unternehmen Erntefest II*
02/06 – 02/26/43	*Unternehmen Hornung* [old name for February]
04/01 – 04/04/43	*Unternehmen Lenz-Süd* [Lenz South]
04/08 – 04/31/43	*Unternehmen Lenz-Nord* [North]
04/16 – 04/24/43	*Unternehmen Zauberflöte* [Magic Flute]
04/28 – 05/10/43	*Unternehmen Draufgänger* [Daredevil]
05/22 – 06/21/43	*Unternehmen Cottbus*

Renamed ***SS-Sonderbataillon "Dirlewanger,"*** the unit had, as of June 8, 1943, about 700 members and was structured as follows:

1 *deutsche Kompanie* (150 men)
1 *deutschen Kradschützen-Zug* [motorcycle platoon] (40 men)
3 Russian *Kompanien* (450 men)
1 *Artillerie-Batterie* (40 Germans and 40 Russians)

As of November 5, 1943, the *SS-Sonderbataillon* was deployed at the front for the first time, southwest of Newel, at Dretun on the border with Russia. In early October 1943, the Red Army had broken through in a previously quiet sector of a *Luftwaffe-Feld-Division* east of Newel, at the juncture between *Heeresgruppe Nord* and *Mitte* and had occupied the transport hub of Newel. *Kampfgruppen* were rapidly pulled together, intended to stop the enemy. After heavy fighting, in early November 1943, more troop reinforcements including *SS-Sonderbataillon "Dirlewanger"* were sent to the front.

This front deployment ended in mid-February 1944. Between April 16 to May 12, 1944, the unit was used for *Unternehmen Frühlingsfest*. After this, the unit was expanded into a *Regiment*, which had been ordered since August 1943, by commandeering hundreds of so-called professional criminals and asocial types from the concentration camps.

SS-Sonderregiment "Dirlewanger"

On August 10, 1943, the *SS-FHA* announced:

"I.) On the orders of the Reichsführer-SS, SS-Sonderkommando 'Dirlewanger' is to be expanded to Regiment strength.

II.) Provision of personnel:
*1. Only convicts from the KL [***Konzentrationslager: concentration camps]** *are to be assigned as personnel.*
2. The prisoners are to be provided with clothing and equipment, as per V. Bl. [Verordnungsblatt: written regulation] of W-SS No. 16 of September 1, 1941 para. 348 by the delivering KL. Any lacking clothing and equipment is to be provided by SS-FHA, Amt [Dept.] IV.

III.) Provision of materiel:
1. Weapons, equipment, vehicles and horses are to be provided from captured supplies.
2. KSTN [Kriegsstärkenachweisung: war strength record] and KAN [Kriegsausrustungsnachweisung: war equipment record] and regulations assigned without request by SS-FHA, SS-FHA, Amt II, Org/StAN [Organisationsplan/Stärke- und Ausrüstungsnachweisung: Table of Personnel Strength and Equipment] and/or by regulations and training departments.

IV.) Missing Feldpost numbers allocated on request by the SS-FHA, SS-FHA, Amt II, Abt. I C/Fp.

V.) Responsible for implementation of paragraph I.) is Kdr. of SS-Sonderkommando 'Dirlewanger.' Execution to be reported to SS-FHA, Amt II, Abt. Org."

This order already said a great deal about the ongoing situation: 500 concentration camp inmates most of them former Kapos were to, using captured weapons, make up for German losses at the front. On February 8, 1944, still designated as a *Bataillon*, the unit had:

Führer	***Unterführer***	***Männer***	**Total**
6	44	209 (Gr)/201 (for.)	460
1.3%	9.6%	89.1%	100%

In mid-June 1944, the former concentration camp inmates reached the Usda area (30km east of Stolpce) and there formed mainly the *II. Bataillon* of what was now *SS-Sonderregiment "Dirlewanger."* On June 30, 1944, *SS-Standartenführer* Dirlewanger reported a strength of:

Führer	***Unterführer***	***Männer***	**Total**
17	87	867	971
1.75%	8.96%	89.29%	100%

The poacher Georg Höfer was drafted into SS-Sonderkommando "Dirlewanger."

III

ᛋᛋ-Soldbuch

zugleich Personalausweis

Nr. 53

für

den .... (Dienstgrad)

ab .... (Datum) .... (neuer Dienstgrad)

ab ....

ab ....

Georg Höfer (Vor- und Zuname)

Beschriftung und Nummer der Erkennungsmarke – 9 – Wachkp./ᛋᛋ-Gren. Ers. Btl. Ost

Blutgruppe ....

Gasmaskengröße ....

Wehrnummer ....

ᛋᛋ-Vordruckverlag W. F. Mayr, Miesbach 15277

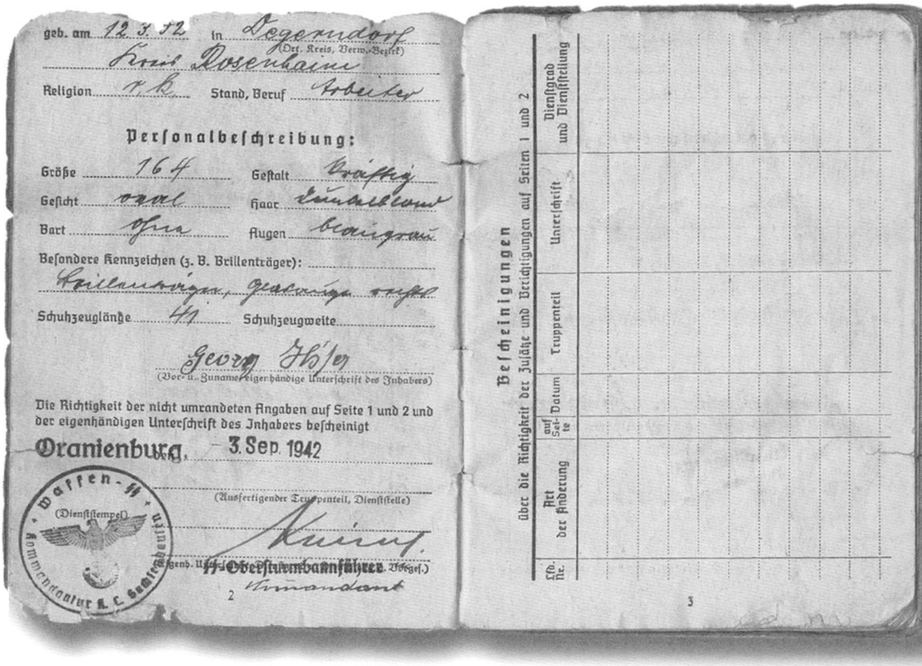

geb. am 12. 3. 12 in Degerndorf (Ort, Kreis, Verw.-Bezirk) Kreis Rosenheim

Religion r. k. Stand, Beruf Arbeiter

Personalbeschreibung:

Größe 164 Gestalt kräftig

Gesicht oval Haar dunkelblond

Bart ohne Augen blaugrau

Besondere Kennzeichen (z. B. Brillenträger):

Schuhzeuglänge 41 Schuhzeugweite

Georg Höfer (Vor- u. Zuname, eigenhändige Unterschrift des Inhabers)

Die Richtigkeit der nicht umrandeten Angaben auf Seite 1 und 2 und der eigenhändigen Unterschrift des Inhabers bescheinigt

Oranienburg, 3. Sep. 1942

(Ausfertigender Truppenteil, Dienststelle)

(Dienststempel) Waffen-SS Kommandantur K. L. Sachsenhausen

SS-Obersturmbannführer Kommandant

2

Bescheinigungen

über die Richtigkeit der Zusätze und Berichtigungen auf Seiten 1 und 2

Lfd. Nr.	Art der Änderung	auf Seite	Datum	Truppenteil	Unterschrift	Dienstgrad und Dienststellung

3

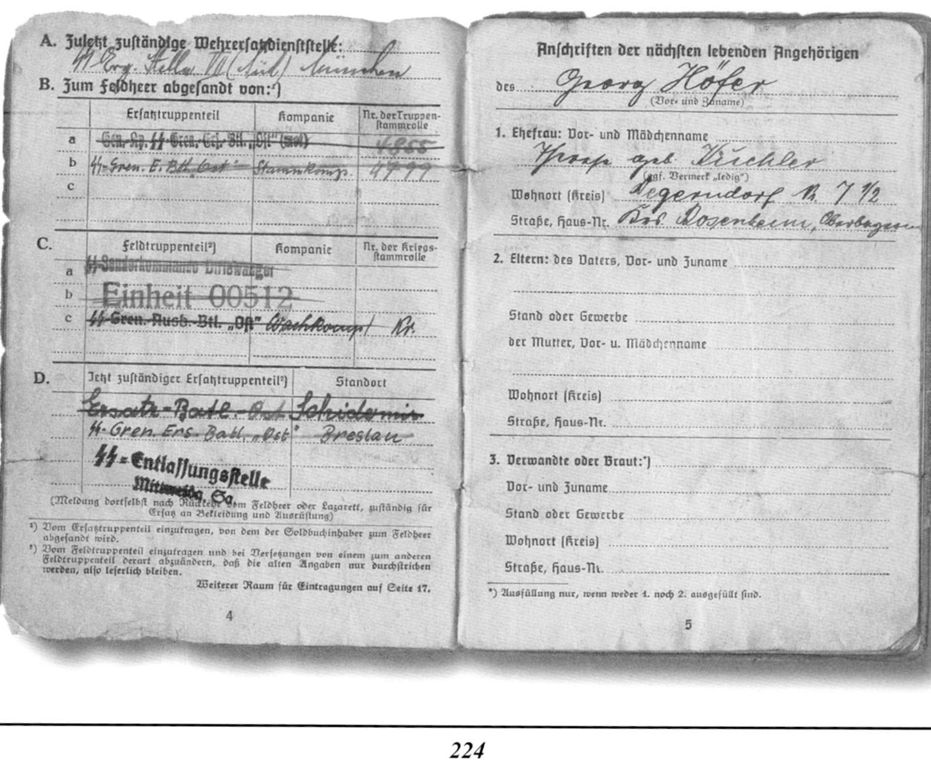

A. Zuletzt zuständige Wehrersatzdienststelle: SS-Erg.-Stelle VII (Süd) München

B. Zum Feldheer abgesandt von:[1])

	Ersatztruppenteil	Kompanie	Nr. der Truppenstammrolle
a	~~Gen.-Kp. SS-Gren.-Ers.-Btl. „Ost" (mot)~~		~~4855~~
b	SS-Gren. E. Btl. „Ost"	Stammkomp.	4799
c			

C.

	Feldtruppenteil[2])	Kompanie	Nr. der Kriegsstammrolle
a	~~SS-Sonderkommando Dirlewanger~~		
b	~~Einheit 00512~~		
c	~~SS-Gren.-Ausb.-Btl. „Ost"~~	~~Wachkomp.~~	Kr.

D.

Jetzt zuständiger Ersatztruppenteil[2])	Standort
~~Ersatz-Batl. Ost~~	~~Schieratz~~
SS-Gren. Ers.-Batl. „Ost"	Breslau
SS-Entlassungsstelle Mittweida Sa.	

(Meldung dortselbst nach Rückkehr vom Feldheer oder Lazarett, zuständig für Ersatz an Bekleidung und Ausrüstung)

[1]) Vom Ersatztruppenteil einzutragen, von dem der Soldbuchinhaber zum Feldheer abgesandt wird.

[2]) Vom Feldtruppenteil einzutragen und bei Versetzungen von einem zum anderen Feldtruppenteil derart abzuändern, daß die alten Angaben nur durchstrichen werden, also leserlich bleiben.

Weiterer Raum für Eintragungen auf Seite 17.

4

Anschriften der nächsten lebenden Angehörigen

des Georg Höfer (Vor- und Zuname)

1. Ehefrau: Vor- und Mädchenname Josefa geb. Kirchler (ggf. Vermerk „ledig")

Wohnort (Kreis) Degerndorf Nr. 7 1/2

Straße, Haus-Nr. Krs. Rosenheim, Oberbayern

2. Eltern: des Vaters, Vor- und Zuname

Stand oder Gewerbe

der Mutter, Vor- u. Mädchenname

Wohnort (Kreis)

Straße, Haus-Nr.

3. Verwandte oder Braut:*)

Vor- und Zuname

Stand oder Gewerbe

Wohnort (Kreis)

Straße, Haus-Nr.

*) Ausfüllung nur, wenn weder 1. noch 2. ausgefüllt sind.

5

Already two weeks later, the two *Bataillone* pulled back towards Lida (distance about 250km) in the German retreat from Byelorussia. In early July they were involved in fierce fighting with strong Red Army Infantry forces. Moving by way of Grodno, which was taken by Soviet troops on July 16, 1944, the *SS-Sonderregiment* streamed back to *Ostpreußen* and reached the Olecko-Elk [German: Treuburg-Lyck] region.

On August 1, 1944, the Polish Underground Army (*Armia Krajowa*) uprising broke out in Warsaw on orders of the Polish government-in-exile in London. The Western-oriented politicians feared for their positions of power in a post-war Poland.

Since the existing German forces in Warsaw were not sufficient to put down the uprising, the *SS-FHA* sent additional military units, including the *SS-Sonderregiment Dirlewanger* in a strength of 865 men, to march to the *9. Armee*, in command in Warsaw.

Under command of the leader of *Höhere SS- und Polizeiführers Warthe, SS-Gruppenführer* Reinefarth, *SS-Sonderregiment "Dirlewanger"* was involved in

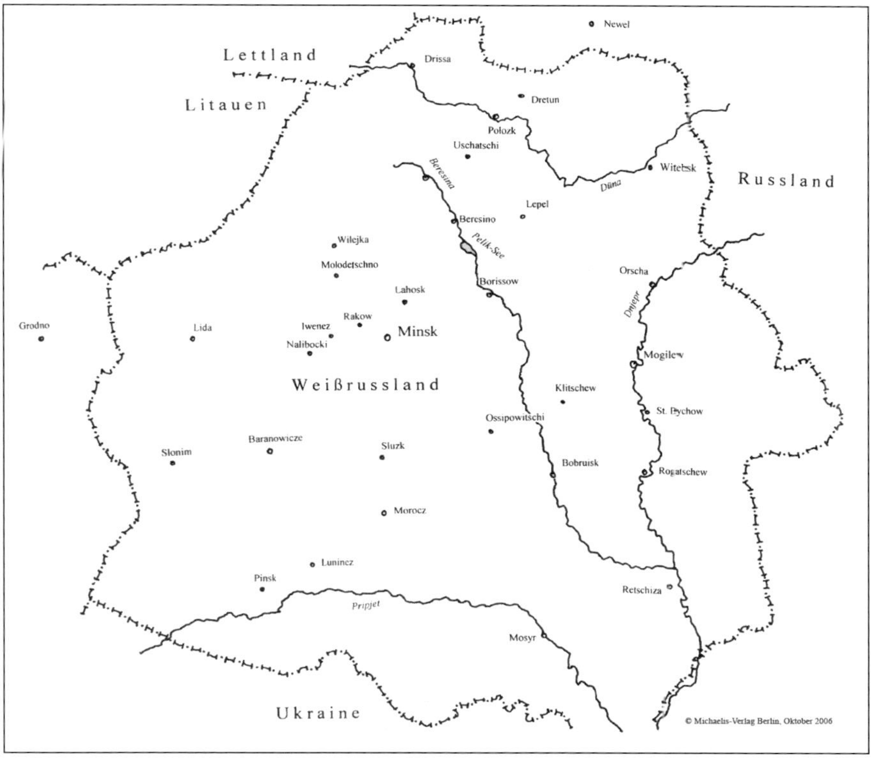

Area of operations of SS-Sonderkommando "Dirlewanger."

Members of the Kradschützen-Zug of SS-Sonderbataillon "Dirlewanger."

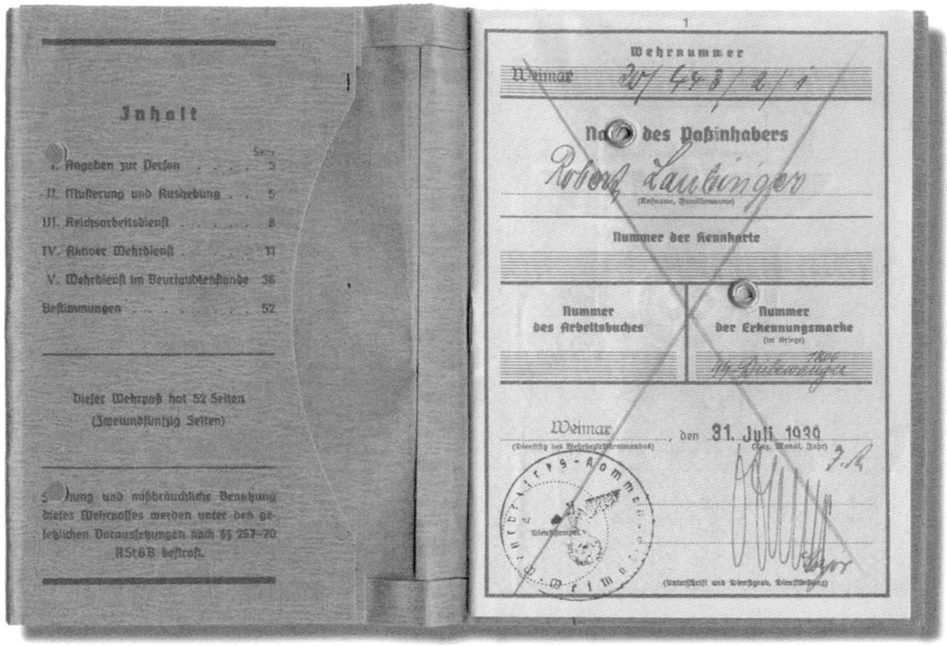
Inhalt

Seite

I. Angaben zur Person 3

II. Musterung und Aushebung . . 5

III. Reichsarbeitsdienst 8

IV. Aktiver Wehrdienst 11

V. Wehrdienst im Beurlaubtenstande 36

Bestimmungen 52

Dieser Wehrpaß hat 52 Seiten
(Zweiundfünfzig Seiten)

Fälschung und mißbräuchliche Benutzung dieses Wehrpasses werden unter den gesetzlichen Voraussetzungen nach §§ 267–70 RStGB bestraft.

1

Wehrnummer

Weimar 20/44/3/2/1

Name des Paßinhabers

Robert Laubinger

(Rufname, Familienname)

Nummer der Kennkarte

Nummer des Arbeitsbuches

Nummer der Erkennungsmarke (im Kriege)

Weimar, den 31. Juli 1939

(Dienststelle des Wehrbezirkskommandos) (Tag, Monat, Jahr)

(Unterschrift und Dienstgrad, Dienststellung)

Robert Laubinger was imprisoned as a gypsy in KL Sachsenhausen. In September 1942 he was drafted into SS-Sonderkommando "Dirlewanger."

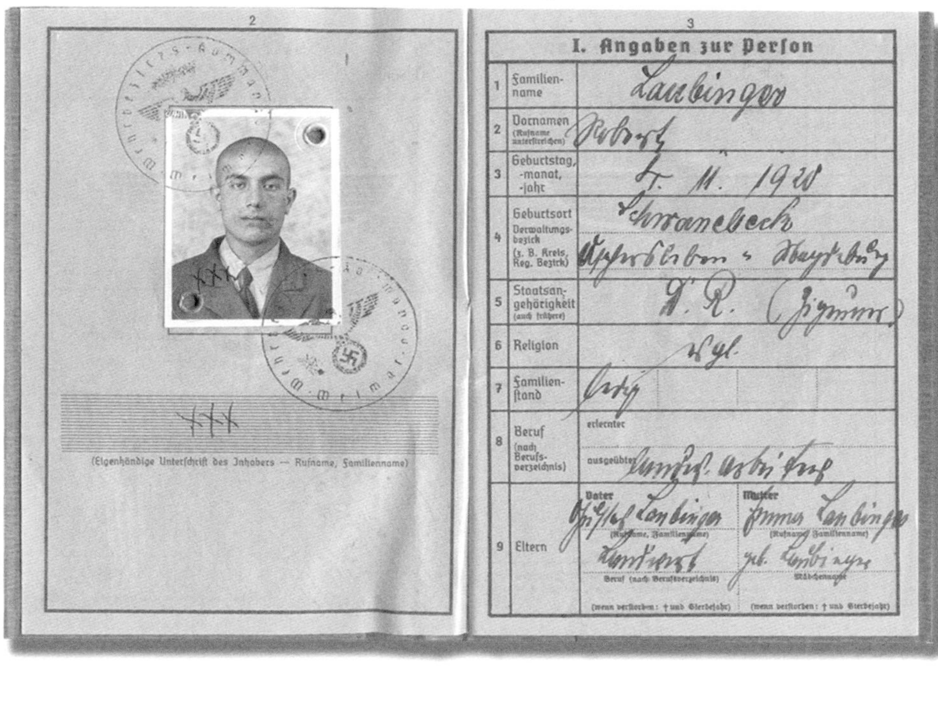
2

xxx

(Eigenhändige Unterschrift des Inhabers — Rufname, Familienname)

3

I. Angaben zur Person		
1	Familienname	Laubinger
2	Vornamen (Rufname unterstreichen)	Robert
3	Geburtstag, -monat, -jahr	7. 11. 1920
4	Geburtsort Verwaltungsbezirk (z. B. Kreis, Reg. Bezirk)	Schwanebeck, Oschersleben – Magdeburg
5	Staatsangehörigkeit (auch frühere)	D. R. (Zigeuner)
6	Religion	evgl.
7	Familienstand	ledig
8	Beruf (nach Berufsverzeichnis)	erlernter: — ausgeübter: Landwirtsch. Arbeiter
9	Eltern	Vater: Gustav Laubinger (Rufname, Familienname), Landwirt (Beruf (nach Berufsverzeichnis)); Mutter: Emma Laubinger (Rufname, Familienname), geb. Laubinger (Mädchenname)

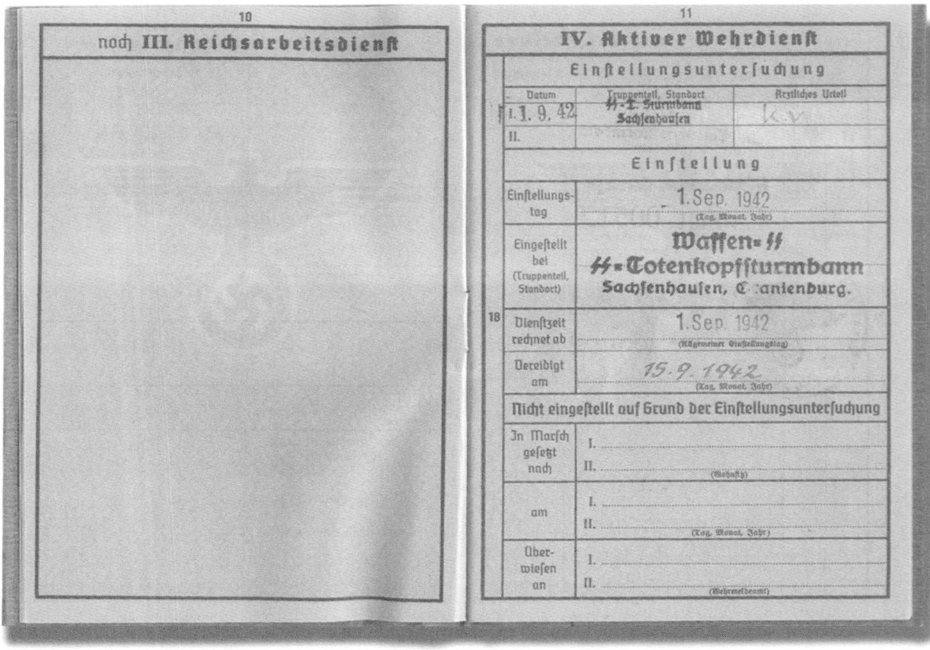

10

noch III. Reichsarbeitsdienst

11

IV. Aktiver Wehrdienst

Einstellungsuntersuchung

	Datum	Truppenteil, Standort	Ärztliches Urteil
I.	1. 9. 42	SS-T. Sturmbann Sachsenhausen	k.v.
II.			

Einstellung

Einstellungstag	1. Sep. 1942 (Tag, Monat, Jahr)
Eingestellt bei (Truppenteil, Standort)	Waffen-SS SS-Totenkopfsturmbann Sachsenhausen, Oranienburg.
Dienstzeit rechnet ab	1. Sep. 1942 (Allgemeiner Einstellungstag)
Vereidigt am	15. 9. 1942 (Tag, Monat, Jahr)

18

Nicht eingestellt auf Grund der Einstellungsuntersuchung

In Marsch gesetzt nach	I. / II. (Wohnort)
am	I. / II. (Tag, Monat, Jahr)
Überwiesen an	I. / II. (Wehrmeldeamt)

On January 14, 1943, Laubinger was killed in Unternehmen Franz.

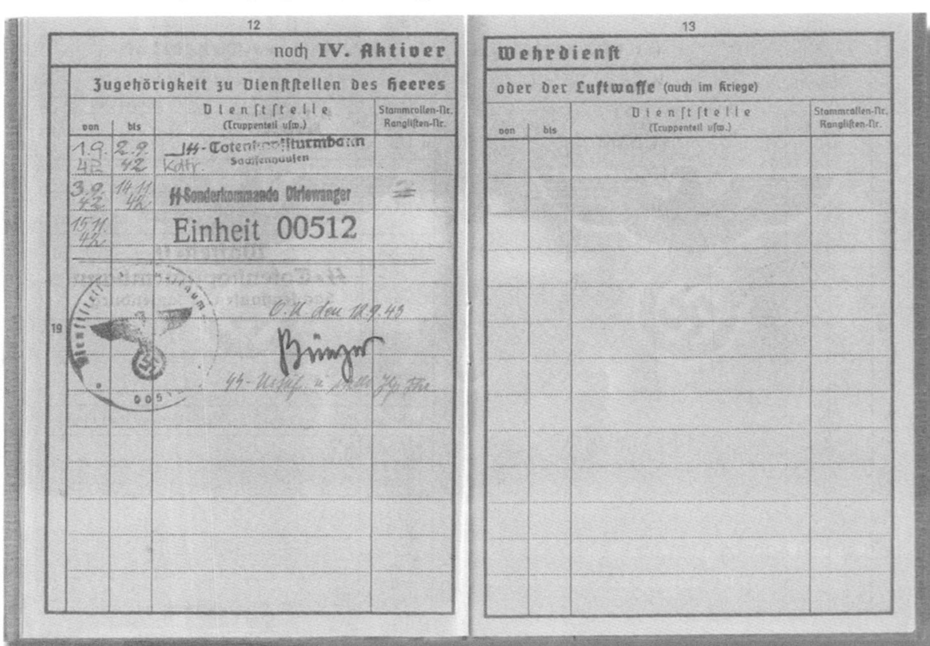

12

noch IV. Aktiver

13

Wehrdienst

Zugehörigkeit zu Dienststellen des Heeres oder der Luftwaffe (auch im Kriege)

von	bis	Dienststelle (Truppenteil usw.)	Stammrollen-Nr. Ranglisten-Nr.
1.9. 42	2.9. 42	SS-Totenkopfsturmbann Sachsenhausen Kdtr.	
3.9. 42	14.11. 42	SS-Sonderkommando Dirlewanger	=
15.11. 42		Einheit 00512	

O.U. den 18.9.43

Bünger

SS-Ustuf. u. [illegible]

19

all major operations to quell the revolt. Their first engagement started August 5-11, 1944, pushing from the west through the city center, eastwards to the Vistula. This operation split the uprising area into northern and southern encircled pockets. Reinforced by prisoners from a number of *Wehrmacht* penal institutions, the German forces overpowered the northern pocket in the Warsaw old town between August 19-26, 1944. A former member recalls:

> *"I was a Luftwaffe soldier and landed, after I had let myself get into some debts, in the Wehrmacht Anklam prison. In August 1944, I and some others joined SS-Sonderregiment 'Dirlewanger' and was used in the house-to-house fighting in Warsaw. There I saw the collar patches on their tunics: two crossed rifles on a Stielhandgranate [stick grenade]. The things I heard after I asked what these meant, were of the worst possible sort. Dirlewanger was a pig; later, in Slovakia he had wooden bunkers built, and anyone who did not carry out his orders had to stand in them for hours. Actually, I only fought for the SS men!"*

Fighting followed from September 3-10, 1944, to the south of the so-called Vistula district and from September 11-23, 1944, in the Mokotow district. On September 20, 1944, the *Regiment* was reinforced with 1,500 *SS* and *Polizei* prisoners from the Gdansk Matzkau prison camp, and deployed between September 29 to October 2, 1944, in the Zoliborzn district. The *Wehrmachtbericht* reported the next day:

> *"The insurgency in Warsaw has collapsed. After weeks of fighting that led to the almost total destruction of the city, the remnants of the insurgents, abandoned by all sides, have ended their resistance and capitulated."*

A few days after the end of the Warsaw Uprising, the *SS-Sonderregiment* was ordered to Slovakia to take part in the crackdown on the national uprising there. There was a coup attempt at the end of August 1944 in Slovakia, which had been independent since March 1939. The military leadership, in an accord with the Czech government-in-exile in London and the left-wing Slovak National Council, intended to topple the pro-German President Dr. Tiso and take power.

Some 4,500 partisans launched attacks and bombings; ethnic German villages were among those attacked and their inhabitants were shot. Since Dr. Tiso had little support in the Slovak Army, he asked Hitler to send German troops. By the end of September 1944, *SS-Obergruppenführer* Hoefle, who had been mandated to suppress the uprising, was able to provide around 11,000 men to launch an offensive on October 1, 1944. Since the Slovak Army's attitude to the German mission was unclear, the crackdown on the uprising had been put off. On October 5, 1944, Himmler approved more troop reinforcements, including the delivery of *SS-Sonderregiment*s *"Dirlewanger."*

Ten days later, the units, transported by rail, arrived in Rosenberg and replaced *SS-Kampfgruppe Schäfer*, which was sent back to the *18. SS-Freiwilligen-Panzer-Grenadier-Division "Horst Wessel"* in southeastern Slovkia. The French *SS* volunteers had seen its first operation on the *Ostront* in this formation's sector, in August 1944.

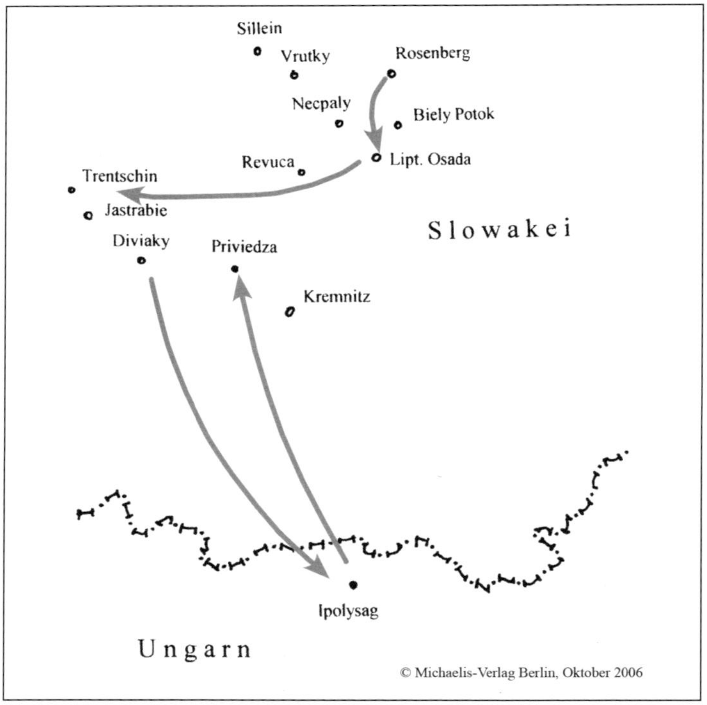

The offensive began against the insurgents on October 18, 1944. *SS-Sonderregiment "Dirlewanger"* was deployed on the northern front between Biely Potok and Necpaly. In heavy fighting, the units were able to reach the Liptovska Osada region. On October 26, 1944, the so-called 1st Czechoslovak Army began to disintegrate. The next day, Slovak Commander Viest ordered his troops to abandon regular resistance and shift to guerrilla warfare. The *Wehrmacht Oberkommando* announced on November 8, 1944: *"The organized insurgency in Slovakia has collapsed and been shattered."*

After this operation, *SS-Sonderregiment "Dirlewanger"* was transferred to Revuca to be reinforced to *Brigade* strength. In contrast to what it did in Warsaw, the *Regiment* took no special role in Slovakia. This was partly because it was weakened in the previous heavy fighting in the Polish capital, as well as due to the composition of the troops.

SS-Sturmbrigade "Dirlewanger"

After some 500 inmates (so-called professional criminals and asocial types) were drafted from the various *KL* to the *SS-Sonderregiment* at the beginning of 1944, there was a second round of drafts in the autumn of 1944. This time, the *Kl Kommandanten* were to pick political prisoners. A total of 1,910 prisoners were supplied, by way of the *Ersatzkompanie,* by mid-November 1944 to *SS-Sturmbrigade "Dirlewanger,"* as the special unit had been reclassified. Walter Christensen entered the *SS-Sturmbrigade* as a prisoner of *KL* Neuengamme:

> *"[One day] I was called and had to come to the office. Two or three tables had been built there, behind which SS men were sitting. They looked at us: how big, what hair color, etc. and then we had to go to the infirmary to check our fitness for combat. Then we took off our prisoner jackets and put on SS tunics. We were photographed and because not all the photos worked, that was all repeated over again all night. The next day, they pulled us together and gave us some perks, and even called us comrades. In the SS camp, we could buy anything we wanted: Beer, cigarettes, etc. We were then dressed, so most of the SS had to give up their second uniforms for us. After we had been taken care of in the SS canteen I must say that we got a decent meal for the first time in Bergedorf, they put us on the train to Berlin in the evening and from there to Krakow.*
>
> *We arrived to a cloister in Fischergasse, and were soon in touch with the nuns. We gave them bread and they brought us fruit in return.*
>
> *From Krakow we went to Rosenberg and Diviaky in Slovakia. We got our quarters in an empty factory, then the Bataillonskommandeur came to us, and told us that he was glad I heard this for the first time that we had enlisted voluntarily."*

In late November 1944, the *SS-Sturmbrigade*, with:

Brigadestab
SS-Sturm-Regiment 1 (I. – III. Bataillon)
SS-Sturm-Regiment 2 (I. – III. Bataillon)
SS-Artillerie-Abteilung
SS-Nachrichten-Kompanie
SS-Pionier-Kompanie
SS-Sanitäts-Kompanie
SS-Feldersatz-Bataillon
SS-Versorgungstruppen
SS-Veterinär-Kompanie

Dr. Oskar Dirlewanger

was placed under command of the German *Befehlshaber* in Slovakia and moved to the Trencin-Jastrabie area. As Soviet troops were advancing on the strategically important Ipolyság, by way of Balassagyarmat on December 9, 1944, the German *Befehlshaber* was ordered to use his forces to secure the narrow passage at Ipolyság. Although *SS-Oberführer* Dirlewanger pointed out that most of his *Brigade* consisted of former political prisoners, the newly formed *SS-Sturmregiment 2* was deployed in the *HKL* on December 12, 1944. This led to a fiasco: after some 600 *SS-Sturmbrigade "Dirlewanger"* members defected to the Red Army, it was able to push through the German front without any significant fighting.

Because the formation had essentially broken down, the troops were initially assembled at Prividza. However, since the Red Army had already reached the Oder by the end of January 1945, it was soon transferred to *9. Armee (Heeresgruppe Weichsel*) on February 2, 1945.

The *Brigade* reached Guben by rail by February 12, 1945, and was placed under command of *Divisionsstab z.b.V. Matterstock* of the *XXXX. Panzer-Korps*. The *OKW* intended to build a defensive line along the Bober and destroy the enemy forces that had already crossed the river. Along with elements of *25. Panzer-Grenadier-Division, SS-Sturmbrigade* elements were also in the fighting around Naumburg. The *KTB OKW* reported on February 16, 1945: *"The enemy was rebuffed at Naumburg. The Brigade 'Dirlewanger' [is] in the fighting at Naumburg."*

At the same time, other elements of the *SS-Sturmbrigade* were able to retake Sommerfeld. The *KTB* reported: *"Sommerfeld was won back by Gruppe 'Dirlewanger.'"*

A few days later, the *XXXX. Panzer-Korps* retreated over the Neisse and tried to occupy new positions there. Already by February 22-23, 1945, there was street fighting in Guben and Forst – the Red Army intended to establish bridgeheads here for their operation against Berlin. When the fighting abated, *SS-Sturmbrigade "Dirlewanger"* was raised to a *Division*.

36. Waffen-Grenadier-Division der SS

Hitler had ordered the expansion of the *Brigade* to an *Infanterie-Division 45* as early as February 14, 1945, with reinforcements from various *Heer* units. At *SS-Truppenübungsplatz* Kurmark (about 25km west of Guben), the formation was to be structured as follows:

Divisionsstab
Waffen-Grenadier-Regiment der SS 72 (I. – II. Bataillon)
Waffen-Grenadier-Regiment der SS 73 (I. – II. Bataillon)
Grenadier-Regiment 1243 (Heer)

SS-Artillerie-Abteilung 36
SS-Nachrichtentruppe 36
SS-Feldersatz-Bataillon 36
Heeres-Panzerjäger-Abteilung 681
    2 Kompanien (each 8 *Pak* 8.8cm *mot. Z.* [*motorisiert Zug*: motorized platoon])
Panzer-Abteilung 1 (Stahnsdorf)[55]
    2 Kompanien (each 14 *Sturmgeschütze*)
Heeres-Pionier-Brigade 687 (Heer)

In fact, the formation was given no training as a unit at *SS-Truppenübungsplatz* Kurmark, since the great majority of *SS-Sturmbrigade "Dirlewanger"* remained in positions on the Neisse. Instead, the *Truppenübungsplatz* served primarily as an assembly point for the commandeerd *Heer* units, as well as, inter alia, for about 400 new *SS-Bewährungsschützen* [probationary Privates] from Duplowitz-Bohemia.

On March 17, 1945, units of the *35. SS-Polizei-Grenadier-Division* took over the Guben positions of the troops, still designated as an *SS-Sturmbrigade*; they in turn, replaced the *72. Infanterie-Division* between Horno and Forst. There they were first used to extend the *Panzersperren* [anti-tank obstacles] and placed under command of *V. Armee-Korps (4 Panzer-Armee)*. Since the expected *Heer* units did not arrive, except for *Heeres-Pionier-Brigade 687*, the unit was only led in the *Korps* as a *Kampfgruppe/36. Waffen-Grenadier-Division der SS*.

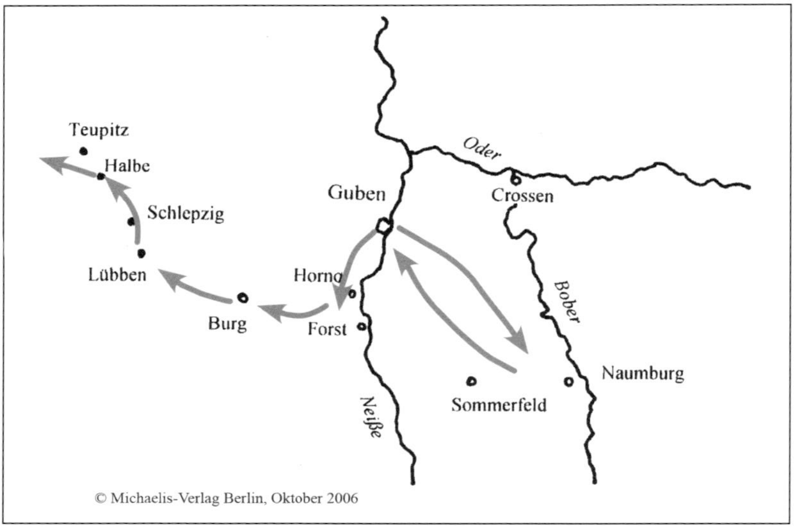

[55] An *ID 45* had no *Panzer-Abteilung*. Since this formation was equipped with *Sturmgeschützen*, it was, like *Heeres-Panzerjäger-Abteilung 681*, fitted out like a *Panzerjäger-Abteilung 45*.

On April 19, 1945, the Red Army launched an offensive along the front in this sector and took some 1,000 soldiers from the *Kampfgruppe* as well as the *342. Infanterie-Division* prisoner in the fighting at Forst.

When the enemy succeeded in encircling the *9. Armee* in the Guben-Mülrose-Fürstenwalde-Königswusterhausen-Lübben area two days later, *Kampfgruppe/36. Waffen-Grenadier-Division der SS* – except for the *II. /Waffen-Grenadier-Regiment der SS 73*, under the command of *35. SS-Polizei-Grenadier-Division* – marched towards Burg on April 24, 1945, without encountering any fighting. From there, by way of Lübben, the men reached Schlepzig at dawn on April 26, 1945. With no further involvement in combat, the troops began to disband.

The breakout of the whatever remained of *9. Armee* from the Halbe pocket on April 28, 1945, led to infernal scenes. Elements of the *Kampfgruppe*, joined up with *Heer* formations and countless civilians, attempted to get through the Baruther forest at Dobbrikow, to reach the *12. Armee*. Since any further fighting was senseless, they attempted to cross the Elbe. Some did this at Tangermünde and others by themselves. The widow of a *Bewährungsschütze* recalls:

> *"In 1940, my husband was drafted, as a convicted poacher, into SS-Sonderkommando 'Dirlewanger' and by 1945 even reached the rank of SS-Oberscharführer. If I remember correctly, he'd already gotten home in early May 1945 – he was never a prisoner of war!"*

While *SS-Sonderkommando "Dirlewanger"* might have been relatively useful in rear area deployments in Byelorussia, the *Brigade* and later *Division* showed itself to be nothing more than a makeshift, improvised unit in front line deployment. It was used in Warsaw, leading to enormous losses, which were tacitly accepted by the German leadership, as the men mostly had no civil rights anyway.

Kommandeure:
07/40 – 01/45 *SS-Oberführer* Dirlewanger
02/45 – 04/45 *SS-Brigadeführer* Schmedes

Feldpost numbers:

Divisionsstab	00 512
Ersatz-Kompanie	21 545
Waffen-Grenadier-Regiment der SS 72	02 610
I. Bataillon	05 322
II. Bataillon	06 260
III. Bataillon	04 677
Waffen-Grenadier-Regiment der SS 73	03 426
I. Bataillon	07 138
II. Bataillon	05 935
III. Bataillon	04 242

38. SS-Grenadier-Division "Nibelungen"

On March 25, 1945, Hitler ordered the *Ersatzheer* [Reserve Army] to the front lines. Two days later he ordered the formation of three new *Divisionen* for the Western and other front from these troops. Among those ordered to be organized was the ***SS-Division Junker-Schule***, [Officer Candidate School] led by the *Kommandeur* of *SS-Junkerschule* Tölz, *SS-Obersturmbannführer* Schulze, in the area of Freiburg-Feldberg-Todtnau.

The 18th *Kriegs-Junker-Lehrgang* [war-time officer training course] class, including the teaching staff, formed the *Führerkorps*, while the *Unterführerkorps* was formed from the 4th (Germanic) preparatory course class. The lower ranks were to be members of the class of 1928, who came from the Jagdstzell-Württemberg *RAD [Reichsarbeitsdienst*: Reich Labor Service], two *Wehrmacht Ersatz-Bataillonen* and the Adolf Hitler schools in Sonthofen and Jihlava.

Organized as an *Infanterie-Division 1945* in the truncated *I.* structure (authorized strength: 8,800 men), the unit was intended to comprise:

Divisionsstab
SS-Grenadier-Regiment 1 (later *95*) *(I. – III. Bataillon)*
SS-Grenadier-Regiment 2 (later *96*) *(I. – III. Bataillon)*
SS-Grenadier-Regiment 3 (later *97*) *(I. – III. Bataillon)*
SS-Panzerjäger-Abteilung 38
SS Artillery Regiment 38
SS-Pionier-Bataillon 38
SS-Nachrichtentruppe 38

On April 9, 1945, the formation, now designated as ***38. SS-Grenadier-Division "Nibelungen,"*** consisted of:

2 *stark*
3 *mittelstark*
1 *durchschnittlich* [average]
1 *schwach* [weak]
Grenadier-Bataillonen with a combat strength of 2,875 men.

While it was at least possible to organize the troops, in terms of personnel, from the available recruits, the *Division* still had to be fitted out with uniforms, weapons and equipment. *SS-Pionier-Bataillon 38* was to be organized in Freudenstadt (Schwarzwald [Black Forest]). *SS-Panzerjäger-Abteilung 38* was pulled together starting April 16, 1945, at Weiden (Oberpfalz), from the remnants of the shattered *SS-Panzerjäger-Abteilung 6* and the newly available *Jagdpanzer Hetzer.* The *SS-Artillerie-Lehr-Regiment* [Training Regiment] in Beneschau formed the *I.* and

III. Abteilung of *SS-Artillerie-Regiment 38*. The *II. Abteilung* was pulled together from the just-organized *III. /SS-Artillerie-Regiment 4*.

When the French and American forces went on the offensive at the Upper Rhine, the Germans started their retreat between the Schwarzwald and Upper Danube on April 10, 1945. As the Allied forces approached the *38. SS-Grenadier-Division* formation area, the *Divisionskommando* was ordered on April 17, 1945, to complete the process at *Truppenübungsplatz* Grafenwöhrg. The first units arrived at Dachau by rail two days later, to organize outfitting and especially getting uniforms there. Up to this point, most recruits were still wearing their *HJ [Hitler Jugend*: Hitler Youth] or *RAD* uniforms.

Since U.S. troops had already reached the Nuremberg area, the *Division* was not sent to Grafenwöhr, but rather – without any unit training – sent to the *XIII. SS-Armee-Korps*. Here, by April 16, 1945, *SS-Panzerjäger-Abteilung 38* and the two *Artillerie-Abteilungen* from Beneschau were under the command of the *17. SS-Panzergrenadier-Division "Götz von Berlichingen"* near Neumarkt.

The first *Division Grenadiere* reached the region south of the Danube on April 21, 1945, and occupied a prepared rear position for the retreating *17. SS-Panzergrenadier-Division* in the Bad Abbach-Kelheim-Neustadt-Vohburg sector. Here, the *38. SS-Grenadier-Division* was sent the only still-operational *Abteilung* of *Waffen-Artillerie-Regiment der SS 26 (ungarische Nr. 2)* and the Polizei-Bataillon Siegling – made up of German *Rahmenpersonal* from *30. Waffen-Grenadier-Division der SS (weißruthenische Nr. 1)*. *SS-Artillerie-Regiment 38* had thus reached its authorized strength, with three *leichte* and one *schwere Abteilungen*. The three *Grenadier-Regimenter* also had eight *Bataillone*.

On April 25, 1945, the *38. SS-Grenadier-Division* was placed under command of *17. SS-Panzergrenadier-Division*. The young men, who had just been drafted barely four weeks earlier, now faced combat. As the enemy rapidly succeeded in establishing bridgeheads over the Danube, the German forces were ordered to retreat over the Isar on April 28, 1945. Since the *17. SS-Panzergrenadier-Division* had moved away towards Augsburg, *SS-Gruppenführer* Lammerding took over leadership of the *38. SS-Grenadier-Division* in the Freising-Moosburg-Landshut line.

Here, on April 29, 1945, the *Division* was reinforced by *SS-Kampfgruppe* Hersche, formed from the French *SS-Grenadier-Ausbildungs- und Ersatz-Bataillon*. This gave three *Bataillone* to each of the three *Grenadier-Regimenter*. The *38. SS-Grenadier-Division "Nibelungen"* occupied positions at Wasserburg on May 2, 1945, and then marched on towards the Chiemsee. Constantly harassed by U.S. troops, the German troops retreated towards the southeast.

On May 8, 1945, the units had reached Oberwössen, near Reit im Winkel, where they surrendered to the American forces. Thus ended the only a few-days-long existence of the *38. SS-Grenadier-Division*. Most of the men got their only military training in the *Hitler Jugend* or the *RAD* and were far from fit for duty in

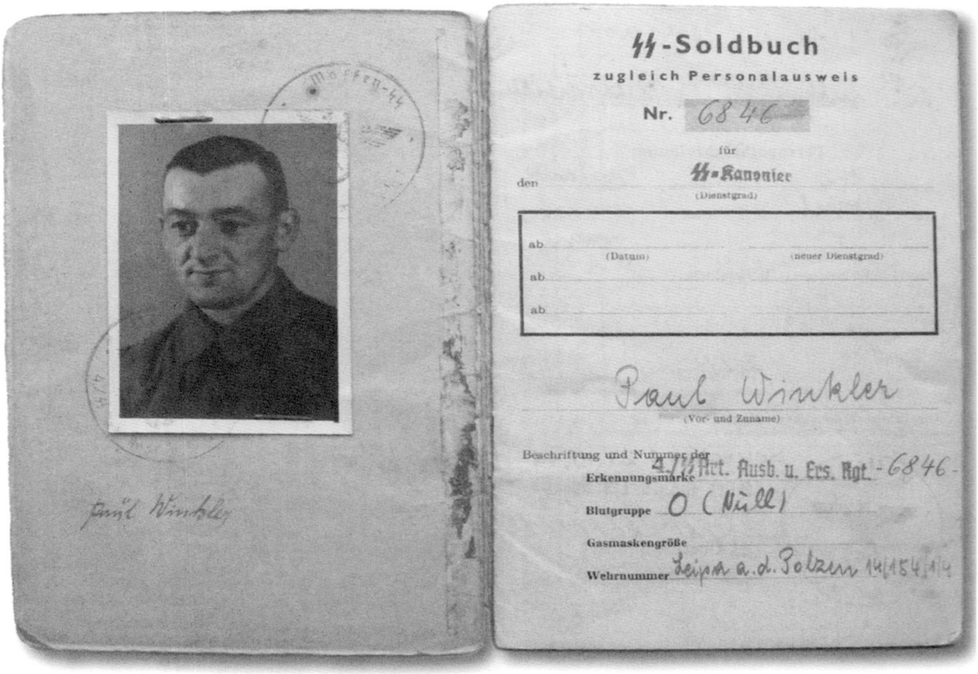
Paul Winkler

ϟϟ-Soldbuch
zugleich Personalausweis
Nr. 6846
für
den ϟϟ-Kanonier
(Dienstgrad)

ab (Datum) (neuer Dienstgrad)
ab
ab

Paul Winkler
(Vor- und Zuname)

Beschriftung und Nummer der Erkennungsmarke 4/ϟϟ Art. Ausb. u. Ers. Rgt. -6846-
Blutgruppe O (Null)
Gasmaskengröße
Wehrnummer Leipa a.d. Polzen 14/154/1/4

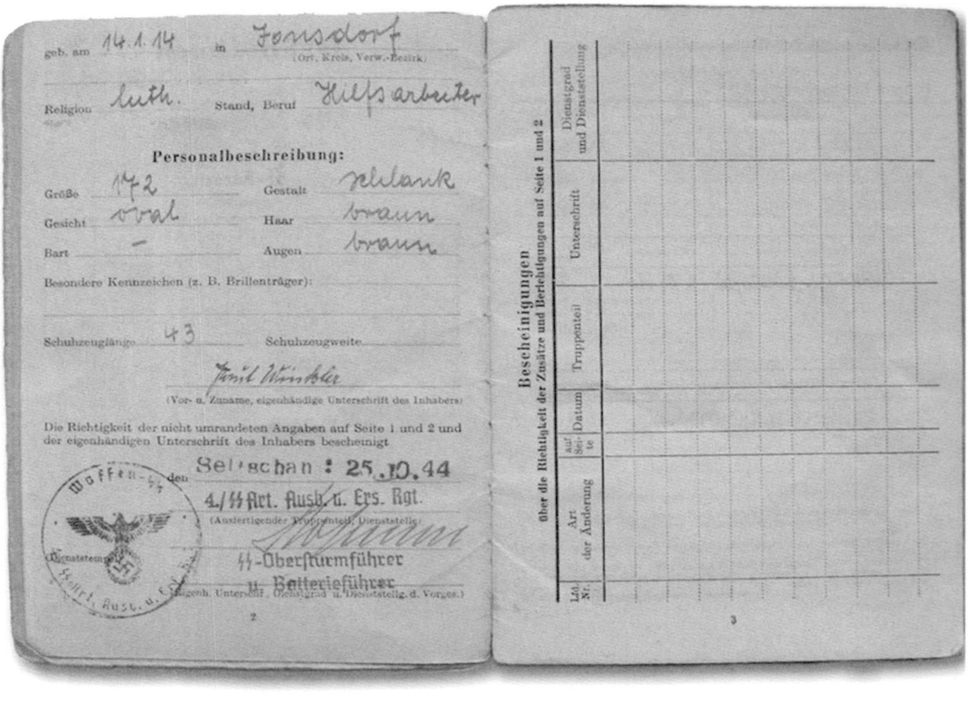
geb. am 14.1.14 in Jonsdorf
(Ort, Kreis, Verw.-Bezirk)
Religion luth. Stand, Beruf Hilfsarbeiter

Personalbeschreibung:

Größe 172 Gestalt schlank
Gesicht oval Haar braun
Bart – Augen braun
Besondere Kennzeichen (z. B. Brillenträger):

Schuhzeuglänge 43 Schuhzeugweite

Paul Winkler
(Vor- u. Zuname, eigenhändige Unterschrift des Inhabers)

Die Richtigkeit der nicht umrandeten Angaben auf Seite 1 und 2 und der eigenhändigen Unterschrift des Inhabers bescheinigt

Selčan, den 25.10.44
4./ϟϟ Art. Ausb. u. Ers. Rgt.
(Ausfertigender Truppenteil, Dienststelle)
ϟϟ-Obersturmführer u. Batterieführer
(Eigenh. Unterschr., Dienstgrad u. Dienststellg. d. Vorges.)
Dienststempel
2

Bescheinigungen
über die Richtigkeit der Zusätze und Berichtigungen auf Seite 1 und 2

Lfd. Nr.	Art der Änderung	auf Seite	Datum	Truppenteil	Unterschrift	Dienstgrad und Dienststellung

3

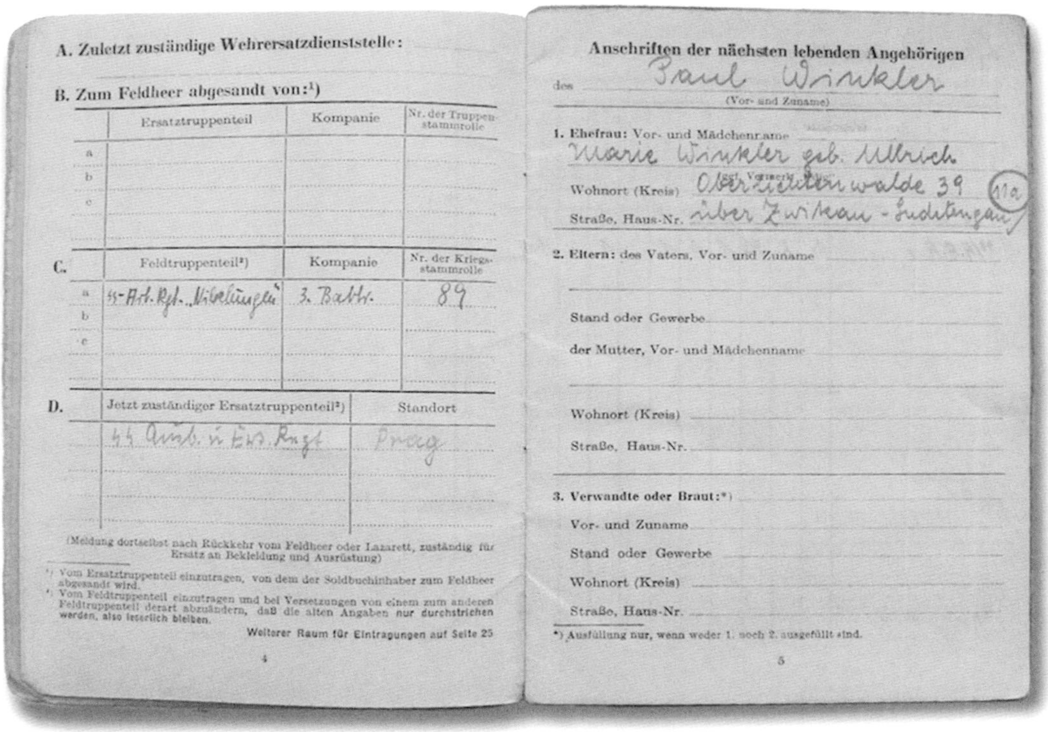
A. Zuletzt zuständige Wehrersatzdienststelle:

B. Zum Feldheer abgesandt von:¹)

	Ersatztruppenteil	Kompanie	Nr. der Truppenstammrolle
a			
b			
c			

C.

	Feldtruppenteil²)	Kompanie	Nr. der Kriegsstammrolle
a	SS-Art. Rgt. Nibelungen	3. Battr.	89
b			
c			

D.

Jetzt zuständiger Ersatztruppenteil²)	Standort
SS Ausb. u. Ers. Rgt.	Prag

(Meldung dortselbst nach Rückkehr vom Feldheer oder Lazarett, zuständig für Ersatz an Bekleidung und Ausrüstung)

¹) Vom Ersatztruppenteil einzutragen, von dem der Soldbuchinhaber zum Feldheer abgesandt wird.
²) Vom Feldtruppenteil einzutragen und bei Versetzungen von einem zum anderen Feldtruppenteil derart abzuändern, daß die alten Angaben nur durchstrichen werden, also leserlich bleiben.

Weiterer Raum für Eintragungen auf Seite 25

4

Anschriften der nächsten lebenden Angehörigen

des Paul Winkler
(Vor- und Zuname)

1. Ehefrau: Vor- und Mädchenname Marie Winkler geb. Ulbrich

Wohnort (Kreis) Oberzeitzenwalde 39

Straße, Haus-Nr. über Zwickau - Sudetengau

2. Eltern: des Vaters, Vor- und Zuname

Stand oder Gewerbe

der Mutter, Vor- und Mädchenname

Wohnort (Kreis)

Straße, Haus-Nr.

3. Verwandte oder Braut:*)

Vor- und Zuname

Stand oder Gewerbe

Wohnort (Kreis)

Straße, Haus-Nr.

*) Ausfüllung nur, wenn weder 1. noch 2. ausgefüllt sind.

5

Paul Winkler was born on April 14, 1914, in Jonsdorf, near Zittau and drafted at Selschan on October 25, 1944, into the SS-Artillerie-Ausbildungs- und Ersatz-Regiment. In mid-April 1945, elements of the Ersatz-Regiment were used to organize SS-Artillerie-Regiment "Nibelungen." Assigned to the 18. Batterie, Winkler took part – in the sector of 17. SS-Panzergrenadier-Division "Götz von Berlichingen" – in the defensive battles against U.S. troops.

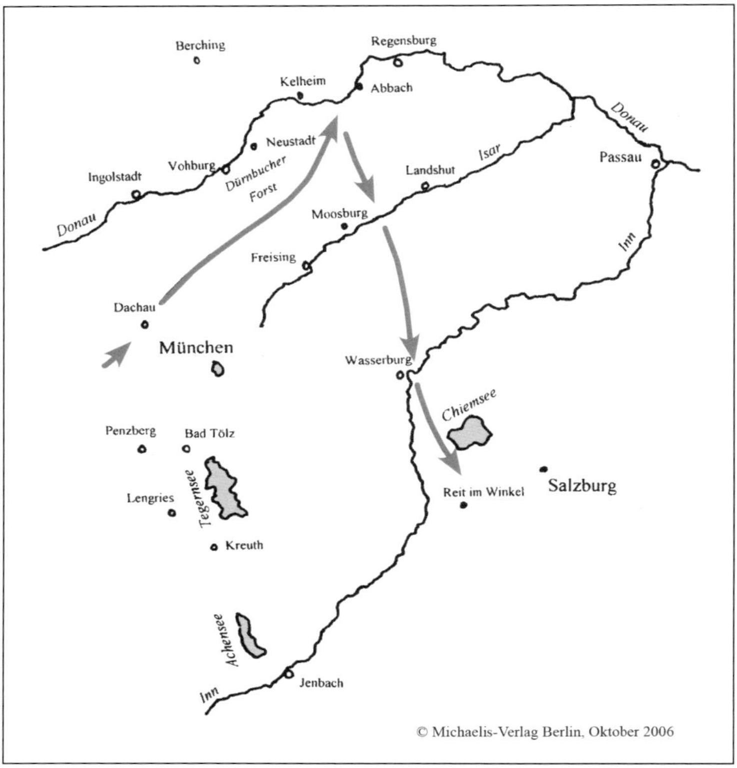

a *Division*. It is interesting that it had full-scale organization, with an *Artillerie-Regiment* as well as a *Panzerjäger-Abteilung*. Since, however, the *Division* was pulled together without any unit training, this was a formation in purely nominal terms only.

Former *SS-Untersturmführer* Netz remembers the situation at the time:

"The members of the current Führerlehrgang [officer training course class] at SS-Junkerschule Tölz, including myself, were informed in March 1945 that they were to form the lower-ranking officers for an SS-Division which was being organized. We were close to completing the course and had passed the final exams – giving me the rank of: SS-Standarten-Oberjunker [graduate officer candidate]. From Tölz, we went to the Schwarzwald. I was quartered at Hinterzarten. After a few days – probably in March 1945 – I was given about forty recruits, 16-18 years old, for training. They had been assigned to the Waffen-SS by the Wehrmacht and were very happy with this shift. The situation in their previous units must have been bad, according to

their descriptions. They liked the tone of things with us better. As I recall, almost all former Hitlerjugend were very enthusiastic. Unfortunately I did not get any Unterführer, whom I would have urgently needed for terrain and weapons training. So I made three former HJ-Führer into Gruppenführer [squad leaders]. This at least made it possible for us to get our rations and maintain the duty roster in a timely way. But I had to deal with the duty myself, as the sole 'activities organizer.' Our Kompanie head was SS-Obersturmführer Miiller, who had already been my Inspektionschef at the Junkerschule. SS-Sturmbannführer Schmidt – who was also from the Junkerschule – was Regimentskommandeur.

At the beginning of April 1945, we took a train to Dachau, where the recruits were outfitted from head to toe, so that they finally felt that they were real Waffen-SS men! It moves me even today, when I think of the enthusiasm and zeal of those young people.

Then we were transported further by rail, towards the northern Danube Bend near Abensberg. During the day, there were constant Jabo [Jagdbomber: fighter bomber] attacks by the Amis [German slang for Americans]. Because our locomotive had been shot up, we were unloaded on the way and had to go on by foot. I was assigned a sector on the right bank of the Danube, where I was supposed to prevent the Americans from crossing the river. I still had no trained, front-experienced Unterführer for a Gruppenführer, nor even a Zugtruppführer. Up until we were taken prisoner, I never saw anyone of that particular species face-to-face, nor saw nor heard anything of schwere Waffen, which could have supported my combat mission.

Under these circumstances, I thought it right to issue some practical orders to my forty 'Hansels,' and they went like this: Avoid any involvement in any contact with the enemy. It was clear that I could not prevent the vastly superior Ami forces from extracting a terrible toll for anything that might annoy them. Unfortunately, the boys, despite my strict instructions to only open fire at my command, were totally undisciplined, and made jokes about shooting at the reconnaissance patrol which had crossed the river. The result: an artillery flyer sighted our position, then a motorized howitzer battery drove onto the opposite bank of the Danube, and the fireworks started under direction from the aircraft. It was astonishing that there was only crop damage, perhaps because of the battery commander only raked his target area line-by-line, which I took advantage of, so that I always directed my young heroes, who were suddenly remarkably obedient again, to where the last hits had kicked up the dirt.

One night (April 27 or 28, 1945), my Zugmelder [platoon messenger] explained to me that he hadn't met a single soldier, at either the Kompanie command post or Bataillion command post. At the same time we had a brush with an American reconnaissance patrol, but it withdrew after the

Erich Netz

Werner Dietsch

Walter Flemming

SS-Junker Günter Adam

Fredo Gensicke

first exchange of gunfire, leaving one dead. After a short consultation with a Junker schoolmate not assigned as a Zugführer, I ordered them to follow the Division, which had apparently moved off. We then marched southwards for two or three days, without encountering the enemy. The boys were slowly getting tired, and to relieve them, I carried a Panzerfaust and the Maschinengewehr along with my service pistol and Maschinenpistole. We never reached the Division. Instead, we were overtaken by an Ami tank in Ergolding on April 30, 1945, so I had to lead the little fellows – still forty of them – into captivity, which I thought was the best solution then and still think so today. So I got them all, I hope intact, back to their mothers. I met one of them later in Nuremberg, where I had been deployed to clear away the rubble. The young man would only address me standing up and with his cap off. I see a bit of respect in that."

Friedrich Bach, sixteen years old at the time, recalls:

"I was born on February 15, 1929, in Alleinstein (Ostpreußen), and in summer 1944, I was 15½ years old and in the 10th grade. Schoolwork, however, had been stopped and we – most of us serving in the HJ – were ordered to dig Panzergräben [anti-tank ditches] south of Wilkomierz. Here, I volunteered to become an officer in the Panzerpioniere [armored engineers]. By mid-October 1944, we were all taken to Angerburg by rail. Together with another Hitlerjugend, I then drove in a moped patrol to an area that had been evacuated, to prevent looting.

On December 14, 1944, our apartment building was bombed and my mother – with me along – was evacuated to Stendal. Here, for a short time, I went back to school (Winkelmann-Gymnasium [academic high school]). After six weeks, all officer candidates – and they were almost all Gymnasium students – were drafted by the Wehrbezirkskommando [military district HQ] and taken to Sonthofen.

At the end of February 1945, we again were getting normal schooling at the Adolf-Hitler-Schule in Sonthofen. Although we were dressed like Adolf-Hitler students, we did not have much close contact with other students. In early April 1945, a Waffen-SS recruiter came to the school and explained how important it was to enlist in the Waffen-SS right now. But only 4 signed up of us about 160 students. But that did not change the fact that we were moved to Tölz shortly after that, and one morning at half past five were dressed in SS uniforms. Classes were stopped and we only did military training. We were all, so far as I can recall, sixteen years old and in Tölz, we were assigned to Panzerjagdgruppen [antitank squads] of 6 to 8 men. As we marched off from Tölz towards Lenggriess, we were organized into the 1./SS-Grenadier-Regiment 95 at the same time. Our Kompanieführer was

SS-Obersturmführer Kniepert, who had been awarded both the EK 2 and the Infanteriesturmabzeichen [Infantry Assault Badge]. We didn't encounter any fighting. Instead, we just marched to Vorderriß. After I had only been on a Spähtrupp patrol just once, we were already released on May 6, 1945, and got seventy Reichsmark severance pay.

I marched back to Lenggriess and from there went on by foot to Adorf in the Vogtland region. I got to Halle by truck and walked on to Köthen. There I stayed with my aunt and collapsed after the grueling march. On June 8, 1945, I took a truck back to meet my mother and little brother in Stenda, where I became an apprentice at a tree nursery."

*Kommandeur*e:
SS-Gruppenführer Lammerding

Feldpost numbers were no longer being allocated.

Appendices

Organizational Structure of an *Infanterie-Division 43*

Authorized strength: 17,193

Divisionsstab 173
3 *Grenadier-Regimenter* (3 *Bataillone* each) 9,179
Artillerie-Regiment 2,536
 I. *Abteilung* [1. – 3. *Batterie* (*leichte Feldhaubitzen* 10.5cm)]
 II. *Abteilung* [4. – 6. *Batterie* (*leichte Feldhaubitzen* 10.5cm)]
 III. *Abteilung* [7. – 9. *Batterie* (*leichte Feldhaubitzen* 10.5cm)]
 IV. *Abteilung* [10. – 12. *Batterie* (*schwere Feldhaubitzen* 15cm)]
Füsilier-Bataillon/Aufklärungs-Abteilung 411
 3 *Füsilier-Kompanien* (one on bicycles)
 1 *schwere Füsilier-Kompanie*
Panzerjäger-Abteilung 555
Pionier-Bataillon 642
 4 *Pionier-Kompanien* (one on bicycles)
Nachrichtentruppe 440
 1 *Kompanie* (*Fernsprecher* [telephone])
 1 *Kompanie* (*Funker* [Radio])
Nachschubführer [Supply Officer] 2,443
 3 *Werkstatt* [Workshop] *-Kompanien*
 1 *Nachschub-Kompanie*
 9 small *Nachschub-Kolonnen* [supply columns]
 3 large *Nachschub-Kolonnen*
Verwaltungsdienste [Administrative Services] 212
 1 *Bäckerei* [Bakery] *-Kompanie*
 1 *Schlächterei* [Butcher] *-Kompanie*
 1 *Verpflegungsamt* [Ration Office]
Sanitäts-Abteilung 368
 2 *Sanitäts-Kompanien*
 1 Kranken*k*raftwagen [Ambulance] *-Kompanie*
Veterinär-Kompanie 234

Organizational Structure of an *Infanterie-Division 44*

Authorized strength: 12,772

Divisionsstab 227
3 *Grenadier-Regimenter* (2 *Bataillone* each) 5,961
Artillerie-Regiment (organized as an ID 43) 2,013
Divisions-Füsilier-Bataillon 708
  3 *Füsilier-Kompanien* (one on bicycles)
  1 *schwere Füsilier-Kompanie*
Panzerjäger-Abteilung 484
  1 *schwere Kompanie* (*mot.Z.*) (12 *Pak* 7.5cm)
  1 *Sturmgeschütz-Batterie* (10 *Geschütze*)
  Flak-Kompanie (12 *Flak* 2cm) (Sf. [*selbstfahrlafette*: self-propelled mount])
Pionier-Bataillon 620
  2 *Pionier-Kompanien* (one on bicycles)
Nachrichtentruppe 379
  1 *Kompanie* (*Fernspreche*)
  1 *Kompanie* (*Funker*)
Feldersatz-Bataillon 925
Versorgungstruppen 1,455
  1 *Kraftfahr* [Motor Vehicle] *-Kompanie*
  1 *Werkstatt-Kompanie*
  1 *Nachschub-Kompanie*
  1 *Fahr-Schwadron* [Driver Squadron]
  1 *Bäckerei-Kompanie*
  1 *Schlächterei-Kompanie*
  1 *Sanitäts-Kompanien*
  1 *Krankenkraftwagen-Kompanie*
  1 *Veterinär-Kompanie*

Organizational Structure of a *Grenadier-Brigade*

Authorized strength: about 6,000

Brigadestab
Grenadier-Regimenter each with 2 *Bataillone*
Panzerjäger-Abteilung
  1. *Kompanie* (*Pak* 7.5cm *mot. Z.*)
  2. *Kompanie* (no *Sturmgeschütze* III)
  3. *Kompanie* (3.7cm *Flak*)
Artillerie-Abteilung with 3 *Batterien*
Aufklärungs-Schwadron
Pionier-Kompanie
Nachrichten-Kompanie
Feldersatz-Kompanie
Sanitäts-Kompanie
Veterinär-Kompanie

Organizational Structure of an *SS-Sturmbrigade n. A.*

Authorized strength: about 2,000

Brigadestab
I. *Bataillon*
  1. – 3. *Kompanie*)
  4. (*schwere*) *Kompanie*
  5. (*Panzerjäger-*) *Kompanie*
II. *Bataillon*
  6. – 8. *Kompanie*)
  9. (*schwere*) *Kompanie*
  10. (*Panzerjäger-*) *Kompanie*
Brigade-Einheiten
  11. (*Infanteriegeschütz-*) *Kompanie*
  12. (*Sturmgeschütz-*) *Batterie*
  13. (2cm *Flak-*) *Batterie*
  14. (8.8cm *Flak-*) *Batterie*

Rank Equivalents

German	**Foreign Nationals**	***Heer***	
SS-Grenadier [SS-Infantry rifleman]	*Waffen-Grenadier*	*Grenadier*	Infantryman
SS-Sturmmann [SS-Stormtrooper, private first class]	*Waffen-Sturmmann*	*Gefreiter*	Acting Corporal or Private
SS-Rottenführer [SS-Corporal]	*Waffen-Rottenführer*	*Obergefreiter*	Corporal
SS-Unterscharführer [Junior Squad Leader/Sergeant]	*Waffen-Unterscharführer*	*Unteroffizier*	Sergeant
SS-Scharführer [SS-Squad Leader/ rank between Sergeant and Corporal]	*Waffen-Scharführer*	*Unterfeldwebel*	Staff Sergeant
SS-Oberscharführer [SS-First Sergeant]	*Waffen-Oberscharführer*	*Feldwebel*	Technical Sergeant
SS-Hauptscharführer [SS-Master Sergeant]	*Waffen-Hauptscharführer*	*Oberfeldwebel*	Master Sergeant
SS-Untersturmführer [SS-Second Lieutenant]	*Waffen-Untersturmführer*	*Leutnant*	Second Lieutenant
SS-Obersturmführer [SS-First Lieutenant]	*Waffen-Obersturmführer*	*Oberleutnant*	First Lieutenant

SS-Hauptsturmführer [SS-Captain]	*Waffen-Hauptsturmführer*	*Hauptmann*	Captain
SS-Sturmbannführer [SS-Major]	*Waffen-Sturmbannführer*	*Major*	Major
SS-Obersturmbannführer [SS-Lieutenant Colonel]	*Waffen-Obersturmbannführer*	*Oberstleutnant*	Lieutenant Colonel
SS-Standartenführer [SS-Colonel]	*Waffen-Standartenführer*	*Oberst*	Colonel
SS-Oberführer [SS-"Senior Colonel"	*Waffen-Oberführer*	No comparable rank	
SS-Brigadeführer [SS-Brigadier General]	*Waffen-Brigadeführer*	*Generalmajor*	Brigadier General
SS-Gruppenführer [SS-Major General]	*Waffen-Gruppenführer*	*Generalleutnant*	Major General
SS-Obergruppenführer [SS-Lieutenant General]	*Waffen-Obergruppenführer*	*General*	Lieutenant General
SS-Oberstgruppenführer [SS-General]	–	*Generaloberst*	Full General

Sources

Bundesarchiv, Berlin: Miscellaneous personnel files.
Bundesarchiv/Militärarchiv, Freiburg: *Heeresgruppe, Armee* file collections.
Bundesarchiv, Koblenz: *Reichsführer-SS* file collection.

Dallin, Alexander: *Deutsche Herrschaft in Russland,* Düsseldorf, 1958.

Friessner, Hans: *Verratene Schlachten*, Hamburg, 1956.

Haupt, Werner: *Heeresgruppe Nord*, Bad Nauheim, 1966.

—: *Heeresgruppe Mitte*, Bad Nauheim, 1968.

—: *Kurland*, Dorheim, 1984.

Kurowski, Franz: *Endkampf um das Reich*, Friedberg, 1987.

Müller, G.: *Die Geschichte der 207. und 281. Infanterie-Division*, Dortmund, 1958.

Manstein, Erich von: *Verlorene*, München, 1979.

Michaelis, Rolf: *Die Waffen-SS – Mythos und Wirklichkeit*, Berlin, 2006.

—: *Belgier in der Waffen-SS*, Berlin, 2010.

—: *Esten in der Waffen-SS*, Berlin, 2000.

—: *Letten in der Ordnungspolizei und Waffen-SS*, Berlin, 2009.

—: *Russen in der Waffen-SS*, Berlin, 2002.

—: *Ukrainer in der Waffen-SS*, Berlin, 2000.

Neulen, Werner: *An deutscher Seite*, Munich, 1985.

Rürup, Reinhard (editor): *Krieg gegen die Sowjetunion 1941-1945*, Berlin, 1991.

Schramm, Percy (editor): *Kriegstagebuch des OKW 1940-1945*, München, 1982.

Stein, Georg: *Geschichte der Waffen-SS*, Düsseldorf, 1967.

Steiner, Felix: *Die Freiwilligen*, Rosenheim, 1992.

Stöber, Hans: *Die lettischen Divisionen*, Osnabrück, 1981.

Thorwald, Jürgen: *Die Illusion*, Zürich, 1974.

Wagner, Carl: *Heeresgruppe Süd*, Bad Nauheim, n.d.

No author: *Die Wehrmachtberichte*, Munich, 1985.

Additional Rolf Michaelis books from Schiffer Publishing Ltd.

SS-Heimwehr Danzig in Poland 1939 Rolf Michaelis. This is the first book in English on this obscure early-WWII SS unit. In July 1939, SS-Heimwehr Danzig was formed from members of the III./4. SS-Totenkopf-Standarte "Ostmark," as well as from Danzig citizen volunteers. As a unit of the RFSS they reinforced other existing Danzig units for the impending invasion of Poland.
Size: 6"x9" • 140 bw photos • 112pp.
ISBN: 978-0-7643-2943-2 • hard • $29.95

SS-Fallschirmjäger-Bataillon 500/600 Rolf Michaelis. This book is the history of the only Fallschirmjäger-Bataillon of the Waffen-SS during WWII. Formed in 1943 as a Bewährungsverband for special missions (guerrilla operations in the Balkans) the unit was deployed at many focal points of heavy combat on the eastern and western fronts.
Size: 6"x9" • 70 bw photos • 120pp.
ISBN: 978-0-7643-2944-9 • hard • $29.95

The 10th SS-Panzer-Division "Frundsberg" Rolf Michaelis. Division "Frundsberg" was formed at the beginning of 1943 as a reserve for the Allied invasion of France. Their first campaign was in the Ukraine in April 1944. Highly motivated after combat success in Ukraine the unit was then transported back to the west where they fought the Allies in France and Arnhem.
Size: 6"x9" • 100 bw photos • 168pp.
ISBN: 978-0-7643-3099-5 • hard • $35.00

The 11th SS-Freiwilligen-Panzer-Grenadier-Division "Nordland" Rolf Michaelis. Several thousand ethnic Germans in Romania, (the so called Volksdeutscher) were drafted into the Waffen-SS in 1943. They were first used in combat in Croatia, the Oranienbaumer, Estonia, and Latvia. After the Soviet attack in Pomerania they fought in Berlin and were destroyed there.
Size: 6"x9" • 80 bw photos • 152pp.
ISBN: 978-0-7643-3100-8 • hard • $35.00

The 32nd SS-Freiwilligen-Grenadier-Division "30.Januar" Rolf Michaelis. The SS Division "30. Januar" was one of the last SS-Divisions formed during WWII and was almost entirely composed of training units and 16-18 year old boys. With a final strength of 12,000, they fought on the Oder-front south of Frankfurt/Oder. After the Soviet attack on 16 April 1945 they were wiped out in the pocket of Halbe southeast of Berlin.
Size: 6"x9" • 80 bw photos • 128pp.
ISBN: 978-0-7643-3101-5 • hard • $35.00

Russians in the Waffen-SS Rolf Michaelis. From summer 1941, some 100,000 Russians served in the Wehrmacht, mostly as so called Schutzmannschaften under the command of the German Police (Höhere SS- und Polizeiführer) in the eastern occupied areas. The most famous unit was the Brigade Kaminski, established by Bronislav Kaminski in the summer of 1941.
Size: 6"x9" • 100 bw photos • 120pp.
ISBN: 978-0-7643-3348-4 • hard • $29.99

Ukrainians in the Waffen-SS Rolf Michaelis. With the beginning of the Operation Barbarossa more than 100,000 Ukrainians volunteered for the fight against Stalin and communism. These volunteers were put into Schutzmannschafts-Bataillone under the control of the German Police.
Size: 6"x9" • 100 bw photos • 128pp.
ISBN: 978-0-7643-3349-1 • hard • $29.99

Estonians in the Waffen-SS Rolf Michaelis. Thousands of Estonians wanted to take part in the war against Russia. Besides the Schutzmannschaften of German Police in 1942 Himmler built up an Estonian SS-Volunteer Brigade which became later the 20. Waffen-Grenadier-Division der SS (estnische Nr.1).
Size: 6"x9" • 100 bw photos • 120pp.
ISBN: 978-0-7643-3350-7 • hard • $29.99

Cavalry Divisions of the Waffen-SS Rolf Michaelis. A concise combat history of the three Waffen-SS cavalry divisions in WWII: 8th SS-Cavalry Division Florian Geyer; 22nd SS-Freiwilligen Cavalry Division Maria Theresia; 37th SS-Freiwilligen Cavalry Division Lützow. The formation and combat histories of each are discussed in detailed text, along with maps and rare photographs.
Size: 6"x9" • 150 bw photos • 168pp.
ISBN: 978-0-7643-3661-4 • hard • $35.00

Panzergrenadier Divisions of the Waffen-SS Rolf Michaelis. A concise combat history of the six Waffen-SS panzergrenadier divisions in WWII includes: the 4th SS-Polizei Panzergrenadier Division; 11th SS-Freiwilligen Panzergrenadier Division Nordland; 16th SS-Panzergrenadier Division Reichsführer-SS; 17th SS-Panzergrenadier Division Götz von Berlichingen; 18th SS-Freiwilligen Panzergrenadier Division Horst Wessel; 23rd SS-Freiwilligen Panzergrenadier Division Nederland.
Size: 6"x9" • 190 bw photos • 208pp.
ISBN: 978-0-7643-3660-7 • hard • $39.99

The Kaminski Brigade Rolf Michaelis. The political and military movement of Bronislav Kaminski in Russia 1941-44 was an interesting case in the German occupation. His self-defense army reached 10,000 men and fought for at least two years with great success against partisans on the Russian front.
Size: 6"x9" • 100 bw photos • 192pp.
ISBN: 978-0-7643-3765-9 • hard • $39.99

Belgians in the Waffen-SS Rolf Michaelis. In the years between 1940-45, approximately 12,500 Belgians served in the Waffen-SS, a number roughly equal to the strength of an infantry division in 1944. This book describes the major units of the Waffen-SS in which the Belgian volunteers were concentrated, and where they were deployed.
Size: 6"x9" • 90 color/bw photos • 128pp.
ISBN: 978-0-7643-4034-5 • hard • $35.00

Panzer Divisions of the Waffen-SS. Rolf Michaelis. A detailed look at all seven Waffen-SS panzer divisions in WWII: 1.SS-PD "LAH"; 2.SS-PD "Das Reich"; 3.SS-PD "Totenkopf"; 5.SS-PD "Wiking"; 9.SS-PD "Hohenstaufen"; 10.SS-PD "Frundsberg"; 12.SS-PD "HJ." Each unit is presented in detailed history from its formation, combat operations throughout the war, and final disposition at war's end.
Size: 6"x9" • 113 bw photos • 320pp.
ISBN: 978-0-7643-4477-0 • hard • $45.00

Latvians in the Ordnungspolizei and Waffen-SS Rolf Michaelis. Roughly 40,000 Latvians served in the Waffen-SS from 1943 to the end of war in the 15. Waffen-Grenadier-Division der SS (lettische Nr.1) and 19. Waffen-Grenadier-Division der SS (lettische Nr.2). This book is the complete operational history of this little-known unit and includes first-hand accounts, maps, and very rare war-era photographs, and soldbuchs.
Size: 6"x9" • 85 color/bw photos • 112pp.
ISBN: 978-0-7643-4262-2 • hard • $29.99

The Volksdeutschen in the Wehrmacht, Waffen-SS, and Ordnungspolizei in World War II Rolf Michaelis. In WWII, ethnic Germans all over Europe were drafted into the German military from all of the occupied countries. Nearly 650,000 men from all occupied countries were put into the Wehrmacht, Waffen-SS, and Order Police. This book details each country and unit from all service arms and includes rare documents, soldbuchs, and war-era photographs.
Size: 8.5"x11" • 100 color/bw photos • 136pp.
ISBN: 978-0-7643-4261-5 • hard • $39.99

Combat Operations of the German Ordnungspolizei 1939-45: Polizei-Bataillone • SS-Polizei-Regimenter Rolf Michaelis. Covers the little known combat operations of the German Ordnungspolizei during WWII. Discussed are unit formations, personalities, and operations including frontline combat, security duties in occupied countries, as well as the participation of some battalions in ethnic cleansing atrocities. Also included are very rare photos, documents, soldbuchs and maps.
Size: 8.5"x11" • 120 bw photos/maps • 128pp.
ISBN: 978-0-7643-3659-1 • hard • $45.00

The History of the 24. Waffen-Gebirgs (Karstjäger)-Division der SS and the Holders of the Anti-Partisan War Badge in Gold in the Second World War Rolf Michaelis. The 24. Waffen-Gebirgs [Karstjäger]-Division der SS anti-partisan unit was mostly comprised of Yugoslav recruits and operated in the Karst border area of Austria, Yugoslavia, and Italy from 1943 to 1945. This is not only a history, but an examination of the German Anti-Partisan War Badge in Gold and its recipients from the unit.
Size: 7"x10" • 120 color/bw photos • 96pp.
ISBN: 978-0-7643-4802-0 • hard • $24.99

The Third Reich Bravery and Merit Decoration for Eastern Peoples Rolf Michaelis. This book is a rare look at a little known Third Reich badge awarded to volunteers from the occupied eastern territories who served in various German formations. Very rare examples of actual badges, award documents and soldbuchs, and never before seen war era images are presented here.
Size: 7"x10" • 49 bw photos • 56pp.
ISBN: 978-0-7643-4803-7 • hard • $19.99

The German Tank Destruction Badge in WWII Rolf Michaelis. This book provides a concise account of Tank Destruction Badge, and the close-range combating of tanks. In addition to a description of the special badge and the most commonly used weapons, it includes operational accounts by recipients of the badge.
Size: 7"x10" • 90 color/bw photos • 64pp.
ISBN: 978-0-7643-4052-9 • hard • $19.99

The German Anti-Partisan Badge in WWII Rolf Michaelis. Those German soldiers and police members who fought against the partisans were qualified to receive the anti-partisan badge. This concise book discusses the award's three grades and includes rare documents and war-era photographs.
Size: 7"x10" • 24 bw photos • 40pp.
ISBN: 978-0-7643-4260-8 • hard • $19.99

Assault Badges of the German Army in World War II Rolf Michaelis. The German assault badges in their various grades were awarded for participation in specific numbers of combat assaults. This concise book discusses the award's various types and grades and includes rare documents and war-era photographs.
Size: 7"x10" • 61 bw photos • 56pp.
ISBN: 978-0-7643-4257-8 • hard • $19.99

Close Combat Clasps of the German Army in World War II Rolf Michaelis. In 1942 the Wehrmacht established the Close Combat Badge in three grades, and it was awarded to those after a specific number of battles. This concise book discusses the award's various grades and includes rare documents and war-era photographs.
Size: 7"x10" • 50 bw photos • 56pp.
ISBN: 978-0-7643-4258-5 • hard • $19.99

German Wound Badges in World War II Rolf Michaelis. The Wound Badge was awarded in three grades depending on the number and/or type of injuries in wartime. This concise book discusses the award's various grades and includes rare documents and war-era photographs.
Size: 7"x10" • 63 bw photos • 56pp.
ISBN: 978-0-7643-4259-2 • hard • $19.99

The German Sniper Badge 1944-45 Rolf Michaelis. Hitler created the Sniper Badge on August 20, 1944, to impel soldiers to train and be used as snipers. Thus the strategic importance of single combat was stressed in highly stylized propaganda. In this concise history, this badge, as well as the actions of German snipers, is examined and includes color images of badges, weapons, awards, soldbuchs, and war era photos.
Size: 7"x10" • 60 color/bw photos • 60pp.
ISBN: 978-0-7643-4032-1 • hard • $19.99